DATE DUE

JE 22 '95			
JE 3 '03			
MY 18 '06			

DEMCO 38-296

Resolving the Argentine Paradox

Resolving the Argentine Paradox

Politics and Development, 1966–1992

Davide G. Erro

Lynne Rienner Publishers ▪ Boulder & London

Published in the United States of America in 1993 by
Lynne Rienner Publishers, Inc.
1800 30th Street, Boulder, Colorado 80301

and in the United Kingdom by
Lynne Rienner Publishers, Inc.
3 Henrietta Street, Covent Garden, London WC2E 8LU

Library of Congress Cataloging-in-Publication Data
Erro, Davide G., 1970–
  Resolving the Argentine paradox : politics and development,
1966–1992 / by Davide G. Erro.
    p.   cm.
  Includes bibliographical references and index.
  ISBN 1-55587-369-3 (alk. paper)
  1. Argentina—Economic conditions—1945–1983. 2. Argentina—
Economic conditions—1983– 3. Argentina—Economic policy.
4. Argentina—Politics and government—1955–1983. 5. Argentina—
Politics and government—1983– I. Title
HC175.E68   1993
338.982—dc20   92-40793
                                                           CIP

British Cataloguing in Publication Data
A Cataloguing in Publication record for this book
is available from the British Library.

Printed and bound in the United States of America

∞ The paper used in this publication meets the requirements
   of the American National Standard for Permanence of
   Paper for Printed Library Materials Z39.48-1984.

AM and KW:
Thanks

Contents

Illustrations

Tables

Figures

Foreword

José Alfredo Martínez de Hoz

Davide Erro commences *Resolving the Argentine Paradox* by posing a question that has been asked innumerable times by knowledgeable foreigners and visitors to Argentina, as well as by preoccupied Argentines themselves: "How has a country of such great potential, which had such auspicious beginnings, found itself in such utter ruin?"

Erro set himself the task of finding an answer to the paradox, with all the difficulties faced by someone who has not lived permanently in the country during any significant part of the period studied. To overcome this obstacle, in addition to digging up and reading important and select literature written by both Argentines and foreign scholars—some of which was quite difficult to find—he traveled to Argentina several times over the course of three years. During these visits, he was able to interview (in some cases more than once) more than fifty personalities from all quarters of the ideological spectrum, who had either been directly involved in Argentine public affairs (both inside and outside the government) or were preeminent academics known for their studies of the evolution of Argentine political, economic, and social (mainly labor) events during the period.

The author was thus able to get a fairly clear and unprejudiced picture of his subject and avoided the possibility of being considered a "weekend-trip expert." Although in some cases he might be faulted for some lack of insight into certain details, the disagreement one could have does not affect his overall conclusions. In addition, he probably has an advantage over some local analysts in that in seeing the trees he has not obscured his view of the forest.

I myself, as someone who has personally lived through the period in question with great intensity and activity in both the public and private sectors, on the occasion of each of Erro's visits to Argentina was able to appreciate how his understanding of the relevant complex political and economic processes and personalities matured as his research progressed. One of the more important merits of Davide Erro's book is that, unlike so many economic analysts who examine the results of economic programs from a purely economic (and many times theoretical) point of view, he adroitly places them in the political and social context of their times.

The relative importance of politics vis-à-vis economics has been the subject of infinite discussions all over the world. Nevertheless, the interrelation between the two is so great that it can safely be concluded that an economic policy, however good it may be, cannot be successful without a firm and continuous political system to support it. It is also true that political stability can be jeopardized by the lack of an adequate economic policy and its sometimes necessary "courageous" implementation. In this sense, a government's political "sensitivity," or the sacrifice of long-term sound economic objectives in return for short-term "political" profits, can only postpone the moment of facing harsh economic reality.

In other words, when governments or political parties have used the excuse of "excessive political costs" for not facing and finding a solution to basic structural economic problems, the results have proved to be politically more costly than if the decision had been taken to implement the requisite measures at the right moment despite the apparently negative short-term factors. Davide Erro was quick to realize the importance that this interrelationship between politics and economic policy had in the Argentine scenario.

Inflation in Argentina, which began in 1947 after nearly half a century of monetary stability, has been one of the most negative factors in the evolution of the country's economy. Some governments and political parties actually looked upon inflation during certain periods as instrumental to the promotion of growth. Others used it as an instrument for redistributing income. Economic agents and the population as a whole first learned how to live with inflation (that is, how to protect themselves from its effects) and then how to profit from it. In the end, it became a veritable addiction, and most economic actors were loathe to see it disappear and be forced to live without this crutch. Undoubtedly, in many cases profits earned through inflationary windfalls were easier to obtain than those originating in hard work, investment, and productive efficiency. For the economy, this meant that there was more incentive for the redistribution than the creation of income and wealth, which explains the very moderate overall rate of growth between 1966 and 1989. Within this context, one sector inevitably had to grow at the cost of another. The result was a continuous tug-of-war that characterized the whole period. The other main factors—apart from inflation—that caused the stagnation of the Argentine economy were the state intervention policy and the closed economy model, which have their principle origins in the immediate post–World War II period.

In Davide Erro's examination of the successive governments beginning in 1966, he is quick to point out the preeminence each one gave to these factors. Political demagogy (loosely called "populism") sacrificed long-term structural economic objectives for short-term political benefits. In other cases, the anti-inflation policy was grounded only in monetarist policy that did not really attack the structural problems. When these problems were seriously confronted with a policy that could be considered the basic cure for economic stagnation, including inflation, the short-term results many times caused price increases due to price liberalization and deregulation of the economy. A successful balance among all of the factors was difficult to achieve.

The theme underlying Davide Erro's work is the action of the so-called corporatist entities, or organized interest groups, and the lobbying exerted by them on successive governments, in conjunction with changing alliances of these pressure groups with the "power brokers," which put the governments in office. This interaction explains many of the initial successes and later failures of various economic programs, either through lack of continuity caused by loss of support or by the inability to resist opposition to basic economic reform measures from groups jockeying for their own vested interests. Davide Erro concludes that "the failure of corporatism rests in the inability of the power brokers to intermediate between the corporatist entities while simultaneously implementing a rational program geared towards economic restructuring." This conclusion explains the political cycles and the associated changes in regimes and general instability, as well as certain defects inherent in the Argentine political institutional framework. In the author's words, "despite the very different structures and ideologies embodied in each of the governments studied, none of them proved able to implement fully a rational economic plan. . . . Each of the governments, regardless of its policies or structures, seemed unable to break the tragic cycle. The answer offered is that each of these governments confronted an immutable (in the short-term) corporatist structure that blocked rational policymaking."

In June 1989, the mismanagement of economic policy culminated in a monthly inflation rate that, measured by the consumer price index, rose to 200 percent. The hyperinflationary period that the country lived through can be said to have had a positive effect; it scared the population at large and demonstrated the ravaging damage inflation can cause. It has been a successful vaccine since then, and now there is widespread preoccupation to avoid policies or measures that could rekindle the inflationary spiral. In the history of nations as in the lives of men, it is sometimes necessary and salutary to hit rock bottom in order to rebound and continue in the right direction on the right path.

President Alfonsín, unable to cope with the chaotic crisis, voluntarily resigned six months before the expiration of his term in office, allowing President-Elect Menem to take over the reigns of government in mid-July 1989. The change that swept over the country is attributed mainly to the breakdown of corporatism and the lack of other alternatives. In other words, "the corporatist structure continues to crumble on all fronts. The corporatist entities grow increasingly irrelevant and divided. The power brokers grow more cohesive and rational. Democracy is further taking root as all political competitions now occur within this arena. Redistributions and subsidies, the driving forces behind past alliances, are being eliminated. As a result, investment is on the rise, capital is being repatriated, and foreign investors are beginning to return."

There is a lot of truth in Davide Erro's words, but a very important factor that is probably implicit in them should be made explicit in order to explain clearly the break with the past. Since the end of World War II, years of practice and indoctrination of the benefits of state intervention in the economy, practically absolute state ownership of public utilities and public services in general in addition to many productive industries, and the closed economy model resulted in the relative stagnation and lack of modernization and competition in the Argentine economy. It gradually became apparent, therefore, that this was not the right path to growth and progress. Certainly many industries and sectors benefited from state welfare handouts such as high protectionism, subsidies, and so on, but the overall economy did not.

The two major political parties had embraced these mistaken policies. Only some minority leaders and enlightened individuals had the courage to speak out against the conventional wisdom, which was deemed to be more "patriotic." During some periods, government policies were reversed mainly to tackle inflation, as in 1967–1969, with successful results that lack of policy continuity ultimately thwarted. During the five-year period from March 1976 until March 1981, an economic program was announced and implemented to attack not only inflation but also the basic structural deformations and bottlenecks of the economy caused by state ownership, excessive regulation, and the closed economy model. At the end of that period, the fruits of the initial and most difficult structural reforms effected and measures taken were prevented from maturing fully, a fact that became evident with another case of lack of continuity and the reversal of those policies.

Nevertheless, the decline of the economy over the next ten years and the breakdown of the state enterprises and utilities that were unable to provide the required basic services, together with the practical bankruptcy of the state and finally hyperinflation, brought to light the stark reality of the failure of the welfare state, of the closed economy model, and of inflation to promote growth and general improvement of the standard of living. Thus the seeds that had so laboriously been sown during earlier efforts were not lost, and blossomed in the form of a gradual change in the mentality of the population as a whole. Sick and tired of empty ideological debate and the favoritism shown to certain sectorial interests over the general weal, the people began to demand a change in policy in the right direction and, for the first time in modern Argentine history, used their voting power at the polls to chastise those leaders who had not realized the need to adapt their political and economic policies to the requirements of modern progress.

When Dr. Carlos Saúl Menem became president in July 1989, he was quick to recognize the change of mood of the population. He adopted the policies of state reform, privatization of public enterprises, deregulation, and the opening up of the economy and promotion of competition, together with a strong anti-inflationary program. These policies, backed by the president's political decisiveness and the public's strong political support, in essence represent the break with the past and the breakdown of corporatism that the change in mentality of the population has brought about.

Davide Erro's book was written during the initial stage of this fundamental alteration of the Argentine picture. If the right policies are implemented with forceful decision and unwavering continuity, the solution to the "Argentine Paradox" will have been found.

Acknowledgments

Many people were instrumental in helping hone the ideas in this book. Nancy Bermeo, my adviser at Princeton University, not only pointed me in the right direction at the beginning of my research, but also offered numerous and often pointed criticisms as my work progressed; as disheartening as they might have been at first, they were always well calculated to make my work more coherent. Atul Kohli, a professor at Princeton's Wilson School, offered tremendous insights into economic development. Professor Paul Sigmund, also at Princeton, offered support and encouragement without which I never would have found the energy to transform an academic work into a book. I am also indebted to many in Argentina. Professors Juan Carlos Torre, Alfredo Juan Canavese, and Marcelo Cavarozzi were generous with their time and their own theories regarding the Argentine Paradox; to a greater or lesser extent, all of their theories have either influenced this book or been incorporated in it. Almost everyone I interviewed was very helpful, but special thanks to Orlando J. Ferreres, Alberto L. Grimoldi, Juan Carlos Herrera, and Jorge Vives.

The Woodrow Wilson School, as well as Princeton University generally, was an ideal place to produce this work. I am deeply indebted and thankful for the stimulating atmosphere, the resources (including several grants that allowed me to go to Argentina to conduct the bulk of my research), and all the people that make the institution what it is. Finally, I must recognize the Horace Mann School and two particular mentors, Murray Mogel and Carlo Puca.

Davide G. Erro

Introduction

Each individual page of Argentine politics has been filled with passions, ideals, and great desires. It seems as though this emotionality is a central and possibly defining characteristic of not only the country's politics, but also its psyche. The Radicals' first ascent to power, Juan Perón's populist movement, and the recent Malvinas/Falkland War, as examples, are separated by over half a century, very different political viewpoints and circumstances, and vastly differing social structures. All the same, each of these occurrences, as well as many others, had a very similar "flavor." The majority of Argentines felt during each of these times that a new and fundamental change was occurring, something akin to a new awakening. Each endeavor in Argentine politics promised to place this Latin American nation in a new and more privileged place in world history. A new justice and national prominence were promised, generating widespread and sincere acclaim from the Argentine citizens.

If the individual governments and political movements were generally greeted with great energy, this excitement transformed itself into sorrow, confusion, and possibly anger as each page of Argentina's history was written. It might be said that as Argentine politics becomes Argentine history, fervor and self-assurance transform into lethargy and self-criticism. As one looks back, one sees only missed opportunities. Moreover, each period of Argentine history inflicted great costs, economically, socially, and personally; and for what? In studying Argentine history, one cannot but feel regret and confusion: all the energy spent, all the blood spilled in search of ideals, has brought little except more suffering.

It is not easy to explain why this dichotomy exists between expectations and results, why the great passions caused only great failures. The question, indeed, is simply a restatement of another that has long plagued Argentines and academics alike: How has a country of such great potential, which had such auspicious beginnings, found itself in such utter ruin? It is difficult to answer what may be termed the Argentine Paradox, but it seems clear that the ideals and great passions unleashed during the various periods of Argentine

1

history have led to the disastrous conclusions. In other words, the optimism during so many of the political processes actually led to their failure and the resultant generalized pessimism about the country.

After so many broken dreams, however, perhaps Argentina has finally stopped looking for a savior, a quick fix to all problems. This change, far more important than any of the "revolutions" claimed in the past, may foster a fundamental change of course, a new political stability, and, finally, a return to economic growth.

At the beginning of this century, Argentina was one of the so-called countries of new settlement, together with Australia, Canada, New Zealand, and, to a lesser extent, the United States. These countries all had vast tracts of fertile land and a relatively small population made up largely of recent European immigrants. It was thought that these conditions were ideal for stable republican governments and prolonged rapid economic growth. Indeed, these were the very prospects that attracted the steady flow of immigrants.

A century later, the prediction of political stability and economic growth has been borne out in each of the countries except Argentina, for which people had the highest of hopes. In the 1890s, Argentina was the sixth richest country in the world in per capita terms. There is agreement that all progressed well through the 1920s. The economy grew briskly and the political situation, although not consolidated due to fraud and exclusion of large sections of the population, was stable. Indeed, on all levels Argentina fared quite favorably with the other countries of recent settlement.

The Great Depression and the subsequent breakdown in international trade quite naturally caused economic hardship in this nation that was highly dependent on exporting agricultural products and importing industrial goods. However, it would be unfair to say that Argentina lost its way during this decade of world economic crisis. Indeed, the Great Depression had far less of a detrimental effect on Argentina than on most other countries, including the United States, most of Europe, and Latin American neighbors such as Brazil.

World War II, the next major world crisis, in no way harmed the country's prospects. Argentina remained neutral until the very end of the international conflict, allowing the country to sell its sought-after agricultural products to any of the warring European powers for immense profits. The decision to join the Allies when their victory became imminent assured Argentina a place at the peace negotiations as well.

However, the period just before and during World War II coincided with the development of Peronism in Argentina. Whereas the 1940s were quite profitable for Argentina, as they were for the other recently settled countries, the Latin American nation began to diverge from these other countries politically. Indeed, the growth of Peronism and the changes this movement wrought on Argentine society have often been blamed for the subsequent and precipitous decline of Argentina in the following decades. Clearly, General Juan Perón had a tremendous effect on Argentine development, both economically and politically. Just as important, this movement fundamentally differentiated Argentina from the other countries of recent settlement. There is no doubt that much of the political instability and economic sclerosis in the years following Perón's overthrow in 1955 directly related to the policies implemented and forces mobilized by the general.

One cannot blame all of Argentina's subsequent problems on Perón's movement. Although very different from the political figures in Australia and Canada, Perón can certainly be compared to Getulio Vargas in Brazil or Francisco Franco in Spain as well as to several other populist leaders. These other histories would suggest that the overthrow, or, in the extreme, the death of such a leader would allow for the re-creation of stability and rational economics. Neither the overthrow of Perón in 1955 nor his death in 1974 led to such changes. The problems afflicting Argentina went beyond the political divisions wrought by the *caudillo*.

Indeed, the period from 1966 until 1989, examined herein, marks an actual deterioration on both the political and economic scenes as compared to any preceding periods of Argentine history, including Perón's first tenure in government and the years immediately after his downfall. During these years, political crises became commonplace. Despite intermittent short periods of economic growth, this time was marked by the most rapid economic decline the country ever experienced. It is fair to say that these two-and-a-half decades represent the culmination of all of Argentina's then existing problems.

As will be seen in the body of this work, it is not for a lack of ideas, sacrifice, or determination that this black period in Argentine history followed. Quite the contrary, many different political structures and economic ideologies were attempted to resolve the nation's problem. Sacrifice was demanded of all groups: at various times the workers were given lower wages in order to pay for a new future, the agricultural elite was forced to reduce profit margins to pay for industrial development, many national industries went bankrupt in the name of greater efficiency and a better distribution of resources. Numbers of young people were encouraged if not forced into exile for political or economic reasons as a necessary or inevitable consequence of the policies effected. Worst of all, tens of thousands of lives were lost, from unionists to businesspeople, from leftists to rightists, from underclothed draftees sent to the Malvinas/Falkland War to many an innocent individual caught in the crossfire. This work attempts to offer an explanation as to why political and economic initiatives failed.

The failures, however, have cooled the passions and the search for ideals that thus far rendered discussion and agreement among the various groups of Argentines impossible. With a bit of luck, this change in outlook regarding current politics will allow one to look back on Argentine history in several years not with sorrow and confusion but rather with pride and understanding.

1

The Crisis of Argentine Political Economy and the Breakdown of Corporatism, 1966–1989

In 1966, Juan Carlos Onganía ascended to the Argentine presidency. In 1973, Juan Domingo Perón followed him. Similarly, Jorge Videla ascended in 1976 and Raúl Alfonsín in 1983. Each of these presidents came to power advocating fundamental changes in the structure and workings of Argentine politics, economics, and even society. These changes were supposed to be geared toward creating political stability and fostering sustained economic growth, both of which had been long lacking in the country. Each man came to power with an extended mandate (at least five years) during which time these changes were to be effected. Finally, each of these four men utterly failed: All of the governments ended abruptly during periods of political chaos and economic crisis.

Each of these governments has been well studied. The Onganía presidency, for example, is the basis of the bureaucratic authoritarian model proposed by Guillermo O'Donnell, the focus of William C. Smith's work on Argentine political economy, and the subject of a slew of articles. Literature on the other governments is just as abundant. It might be claimed that the reasons for the failure of each of these governments are "understood," at least as well as can be expected in political science; one and often several explanations exist for the failure of each of these governments. The explanations are couched in theoretical arguments but none of the individual explanations seems to apply to all of the governments between 1966 and 1989. The implication appears to be that the causes of each of the failures were particular to each of the individual governments. However, many questions remain.

In order to better resolve these questions, the whole period should be studied as a distinct unit. The particular problems confronted and aims proposed by these governments, although seemingly different, are fundamentally the same. Whereas the governments between 1955 and 1966 (with the notable exception of Arturo Frondizi's discussed below) did not call for, much less attempt to effect, a fundamental restructuring of Argentina, each of these four presidents did. On the political side, each of these presidents wanted to impose a certain political outlook on the nation as a part of the restructuring. Their governments often attempted to force interpretations of history, moral values, and political ideology on the population at large.

Even more clear was the fact that each of these men wanted a complete restructuring of the Argentine economy. It was clear to many at the time, and to all in retrospect, that Argentina had come to an economic impasse; the country's economy did not lead to or encourage investment. Each of the presidents realized this problem, and a central aspect of all of these governments became the resolution of the economic stagnation. Various attempts were made to find a new mode of capital accumulation. The solutions each of the presidents offered, it must be emphasized, had tremendous implications for the structure of the economy and the income of all economic groups. Had any solutions been successful, certain economic groups would certainly have prevailed over others in a process of economic realignment.

Moreover, the issues confronted during the 1966–1989 period were far broader and more penetrating than in the preceding years. These governments saw Argentina's problems as being more complex and deep-rooted than was commonly assumed during other periods. It was thought, as stated above, that part of the remedy rested in new, bold, and comprehensive economic policies. At the same time, these governments advocated altering the very social and cultural underpinnings of the nation. Such policies, which took any form from propaganda to violent repression, were in part geared towards reintegrating the Peronist voice, excluded for over a decade following Juan Perón's exile. This goal was a perennial one in Argentina and resembled that of all preceding governments. The policies themselves, however, contrast markedly with the previous flimsy political attempts to reintegrate the Peronists through various political alliances and limited conscriptions of political candidates. The policies implemented by these four governments were geared toward getting to what were considered the roots of the problems, instead of merely counteracting the results. These were to be "serious" governments with clear goals, wide powers, and tremendous consequences. Indeed, the slogans of the governments studied—*la Revolución Argentina, la Reconstrucción Nacional, el Proceso de Reorganización Nacional,* and *el Tercer Movimiento Histórico*—reflect the peculiar character shared by all of them.

The reasons for studying these four governments as a unit become all the more clear when one realizes that there are three important similarities shared by all of them. Just as important, these similarities also begin to suggest that the reasons for each of these governments' failures are not particular to themselves. First, all of these regimes came to power with widespread popularity and support that cut across interest groups and social and economic classes, as will be shown in the following chapters. It must be emphasized that this contrasts with the preceding governments. From the beginning of the century until Perón's overthrow in 1955, governments tended to have limited support from only certain economic groups or classes, a support that tended to split Argentine society into two factions, generally of approximately the same power. Hipólito Yrigoyen, the founder of the Radical Party who then became president, crystallized through his political actions the tensions between the old "oligarchy" and the new middle classes. Perón was famous for dividing Argentine society into pro- and anti-Peronists, both of which had similar levels of power. From 1955 until the period studied, on the other hand, governments had only minimal support, but support which, compared to the previous period, cut across social classes. President Arturo Illia (1963–1966), for example, was elected with a plurality of only approximately 25 percent of the votes—hardly a strong mandate. The governments to be studied here were not saddled with these weaknesses.

Second, at the beginning of each of these governments, there was widespread agreement among politicians, economists, and society at large that significant changes had to occur in the political and economic spheres. In other words, society offered government the go-ahead to implement policies that might overhaul Argentina politically and economically. Indeed, this acceptance of the need for such policies led almost all groups, as will be seen in the following chapters, to accept short-term sacrifices in the hopes of long-term gains.

Third, each of these governments came to power with an extended mandate, generally of five years. Such a period of time should be sufficient to implement fully any set of policies. Clearly, these three conditions, particularly taken together, were highly advantageous for an incoming government with the hopes of implementing la Revolución Argentina or el Tercer Movimiento Histórico.

The two main differences between these governments are just as important, however. First, the structures of regimes were widely divergent. General Onganía came to power through a military coup, although he himself had already retired from active service; his government corresponds to a variation of a bureaucratic authoritarian regime. Perón, a highly charismatic leader of fundamental importance in Argentine history, came to power through the mobilization of his core followers, which resulted in elections he went on to win; his government might be termed a mass-movement democracy. The Videla government was yet another attempt at bureaucratic authoritarianism, this time under the direct control of active military officers. Finally, Alfonsín, also very charismatic, was democratically elected in a very competitive election.

Second, the policies implemented by these governments were just as diversified as the types of regimes themselves, ranging from populistlike economic policies under Perón to conservative ones under Videla. In other words, in analyzing Argentina's problems, each of these governments came up with different supposed problems and potential solutions.

The initial popularity and agreement that greeted these governments suggest that they each had an advantageous social and political climate in which to attempt their policies. The different policies were based on dissimilar assumptions and ideologies, at least one of which should have been "correct." Given these factors, one of these governments should have been successful at reforming Argentine politics and economics. The juxtaposition of these factors leads to a central question: Were the problems that caused the failure of these governments distinct for each one, as the existing literature seems to imply,[1] or continuous throughout the twenty-three-year period? The question becomes even more intriguing when one notes that there is now growing agreement that all of the initial economic programs were rational as proposed and could have been successful in promoting sustained growth had they been fully implemented for an extended period of time. In other words, the economic failures cannot be attributed simply to a series of incoherent economic plans.[2]

The answer to the above question, as the evidence thus far presented implies, is quite definitely the second alternative: There were continuous structural problems that blocked the implementation of any economic and political strategy during the whole period here studied. What were these structural impediments? More generally, why has Argentina been unable to implement a viable development strategy and to promote political stability? This study attempts to answer those questions.

The Tragic Cycle

Each of the four governments ended in crisis. It was repeatedly assumed that these periods represented the total breakdown of the political and economic structure. "When the military took power in 1976, the whole economic and political system had broken down. We had to build it up from nothing—there was no alternative,"[3] is a statement that exemplifies the feelings surrounding a regime change. This recurring conclusion was supported by the overtly radical changes in the type of regime and economic policies after each crisis. Upon closer examination, however, a cycle can be discerned that is common to all four governments:

The first phase: A consensus grows among important interest groups and society at large that the political system must be overhauled in order to ensure political stability and economic prosperity. The important interest groups or "primary corporatist entities" congregate around a particular "power broker" capable of taking control of government.

The second phase: The power broker ascends to the government through an unconventional and noninstitutionalized procedure. This is clearly the case for military coups. The same is claimed, however, for the first democratically elected government after a prolonged military regime, all the more so when the elections and the transfer of power occur during political breakdown and economic instability. All the governments here studied were products of such chaotic and atypical circumstances.

The first policies implemented by each of these governments are geared towards satisfying all the corporatist entities, particularly through expansionary economic policy.

The third phase: The original economic policy, due to its disregard for inevitable economic trade-offs, gives rise to growing inflation and distributional conflicts. Far from encouraging investment so needed for economic growth, these policies and the resulting situation actually discourage it. As a result, the economic policy changes course and assumes an independent and ostensibly rational (as compared to political) direction. The economics team, composed of nonmembers of parties—or outsiders—is given autonomy but is required to accomplish immediate and continuous advances on various fronts: reduce inflation, promote growth of the gross national product (GNP), and, theoretically just as important but in actuality less urgent, implement structural reform. These economic criteria become the "objective" measures of the validity of the economic policy. It must be emphasized that no trade-off, even in the short term, is acceptable.

A tentative alliance is created with the goal of effecting higher growth and investment as well as lower inflation. This alliance includes a group of corporatist entities and the government, or, more specifically, the economics team. The alliance excludes the other corporatist entities. It can be termed "tentative" as there is not a complete partnership between the favored entities and the government, especially because special emphasis is placed on not antagonizing the excluded sectors.

The new stability and the rational economic plans foster an initial economic boom based on bringing unused but installed excess industrial capacity on-line.

The fourth phase: As a result of the lack of structural changes and the delayed costs of the economic plans, pressures in the original economic plan mount, forcing more drastic measures. This tension is reflected in some combination of mounting inflation and slowing growth. These measures force the further exclusion of the nonallied sectors and greater tensions within the original alliance.

The fifth phase: Oppositional forces (including certain sectors of the original alliance) begin lobbying the more sympathetic factions within the power broker group. These same interest groups also start opposing government policy within society at large by means of strikes, demonstrations, and so on. The growing opposition to the government and to the economic policies inevitably causes a deterioration of the primary economic indicators (inflation and GNP growth).

The sixth phase: An internal coup occurs, causing a radical shift in economic policy. New strategies are attempted, but the lack of confidence in a government that so recently changed directions blocks the consummation of new partnerships between corporatist entities and the state. Hence, economic policy rapidly degenerates into ad hoc initiatives geared toward staving off an immediate economic crisis. Among the corporatist entities and within society at large, open antagonisms grow as each group attempts to defend its own self-interests; conditions similar to those of praetorianism[4] appear.

The seventh phase: In the midst of political chaos and economic crisis that the government can no longer contain, a new consensus emerges that fundamental political, economic, and even social changes must be effected. The cycle is repeated.

In sum, 1966 through 1989 has been marked by a cyclical formation and breakdown of consensus among corporatist entities and even in society at large.

A model in the form of a comparison is in order both to summarize and to elucidate. Argentina can be seen as a patient going through psychoanalysis. The patient's problems all relate to relatively few fundamental disorders. These disorders keep recurring in very different guises that often obscure rather than clarify the fundamental maladies. Further, in the process of getting "cured," the patient first deteriorates and then slowly emerges from the depths of his crises. What occurred in Argentina was similar. The situation when Onganía was overthrown was mild in comparison to the open political warfare and economic standstill that shrouded the overthrow of the Perón government. The crisis at the end of the Alfonsín presidency was also trivial in comparison: Political violence was nil and the economic crisis was purely financial (hyperinflation). Indeed, I claim that the Alfonsín government demarcates the end of the structural impediments. But what were the fundamental problems that kept reemerging? What fundamental name can we give this neurosis?

There are three central traits that one can discern from this repeated order of events. First, the power broker is unable or unwilling to consummate a complete alliance or "marriage" of interests with a particular economic group: Although some groups are favored over others, never is the government apparatus clearly aiding one group in the economic reorganization of the nation. Second, there is an obvious disparity in the relative powers of the power broker in question and the corporatist entities, the latter being far more powerful, a power that increases with time during each government. Due to this, the corporatist entities are repeatedly able to force the replacement of the economic plan that the power broker has chosen. Third, all of the governments exhibit a clear time constraint, hence implementing policies geared toward simultaneously and immediately promoting both growth and disinflation, despite the inherent trade-off between these two economic indicators; in economic terms, there is a recurring time-consistency problem.

Can a fundamental hindrance confronted by all four governments be honed from these characteristics? Yes—at the most basic level, the problem is a lack of legitimacy, arising mainly from the absence of an institutionalized method of choosing a power broker. What is essential to realize is that there is competition between three brokers for power, each of which, during the period studied, relied on different processes of coming to power: the military coup, popular mobilization, and democratic elections. The fact that each comes to power in a very different method juxtaposed with the fact that they are all viable holders of power results in a lack of legitimacy for all that end up in power; no method of choosing a power broker can be considered fair or correct. This combination of factors allows the population at large, through the various interest groups, first to encourage a power broker to government, and then to undermine that government by criticizing its very method of coming to power and encouraging another power broker to supplant the first through some other process of coming to power. A prime characteristic of this cycle is the complete lack of enduring responsibility or accountability on the part of those that supported changes in governments; instead of being forced to understand where the governments that the interest groups had chosen went wrong, interest groups were repeatedly able to lay the blame on the power broker. New fanciful hopes were pinned on changing governments.

Elections cannot be considered a more acceptable process of choosing a government as the initial support for and legitimacy of the military regimes rivaled that of the new civilian ones. Moreover, as shall be seen, the ostensible processes of coming to power—elections, coups, and so on—are the result of a previously made choice of power brokers, not vice versa; the choice of government occurs in deciding whether to support elections, Perón's return, or a military coup, not in an election booth. It is the interest groups that choose among the power brokers by deciding the process of coming to power; the power brokers themselves never compete on equal terms in the same political arena, such as the ballot box. Within this context, democracy offers little assurance of guaranteed support or acceptance.

In turn, this lack of legitimacy promoted desperate attempts to gain and to retain support, a condition necessary to ascend to and to remain in power. The power broker was, as should already be clear, in a very weak situation compared to the corporatist entities. As a power broker never clearly won a mandate over the other power brokers, the broker in government was constantly dependent on the corporatist entities to remain in power. The power broker is confronted with a never-ending need to pander to the corporatist entities for their support or else to justify the economic program in some other way. The relative weakness blocked a direct confrontation with the corporatist entities, thwarted a total alliance between the power broker and a more powerful entity (lest the power broker lose its own autonomy), and valued favorable economic indicators above the restructuring and long-term prospects of the underlying economy.

Why was there a problem of legitimacy in Argentina? Restated, what factors have led up to the political impasse studied here? To answer this, a brief review of Argentine history is essential.

A Review of Argentine History

For the purposes of this study, Argentine history can be divided into five periods: the liberal period ending in the early part of the century, the incorporation period from the early part of the century until 1955, the political impasse period from 1955 until 1966, the corporatist breakdown period (which is the focus of this book) from 1966 until 1989, and finally the renovation period currently going on.

The liberal period was marked by rapid growth and close integration with the world economy (and particularly that of Britain). The Argentine economy during this period was driven by agricultural exports, a sector that benefited enormously from the comparative advantages offered by some of the most fertile lands in the world. Two problems developed during this period. First was a problem created by the political exclusion of the vast majority of Argentine society. The economic growth attracted an important flow of immigrants, a group that accounted for more than half of the Argentine population at times. It was a common tendency among this group to take up residency, but not to seek citizenship, thus reinforcing their exclusion from civil society. Obviously, the Argentine elite was eager to retain its power and encouraged this situation. The second problem was a recurring foreign accounts deficit, which caused inflation and currency instability. This problem can be traced to the juxtaposition of a high dependence on imported finished goods and of variable export earnings due to the vagaries of world market prices and of crop yields. Difficulties in importing industrial products were reinforced during World War I when Britain, the source of most of Argentina's imports, was unable to satisfy Argentine demand for finished goods.

The incorporation period was marked both by attempts to correct these problems and by political maneuvers to take advantage of them; a "push" and a "pull" dynamic was clearly evident throughout the period.[5] The economic response was the de facto implementation of import substitution. This was seen as a method of reducing dependence on imports and of tempering the foreign exchange crises. The initial phases of import substitution were encouraged by the agricultural elites as a method of fostering more efficient, more profitable, and more stable agricultural exports; there was never emphasis on the export of manufactured goods. Import substitution was further encouraged by the shortage of imports caused by the breakdown of trade during the Great Depression and World War II. Clearly, there was a "push" for import substitution given the economic conditions.

The "pull" was supplied by national political factors. In essence, political actors supported these newly created sectors in order to gain popularity. The Unión Cívica Radical (UCR) or Radical Party was the first to benefit from the growing middle classes. Due to the new importance of this class as well as its significant representation in the military (a bastion of middle-class social mobility), election processes were changed and the Radicals came to power. In essence, the middle sectors were incorporated into society and jointly ruled with the old agricultural elite or oligarchy. This period is now frequently referred to as the Primer Movimiento Histórico. The urban and, even more notably, rural lower classes were still excluded, however. This group offered Juan Perón a tremendous potential resource that was ready to be tapped. In so doing, he changed the dynamics of Argentine politics and society.

Peronism

Juan Domingo Perón began his political ascent by joining a military lodge, the Group of United Officers (GOU). This group was composed of like-minded officers, all middle-ranking like Perón, who were preoccupied with the course of Argentine politics. The group was worried, as had been their fascist counterparts in Europe, about growing labor militancy. Far worse than the immediate effects were the potential ones that were so clearly evidenced, in the GOU's eyes, in the Soviet Union. With communism on the rise on the old continent, socialist, anarchist, and syndicalist immigrants from Italy and Spain were seen as dangerous. Many began to believe that these individuals should be silenced. Their potential followers, the poor and the rank-and-file union members, were to be rendered less susceptible to supporting such deviant ideologues. Many of these officers (including Perón) had been trained in fascist Italy and Germany, political systems for which they had much sympathy. Largely due to this, these officers resisted the growing pressure to join the allied war effort.

The GOU overthrew the government of Ramón Castillo on 4 June 1943. Despite the fact that the outgoing government was "conservative" and had had the support of the old oligarchy or land-owning elites, parts of Argentina's high society supported the coup: A feeling was growing that a new approach had to be taken in order to control and subdue the masses. This support further parallels European fascism, which was originally supported by much of the aristocracy as a method of retaining its power.

The new government, in actions that set the precedent for many others that occurred during the period 1966–1989, proscribed various political parties, banned several newspapers, and arrested many competing leaders. While all of this was occurring, however, internal dissension grew within the ruling GOU, dissension that allowed Perón to augment and to consolidate his power. He was first appointed as the undersecretary of war. Soon thereafter, however, he was put in charge of the central task of gaining control over organized workers as the secretary of labor. It was clear at this point that Perón was an emerging focal point of power.

Perón realized the potential for immense political support among the thus far excluded masses. His strategy for gaining power, moreover, could be rendered all the more acceptable to the powerful classes, which could interpret his actions as geared towards deactivating the socialist and anarchist threat. The labor secretary actively supported sympathetic unions with favorable mediation and fat contracts while repressing the radical or independent-minded unions that did not fall into line. Through a series of political maneuvers, Perón tried to force some sort of unity among the many unions. First, a law was passed that paved the way for single union representation in each industry; whereas in the past, several unions could compete for the support of metal-workers, for example, these unions were slowly consolidated into one. Similarly, Perón tried to further the vertical organization and unity of the various industry unions by forcing them to act together through the newly formed Confederación General de Trabajo (CGT); for example, Perón would often call for patriotic rallies that even the most independent-minded union leaders were hard pressed to resist.

Many within the military were fearful that the newly emerging Peronist movement would go too far, particularly as it seemed that Perón was poised to win the upcoming election slated for 1946. On 9 October 1945, Juan Perón was arrested. However, Peronism had already grown too powerful to be so easily controlled. Perón's supporters called strikes and filled the central Plaza de Mayo demanding their leader's release. The military, fearful of unrest, relented. Perón's election and subsequent accession to the presidency were all but assured.

The new president redoubled his efforts to further his control among the working classes. Rural workers were encouraged to migrate to the cities where they could be more easily organized. An alliance was forged with the national bourgeoisie which, although still weak, accounted for a greater percentage of gross national product (GNP) than agriculture.[6] The traditional populist coalition of the bourgeoisie and the workers both profited as the new president increased wages by 25 percent in 1947 and a further 24 percent in 1948. This was feasible during easy import substitution when increased wages translated into increased demand for locally produced goods. In sum, both groups could simultaneously profit despite inherent tensions between labor and capital; workers profit from the wages and industrialists profit from rapidly expanding demand. This profit comes at the cost of other sectors, however, most notably in Argentina at the cost of agriculture. In one stroke, Perón was able to solve (temporarily) both of the problems of the liberal phase—and he profited handsomely in the political sphere.

Just as the populist economics came at the cost of certain groups and, even more notable, at the cost of future economic well-being, Perón gained political power at an immeasurable political cost to the future of the country. Perón succeeded in splitting Argentine society in half. One group supported Perón. The other would do anything possible to ensure that neither Perón nor any Peronist successor would ever come to power. Argentina was divided into the Peronists and the anti-Peronists. This fracture caused great difficulty in the years immediately following Perón's overthrow, as will be seen below.

It is worth noting, however, that in other ways Perón's presidency, particularly during the latter years, foreshadowed events to occur from 1966 to 1989 and began trends that only grew in magnitude. State policy became associated with economic largesse. Upon assuming the presidency, Perón found Argentina's coffers full from the profitable war-time agricultural sales; this money was lavishly spent on new government jobs, higher wages, military projects, and public contracts that went well beyond even other populist experiments. Moreover, although some populist platforms were actually based on the belief that such policies were the best for encouraging development, this "economic" policy was clearly based on gaining political support. Perón's economic advisers explained that he would later have economic problems, but this did not seem to daunt him in his constant quest for immediate popularity and support. Indeed, economic problems haunted Perón from 1954 onward when he had to implement austerity measures sponsored by the International Monetary Fund (IMF). This was the first time the government knowingly effected bad economic policy in an attempt to gain support. It hoped, of course, that the disaster would strike some distant future government.

Regarding political repression as well, the Perón government surpassed all precedents. Repression of dissidents and adversarial political leaders grew greatly. Workers who did not offer allegiance to the government could be "roughed-up" or fired. The government was quick to censor oppositional newspapers and emit rosy propaganda in the place of the critical articles that had been erased. Intervention in the universities began in earnest for the first time, and packing the judicial system developed into a political art.

By the time Perón had to implement austerity measures, he had lost much of his support. The parts of the old elite class that had supported him as a necessary evil to control worker radicalism had long since abandoned the Peronist bandwagon. The national bourgeoisie grew disenchanted with the recessionary economic policy and the associated increase in foreign penetration of the economy. On the political side, anti-Peronists were eager to exact revenge on the populist leader. Moreover, Perón's highly charismatic wife and political partner, Eva "Evita" Duarte de Perón, died, hence eliminating a source of sympathy and support. As would occur in many of the governments under scrutiny, the president became increasingly radical in his policies and programs so as to mobilize support; for example, Perón challenged the Catholic Church, a very important and large anti-Peronist institution, first by legalizing divorce, and then by fostering a greater division between state and church. As would prove to be the case in later governments as well, however, attempts to mobilize and activate widespread support when the governments' legitimacy began to wane only precipitated and exacerbated the crisis.[7] In September 1955, Perón's fellow military officers offered the president an ultimatum, in effect demanding his resignation, the alternative to which, they made clear, would be civil war. Perón sailed off to Paraguay to begin his eighteen years of exile.

Perón left a radically altered country behind him, however. The incorporation of Argentine society had been completed. The working masses were almost unanimously organized into the union structure. At the same time, the national bourgeoisie's position in the economy and political power had been solidified.

It would be misleading, however, to think that this new political structure was stable. Society had largely been fractured into halves, one favoring and one opposing Perón; this, as will be discussed in the next section, clearly limited political alternatives. Moreover, the state's relationship with several key interest groups remained unclear; in other words, the corporatist structure (to be discussed below) of the nation was at best only partially complete. Labor unions, for example, were largely dependent on the state's actions. However,

> The government's domination over the CGT, though great, was never as complete as Perón would have liked, despite his best efforts to assure it. It is no secret that he had to intervene many times to terminate unauthorized strikes by locals, whose leaders took it upon themselves to improve salaries and working conditions.[8]

Similarly, Perón never progressed much beyond using the relatively blunt instruments of fiscal, monetary, and exchange rate policies to affect the behaviors of the other economic groups. The nebulousness and divisiveness implicit in these circumstances were amplified during the following years of political impasse.

The Political Impasse Period

The political impasse period was ushered in with the military coup against Perón in 1955. The fundamental trait of the whole period (1955–1966) was the inability of all the administrations to find a stable political formula due to the schism Perón created within Argentina. Given the great animosities he fomented, Perón would not be able to return and lead a new government for many years. Without his support, however, no government could count on gaining a widespread base of support. The division of Argentine society into two fairly equal groups, both of which held to their views with passion, meant no political equation allowed for a solid majority.

An alternative would have been to promote a Peronistlike populist movement under another's leadership. Such a solution could have fostered greater consensus around policies similar to Perón's. Due to his attacks on the church, his disregard for political opposition, his inefficient and corrupt government, and his desire to concentrate power in his own hands, many opposed Peronism more because of its leader than because of its content; in other words, for many the populist approach to Argentine politics and economics was not the problem so much as Perón himself. Such an alternative was not then feasible. For the years following Perón's overthrow, the general retained a very committed and large base of support that was completely unwilling to replace its leader; Perón's mystique, powerful even today, was far too great. Indeed, various attempts by several Radical presidents during this period to win over Peronist support failed. As will be seen in Chapter 3, even when Perón himself finally returned to impose his policies once again, he failed. With the passing of easy import substitution, populism itself became infeasible as the tensions between the bourgeoisie and the workers grew too strong. In any case, Perón, clearly a power broker, was effectively blocked from retaining national power in an open and stable way.

Moreover, the military was still unwilling to rule the country during the impasse period. Certainly, military coups had been common and continued throughout the political impasse period. The coups, however, served more as a veto than anything else; the military overthrew a government when the officers (always with varying degrees of support from civilian leaders) felt that the economic and, more important, political objectives and results of the government were harmful to the nation. On a practical level, this almost always meant moves towards reintegrating the Peronists. The goals of the coup leaders, unlike in the subsequent period, were never to take direct control of the government apparatus. The military thus far was unwilling to propose and implement policies, contenting itself with the (often used) ability to veto those of others; the military as a power broker refused even to attempt to choose and to implement policies.

These factors resulted in frequent regime changes, all of which occurred with major limitations on the Peronist voice. A certain pattern set in. Elections would be held in which the Peronists would be proscribed. A faction of the Radical Party would win with a plurality of 20 to 25 percent of the vote (Perón would always order his followers to cast blank ballots, which would typically account for approximately 40 percent of the vote). The new government, in planning for the next series of elections, could either attempt to consolidate the anti-Peronist vote or else try to gain Peronist support generally by legalizing some Peronist political parties and organizations.

Both alternatives were doomed: The former was blocked by other parties that refused subordination, the latter by losing the original anti-Peronist vote or, more frequently, by military coup geared toward continuing Peronist political exclusion. This repeated series of events is now referred to as "the impossible game."[9] The volatility was purposefully augmented by the exiled but still popular and powerful Perón as he battled against his opponents; he did his best to ensure that no government was successful in order to further his hopes of once again returning to power. In essence, the period was marked by rapid changes in government and lack of stability and continuity. Moreover, a legitimacy problem was developing as neither fixed elections nor furtive coups could gain the acceptance, much less support, of Argentine civil society.

The situation was made even more unmanageable and more mercurial because of the economic situation. It became more and more obvious that Argentina had come to a crossroads in its economic development. The incorporation period occurred during progressive phases of import substitution—industrialization, the driving force behind the incorporation of the middle and working classes, was promoted through encouraging the national production of previously imported products. The first stages of import substitution, the so-called easy import substitution, lead to national production of consumer products that do not generally require high levels of technology. This was the key to populism not only in Argentina but throughout Latin America, as higher wages promoted greater consumer demand (for domestically produced consumer goods), hence allowing a meeting of the industrialists' and workers' interests. Now that easy import substitution had been exhausted, however, a new economic plan was necessary for further development or "deepening."

As the economy was still dependent on foreign capital goods and technology, imports were essential. Yet the traditional agricultural exports were being starved off by increasing domestic demand and government neglect, if not outright abuse, of this sector. Under these circumstances, the whole period was marked by rapid increases in GNP growth, followed by foreign sector difficulties, and finally by austerity measures. A "stop-and-go" cycle was clearly visible during these eleven years.[10]

President Arturo Frondizi (1958–1962) made the most serious commitment to resolving the economic quagmire. His period in government, quite atypical for the impasse period, was marked by fast growth and large-scale modernization of the economy. It was during Frondizi's reign that tremendous foreign capital was attracted and new forms of industrialization manifested themselves (the manufacture of automobiles, for example). New economic ventures, such as the first serious attempt to tap efficiently Argentina's large oil reserves, also began during this period. Indeed, Frondizi oversaw a deepening of import substitution and increased flows of investment.

Critically, however, Frondizi was unable to resolve the underlying political impasse. The president's party, Unión Civica Radical Intransigente (UCRI), was, as can be seen from its name, a split-off faction of the Radical Party. Although elected by a commanding plurality for this period (45 percent of the popular vote[11]), the UCRI faced the same limitations posed by "the impossible game." Frondizi attempted to secure reelection by gradually legalizing the Peronist party, and, it was hoped, integrating many of these Peronists into his own ranks. Particularly with Perón agitating from abroad, it was still impossible for this integration to occur without government policy taking on an overly Peronist appearance. Frondizi, as was predictable according to the rules of the times, was overthrown by a military coup towards the end of 1962. This failure subsequently overflowed into the economic field, reversing many of the gains made during these years. The stop-and-go cycle was not eliminated in the Argentine economy during Frondizi's four-year presidency.

The impasse period caused significant and permanent changes in the political sphere, however. Most important was the decoupling of corporatist entities from particular political representatives. This decoupling was gradual, but seems to have been completed, or nearly so, by 1966. The best example was the notable and growing independence of the union movement vis-à-vis the Peronist political structure. Whereas during Perón's presidency the unions were vertically linked to his political apparatus (albeit tenuously so, as explained above), the unions grew astute and adept at defending their own interests during Perón's eighteen years of exile. No longer was it impossible for other political groups to gain support (although generally ephemeral) from the CGT. After so many years of exile, union rank-and-file as well as leaders began to see little value in hoping and agitating for Perón's return— there were easier and more efficient methods of improving work conditions and pay by pressuring other political groups that rotated in power, that is, the Radical Party and the various factions within the military. In sum, unions would bargain for better treatment by offering support for the government, support that was fundamentally conditional as it depended on continued "payment" in the form of economic advantages.

The other pressure groups acted in a similar fashion. The national bourgeoisie solidified its contacts with the military and the other political parties. The old agricultural elite was thus no longer able to depend on the military for either unswerving, daily support or for taking the reins of government, so it was forced to search for other representatives. Foreign business groups, traditionally associated with the agricultural elite, found new champions in men like Frondizi. All of these groups would also offer conditional support to different governments. The transitory quality of the support throughout this period translated into recurring legitimacy crises for the governments. As a reaction, the various political groups, including the military, sought out contacts and sympathies among the pressure groups so as to gain legitimacy and therefore political power. This problem was also to plague the corporatist breakdown period that is the focus of this study.

If legitimacy was the fundamental problem that the Onganía, Perón, Videla, and Alfonsín governments faced, why were they unable to solve the problem? What were the structural impediments to the formation of a solution? The answer lies in corporatism.

Corporatist Theory

Corporatism is a method of representation through unique or "noncompetitive" organizations, each of which corresponds to a specific and definable interest group. A central aspect of corporatism is that the corporatist entities represent as a single unit all actors with similar roles in the economy or in society. Philippe C. Schmitter offers a more precise definition of corporatism

> as a system of interest representation in which the constituent units are organized into a limited number of singular, compulsory, noncompetitive, hierarchically ordered and functionally differentiated categories, recognized or licensed (if not created) by the state and granted a deliberate representational monopoly within their respective categories in exchange for observing certain controls on their selection of leaders and articulation of demands and supports.[12]

Implicit in corporatism is the fact that communication between the corporatist entities and the government is direct. In other words, the corporatist entities pursue their goals through contacts with the government, which, similarly, transmits its policy goals directly to the corporatist entities. Howard Wiarda offers a method of visualizing this structure in Figure 1.1.

These contacts can be and often are institutional; they need not be, however. Often corporatist entities are able to communicate their desires and concerns through social functions where various elites meet, through the media, and, in the extreme, through active resistance such as strikes on the part of unions. Indeed, it is important to keep in mind the fact that relations between the entities and the government have always been largely "behind the scenes" in Argentina; this in no way alters the validity of the fundamental corporatist nature of the political structure. The corporatist structure had been forcibly created with the structure of the economy as all the economic actors within a particular group were fundamentally affected in a similar way by government policies. When one actor from this group communicated with the government, he spoke for all those in his group. Many institutions, official and merely social, allowed these economic actors to converse and prepare a united front; in the extreme, the media itself was enough of a means to foster a cohesion. The fundamental result of this cohesion was the ability to

Figure 1.1   Structure of Corporatist Entities

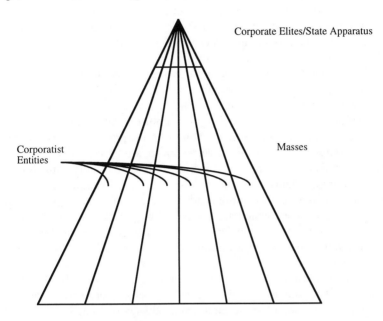

Source: Howard Wiarda, *Corporatism and National Development in Latin America*, Westview Press, Boulder, 1981, p. 36. Reprinted with permission.

mobilize the members of the economic group to support or oppose certain policies. The ability to mobilize in a controlled and planned manner identifiable individuals with common interests rests at the base of corporatism—the processes of communication, both between the government and the groups and among the members of a group, are largely irrelevant. As will be abundantly evidenced, Argentine corporatism was alive and well during the period studied as all of the primary corporatist entities were quite willing and able to mobilize their rank and file.

Corporatist theory assumes that there are two types of actors in political society. First, of course, are the corporatist entities. Second is the authority, generally in control of the state, that acts as a mediator between the various groups—this authority is referred to as the "power broker" in this book. The functioning of a corporatist state depends on the ability of the power broker to decide upon a course of action (one that, needless to say, is economically viable) and then to impose this direction on the various corporatist entities. The state fosters obedience on the part of the corporatist entities through some combination of "inducements" and "constraints."[13] Inducements are generally based on economic advantages—on the redistribution of national income in favor of particular corporatist entities, for example, by higher profit margins or wages. Constraints are far more varied and can include the elimination of financial resources (union dues, for example), revocation of legal status, and, in more extreme cases, physical violence or jailings. It is worth noting that the mixture of inducements and constraints can define the type of corporatism.[14]

The concepts of inducements and constraints lead us to an essential conclusion: All actors of a particular economic group (leaving aside, for reasons that will become obvious, entities not based upon economic agglomerations) are affected similarly—in both outcome and degree—by particular sets of government policies. Moreover, the prominence and returns of economic actors, from workers to corporations, are far more dependent on government policy, or macroeconomics, than on the particular situation of the firm, or microeconomics. As will be seen, for example, the profit margins of the agricultural sector depend far more on the exchange rate and particular (export) taxes, which are controlled by the government, than on investment levels. Given a particular set of economic conditions and policies, it is immediately clear which economic groups will profit and which will lose.

The similar economic situation confronting groups of easily identified and categorized economic actors necessarily creates a corporatist structure as the mutual interests of these actors will always outweigh the mutual interests of any of these actors with an actor of another group. In the same manner, differences in economic well-being among the individual actors due to investment levels and choices will always be minimal compared to differences in income resulting from policy changes. Given these factors, the individual actors will act as a cohesive and easily mobilizable group. The economic structure inevitably results in the formation of corporatist groups. This formation is essential for understanding the durability of the corporatist structure as well as the failure of all of the economic and political programs attempted throughout the years studied.

With the unavoidable cohesion of corporatist entities in mind, it is easier to comprehend many of the other anomalies of corporatism in Argentina. It becomes clearer how the corporatist structure influenced and endured the various governments despite the nebulousness of links between the groups and the state. These links were rendered obscure by various occurrences to be discussed in later chapters, occurrences that included government interventions into many of the corporatist institutions and mergers of institutions that represented different groups. Despite such circumstances, the corporatist groups were able to continue to pressure the governments and to act in decided and cohesive fashion. It would always be clear to the various presidents and ministers of economics which individuals, companies, or institutions represented each entity.

Needless to say, as the economic actors have fewer interests in common with the other actors of their corporatist entity, and as individual actors become less easily identifiable as pertaining to any particular entity, the corporatist structure breaks down. As will be seen in the following chapters, this breakdown occurred gradually during the period studied. The corporatist structure under Onganía, at the very beginning of the period studied, was much sharper and more explicit than it was under Alfonsín, the last government to suffer from this structural quagmire. Indeed, the culmination of the period resulted in a new type of structure under Carlos Saúl Menem, which will be discussed later as a contrast; by 1989, the Argentine Paradox had been resolved.

It should not be forgotten that the relationship between power broker and entity is symbiotic; just as the government attempts to encourage certain comportments on the part of various groups of economic actors through inducements and constraints, the corporatist entities try to persuade or, at times, to force the government to adopt certain outlooks. On the simplest level this occurs through lobbying and propaganda, but often digresses to more forceful and raw processes such as general strikes or refusal to invest in the economy. The dialogue between each entity and the state can be viewed as a negotiation in which each has particular goals and depends on the acquiescence if not outright support of the other.

The idea of negotiation begs a question regarding what relation of power exists between the power broker and the various corporatist entities. Clearly, there is a reciprocal dependence between the two; in other words, autonomy should be viewed as a relative concept within a corporatist framework. A continuum exists, one extreme of which represents state dominance, the other of which represents the ascendance of the corporatist entities; clearly, the equilibrium varies over time and with circumstances. The following chapters will show that the commencement of each government represented a period of relative ascendance of the state over the entities, an ascendance that inevitably reversed by the end of the regime. It is less clear whether the relationship was fundamentally different among the various governments as compared to that within the same government. It might be more apt to say that the corporatist structure merely collapsed at the end by 1989, not that it had evolved. All of a sudden, Menem's government was in a structurally more powerful situation.

Corporatism is nothing more nor anything less than a system of governing, however. Just as with any other system, if implemented correctly, it can work. Why, then, was the 1966–1989 period in Argentina a case of failed rather than functioning corporatism? The answer to this question lies in the relationship between and individual characteristics of Argentina's power brokers and corporatist entities. An analysis of the organizations is now essential.

The Corporatist Entities

Corporatist theory suggests that most interest groups can be amalgamated into a corporatist entity, ranging from labor unions to the Catholic Church. Indeed, Argentina has a wide array of corporatist entities that arguably includes the church, student unions, and legal associations. However, this study will concentrate on four "primary" corporatist entities, which cumulatively represent most economic actors: agriculture, labor unions, the national bourgeoisie, and the international bourgeoisie. The other corporatist entities will be referred to only occasionally. However, the reader familiar with Argentine history should realize in the following chapters that the actions and dispositions of the "secondary" corporatist entities reinforce the results caused by the primary ones. The same course of events analyzed here for the primary entities could be attributed to and modeled for all corporatist entities in a more complete—but complex—study of which political economy were just a single theme. For the purpose of this work, it is less important to understand these corporatist entities' precise outlooks and actions than to realize that they further compromise stability and legitimacy.

It is tricky to determine exactly which official organizations represented each of the corporatist entities due to many of the anomalies discussed in the previous section. Often, there was more than one representative for the entity. Sometimes affiliates of the larger entities took on more importance than the ostensible leader group, complicating the task of deciding which body really represented the corporatist group. The metal-workers union, for example, had at times led the Confederación General de Trabajo (of which it is a member) more than it has followed it. At times, distinct factions within a single organization represented different interests. All the same, the primary corporatist entities were traditionally and fundamentally represented by particular organizations: agriculture by the Sociedad Rural Argentina (SRA), labor unions by the Confederación General de Trabajo (CGT), the national bourgeoisie by the Confederación General Económica (CGE), and the international bourgeoisie by the Unión Industrial Argentina (UIA). For the sake of this work, these organizations will be referred to as the proper representatives of the respective corporatist groups.

All of these corporatist entities shared several key characteristics. Most important among them is the fact that all of these primary corporatist entities were extremely powerful. In essence, each of the four entities had by 1966 refined methods of defending its self-interests in the face of opposition. Of central importance is the fact that each corporatist entity had developed a different method of self-defense; no common institutions, market places, or forums were used—quite the contrary, each entity fought its battles on completely different turfs. One observer of Argentina has explained that each of these groups had a particular and unique "political currency."[15] For example, unions utilized general strikes, whereas the agricultural elite withheld their products. This situation compares to praetorianist conditions, which developed toward the end of each regime studied, where "no agreement exists among the groups as to the legitimate and authoritative methods for resolving conflicts."[16]

A major reason for the efficacy of the corporatist entities' resistance lies in their mobilizing abilities. The individual firms and people these entities represent depend on the larger amalgamations for their standards of living; therefore, these individual actors are willing and even eager to do everything possible to ensure the success of the corporatist entities' strategies. Further, the corporatist entities are well-organized associations that are always actively monitoring, if nothing else, government activity. In sum, the power of the corporatist entities is enhanced by their mobilizing capabilities. A formula can be offered:

$$\text{Power of Corporatist Entity} = \text{Power of Followers} \times \text{Mobilizing Capabilities}$$

It must be noted that the power of the corporatist entities rested in destructive rather than constructive means; in other words, the power of the corporatist entities rested primarily in a threat to disrupt the economy. Few options existed between lobbying a government and actively subverting official policy and national stability. A consequence of this is the fact that the corporatist entities could easily resist and destroy economic policies but could only with great difficulty encourage a chosen or potential course of action. The cost of imposing or opposing policy is the same, but the advantages of pressuring for advantages are far greater than those resulting from blocking redistribution to other corporatist entities. Any proposed redistribution, it is assumed, is paid for by the other three corporatist entities. The advantage to the "winning" group can therefore be denoted as "x," whereas the resultant cost to each of the other entities is only x/3. Clearly, it is more efficient to pressure for a counteracting policy instead of opposing redistribution to another group. The result, as will be seen, is a "Nash sub-equilibrium."[17]

Redistributional demands both result from and largely cause the immense power of the corporatist entities. The distribution of national income in Argentina has had exceptionally wide fluctuations, which are generally caused by government policy. The manipulation of a few central prices by the government can and has caused tremendous variations in income. By altering the exchange rate, wages, or agricultural prices, all traditionally controlled by the Argentine government, certain sectors can immediately and decisively benefit at the cost of others. On the one hand, the corporatist entities have been able to mobilize membership more easily because of the costs involved in losing a political battle. At the same time, the proven power of the corporatist entities has reinforced the demands of the rank and file.

A complete absence of agreement regarding the "correct" distribution of income resulted in a complete lack of a "traditional" or baseline distribution. Each corporatist entity would, quite obviously, accept the most favorable conditions for its group as the "correct" distribution. The result was an enormous shortfall between the expenditure demanded of and the receipts received by the government; one analyst has analyzed this deficit and named it the "potential" budget gap.[18] In a corporatist framework, the type and amount of power held by the entities in conjunction with the tradition of redistribution on the part of the state resulted in a type of corporatism based more on inducements than on constraints.[19] A shift from one to the other would inevitably prove to be quite difficult.

The distributional claims resulted in the politicization of the corporatist entities; each sought to win favor with all of the power brokers in order to promote its political program. The politicization results from the redistributional desires of the entities combined with the fact that they were "de-linked" from any single political power. In other words, to promote their policies best, the corporatist entities sought to convince all political power brokers of the justice and economic value of their views. During the impasse period of Argentine history, most vertical connections between entities (labor unions, for example) and their corresponding political representatives (the Peronist Party) were destroyed. After eleven years of fending for its interests without these links, each corporatist entity had developed contacts with all of the pertinent power brokers. Within each power broker, in turn, there were factions that were sympathetic to each of the corporatist entities.

One final characteristic arises out of these others: The relatively low importance of economic investment (defined as promoting economic returns through the creation of wealth) as compared to political influence (defined as promoting economic returns through the redistribution of income). Capital investment and the promotion of economic growth are decidedly secondary to attempting to affect and to discern decisions regarding economic redistribution. The reasons for this should be clear from the above discussion: (1) the returns from investment are quite small compared to the returns from successfully lobbying for redistribution and (2) any investments are very risky, given the political insecurities. More technically, the expected return of an investment is equal to the value of the investment, assuming it is successful, multiplied by the probability of its success. In Argentina, this last factor is far lower and harder to predict due to the political situation; hence, the expected return is reduced. This reduction results in lower rates of investment. Juan Carlos de Pablo explains the situation as it confronts the typical executive:

> The CEO of the Argentine firm is so busy that he has no time to . . . work. It should be emphasized that this allocation of executive time and creativeness is absolutely rational from the private profit maximization

point of view. The CEO knows that the feasible increase in private profits that comes out of technological improvements, or cost reducing efforts, is far smaller than the increase that arises from knowing better, or knowing before, what the next move of the government is going to be and to act accordingly.[20]

On a concrete level, this meant that wage increases were never linked to productivity increases in Argentina; for similar reasons, the Ford Motor Company had not made the requisite investment in over two decades to update its standard model, the Falcon, a car originally designed in the sixties.

The only way to overcome this aversion to investment in the longer term is by simultaneously effecting policies that will increase the economic returns of investment while assuring a stable and predictable policy for an extended period of time so that the real and perceived risks will be lowered. In the shorter term, as will be seen, constraints must be juxtaposed with inducements, always within the general context of stability. The political stability is particularly important as stable political rules reduce the potential returns—and losses—of influencing or anticipating policy. In other words, the state must at the same time effect a partnership with the bourgeoisie while retaining a certain independence from it so as to avoid being pressured into increasing the bourgeoisie's profits solely through policy changes.

The central point during the period studied, however, is that while the excluded groups immediately lower investment, the favored groups will increase investment only after a significant time lag, given that, as shown in the following chapters, the government could never effectively implement constraints. Before the inducement-based policy will become effective, economic actors must first feel assured of the stability of the changes, a sentiment that can only come with the extended implementation of and support for the policy. All of this is to say that redistribution of income through increasing the profit margins of some groups results in increased resistance to policy (from the excluded groups) but not—in the short term— in increased investment rates even among the favored groups. Increasing profit margins results at first only in an economic transfer and not in increased fundamental economic activity (as defined by potential and not actual GNP). The specific manifestations of each of the above characteristics are clearly visible in each of the primary corporatist entities.

La Sociedad Rural Argentina

La Sociedad Rural Argentina, founded in 1866, is the oldest of the corporatist entities. Throughout the liberal period, the SRA was associated with the highest Argentine classes, the derogatorily named "oligarquía" (oligarchy). Its membership was limited to only 2,500 of the wealthiest owners of Argentina's best agricultural land, the pampas. Clearly, until well into the 1930s, the SRA was a central point of power in Argentina, having provided, for example, half of the cabinet ministers between 1910 and 1943.[21] Throughout this period, agriculture's interests pervaded both the conservative parties as well as the still largely aristocratic armed services.

Over the years, the SRA has remained the most cohesive of the corporatist entities, although it is not nearly so exclusive as it once was. As should be clear in later chapters, however, the SRA has no longer been able to rely on military support for its policies, a fact that has forced this corporatist entity, as the others, to lobby all power brokers. The agricultural sector's power has undeniably declined since the turn of the century as industrialization has progressed and as new classes have been incorporated into Argentine society. The lack of long-term stimuli to invest in Argentina over the past decades is very clearly visible in this sector as the pampas have significantly lower yields than comparable properties in countries such as the United States or Australia. It must be mentioned, however, that this sector was particularly discriminated against during the incorporation period and during Perón's government.

The SRA has very powerful defense strategies, however, that have proven quite effective in destabilizing unfriendly governments. This group's power centers around its ability to withhold products from the market. By withholding agricultural products from the national markets, the SRA can have an immediate and significant effect on the Argentine rate of inflation. Meat production, in particular, plays a central role in this technique, as up to 40 percent of the basket of goods on which the consumer price index is calculated has been accounted for by meat prices. Moreover, the agricultural bourgeoisie has a large degree of discretion regarding when to slaughter herds, particularly as compared to the discretion allowed in bringing perishable agricultural products to market. These factors have largely driven the increasing importance of herd breeding within the agricultural group.

Agriculture is still considered the "traditional" export and accounts for significant foreign currency earnings. Due to this, the SRA can further pressure government either by refusing to export (bring their products to foreign markets) or else by refusing to exchange their foreign currency holdings into Argentine currency. Either of these actions can put tremendous pressure on the exchange rate, which, in turn, is central to inflation and hence to all economic plans. By withholding herds for even one or two months, immense economic damage can be wreaked and therefore political pressure imposed.

The policy goals of the SRA are relatively predictable. The SRA favors high agricultural prices and a low exchange rate as methods to effect a favorable income distribution for this group.[22] Clearly, the SRA is vehemently against the export taxes—taxes that are quite similar to duties but levied on exports rather than imports—often imposed on the agricultural sector starting with Perón's presidency. Wages should also be high so as to stimulate internal demand. On a structural level, the agricultural sector has always been eager for an open economy so as to profit more easily from its international comparative advantage. Finally, the SRA is in favor of minimal government intervention in the national affairs that, for the most part, do not benefit the agricultural sector; indeed, it was generally the SRA that, through export taxes on agricultural products, subsidized such policies that benefited the other corporatist entities.

La Confederación General de Trabajo

La Confederación General de Trabajo, on the other hand, favors policies almost diametrically opposed to those favored by the SRA. The CGT, obviously, favors high wages but disagrees with the SRA on all other counts. The typical workers' standard of living is augmented with cheaper prices. This is effected through a high exchange rate that renders not only imports relatively cheaper, but also foodstuffs (which are based on world prices in dollars).[23] Moreover, on a structural level the CGT favors a closed economy (so that jobs cannot be lost to overseas competition) and widespread government intervention, which benefits workers both directly (through pensions and other transfers) and indirectly (through government contracts, which, in turn, spur demand for labor).

The history of the CGT is also quite distinct from that of the SRA. The former came into existence only in the 1940s during Perón's rise to power. Clearly, its origins are closely linked to the populist movement, as are its goals. Throughout Perón's period in power as well as in subsequent years, the CGT's power grew tremendously. Membership increased from a small unionized base to include nearly all workers in all industries. This trend was strengthened by the growth in the number of jobs in industry, the traditional domain of unions. By controlling union dues and many of the social benefit programs, this organization has also become extremely wealthy.

This innate power has been used to create a well-organized and cohesive corporatist entity with the central ability to mobilize and to finance strikes. Strikes, often in conjunction with factory takeovers, have developed into the prime method of defense for the CGT, and one that is highly effective given that a general strike almost closes down the country. Short of the general strike, the CGT can pressure governments with its control of financial resources and its immense membership that can be called upon for anything from rallies to posting political announcements.

La Confederación General Económica

La Confederación General Económica shares many objectives with the CGT; indeed, it was an alliance between these two groups that formed the backbone of populism. The CGT is in favor of low agricultural prices, implicitly subsidizing the cost of workers, and a high exchange rate, reducing the cost of imported capital- and intermediate goods on which the national bourgeoisie is highly dependent. The CGE also agrees with the unions regarding the structure of the economy: extensive pump-priming intervention on the part of the government increases national demand, and a closed market protects national producers from foreign products. Of course, the CGE and CGT diverge when it comes to wages—the national bourgeoisie supports lower wages.

The general concord of the CGE and the CGT mirrors their similar histories. The CGE was founded during Perón's first presidency. The group became closely associated with Perón and his populist policies: "We were never officially Peronist, but the distinction was at times hard to make. This contrasts with the great plurality of political views now present in the CGE."[24] In other words, as with the CGT, this organization has become "de-linked" from its largely Peronist origins.

As might be expected, the national bourgeoisie defends itself by increasing prices on its products or, if necessary, withholding the products. In this manner, economic bottlenecks and inflationary pressures begin to plague the economy quite quickly. It should be noted that this method has proven highly effective despite various attempts at price controls—when normal markets are regulated, products "disappear," only to be sold on the black market. Moreover, through control of the demand for labor, and hence the unemployment rate, the CGE had often been able to assure its relative prosperity. On a purely political level, the national bourgeoisie had, during the period studied, a powerful rallying call in claiming that its well-being is essential to prevent the denationalization of Argentine industry. Such an appeal resonates with the unions (fearful of losing jobs) and groups (including the military as well as the Peronist and Radical parties) that had felt nationally controlled industry was central for self-defense and economic and political independence.

La Unión Industrial Argentina

The final group is here termed the *international bourgeoisie*. In reality, this group has been far more motley than the name implies, including not only the international sectors (mainly subsidiaries of multinationals), but also the financial sectors (both national and international), international organizations such as the IMF, and the sectors of the national bourgeoisie that are either internationally competitive (parts of the steel-tube industry, for example) or are natural monopolies. All of these sectors share financial stability and economic strength and flourish when integrated with the world economy. Similarly, the international bourgeoisie favors minimal government activity on the domestic front. In yet another similarity with the SRA, this group also favors a low exchange rate. However, the international sectors diverge from the free-market–oriented SRA in favoring low wages and low agricultural prices (further subsidizing labor costs).

Given the diversity of the international bourgeoisie, there are many structures and methods that are used for pressuring government. The Unión Industrial Argentina has been the primary pressure vehicle (and will be referred to in this work as referring to the whole of this group), although there have been other corporatist organizations that are generally used for the most basic level of lobbying the government. However,

> if government policy is unacceptable for a prolonged period of time, lobbying gives way to a wider political battle in which there are many ways to fight. These can include involving, for example, foreign embassies in Argentina, international credit organizations both public and private, and even world opinion.[25]

The UIA was rendered even more powerful because of its sheer importance within the Argentine economy. Many of the most advanced and the most stable companies have traditionally been subsidiaries of foreign industries. More important, any significant deepening of the economic base and export-oriented development strategies require the active participation of this group.

Potential Alliances Between Corporatist Entities

Figure 1.2 offers a visualization of the corporatist entities and their salient characteristics. The potential alliances between any two of the corporatist entities are denoted by the connecting lines. The criterion is the convergence of interests as determined by common economic goals, either of two of the three short-term goals (exchange rate, wages, and agricultural prices) or of one short-term goal and both long-term ones. Such a convergence seems theoretically logical; more important, however, is the existence of empirical evidence of such alliances. Each of the three alliances was attempted during the period studied, and each failed.

The failure of each of the attempted alliances raises many questions. Why didn't the alliances work? To what extent did tensions grow between the colluding interests? In sum, why did these alliances remain potential instead of becoming fully consummated? These questions will all be addressed in the subsequent chapters. A conclusion that will be discussed after the case studies is worth flagging now, however: One of the central reasons for the breakdown of corporatism, that is to say the passing of the structural impediments blocking political and economic development, is the fact that all potential alliances resulted in failure. The breakdown of these alliances proved highly costly to both of the colluding parties as well as to the country as a whole. It might be said that each of the corporatist groups had grown mistrustful of its potential partners, hence impeding the reformation of these alliances. Yet no other alliances are possible. Within the corporatist

Figure 1.2   Characteristics of Corporatist Entities

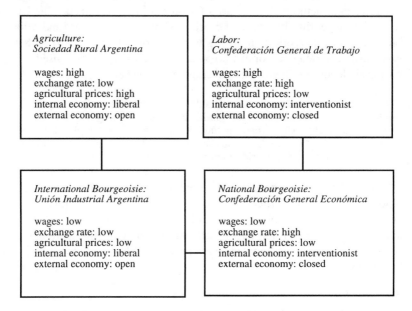

Agriculture:
Sociedad Rural Argentina

wages: high
exchange rate: low
agricultural prices: high
internal economy: liberal
external economy: open

Labor:
Confederación General de Trabajo

wages: high
exchange rate: high
agricultural prices: low
internal economy: interventionist
external economy: closed

International Bourgeoisie:
Unión Industrial Argentina

wages: low
exchange rate: low
agricultural prices: low
internal economy: liberal
external economy: open

National Bourgeoisie:
Confederación General Económica

wages: low
exchange rate: high
agricultural prices: low
internal economy: interventionist
external economy: closed

Note: Lines denote possible alliances.

framework, as should become obvious, an alliance is necessary not only to bring a power broker to government but also to render an economic strategy feasible. Now that these alliances can no longer occur, the very corporatist structure has broken down.

It is essential to note further that all of the possible alliances are at least partially based on the redistribution of income through the manipulation of some combination of the exchange rate, wages, and agricultural prices. Fixing these rates, however, costs the government resources. Moreover, the state also played a more direct role in the redistribution of income through tax changes, state contracts, and benefit programs. The necessary prerequisite for this redistribution is the existence of something to redistribute; in other words, some source of funding must be found in order to be able to implement these policies. In part, the resources for the favored corporatist entities have come from the excluded ones; a clear example is the implicit redistribution of income from workers to industrialists through lowering wages. However, as will be demonstrated, the corporatist system was dependent on the state finding other, more explicit sources of revenues. These funds were needed for everything from paying for subsidies to buying dollars in order to stabilize the exchange rate.

The sources have been varied: from explicit taxes on certain sectors (such as agriculture under Onganía), to domestic savings in bank accounts that yielded negative real interest rates under Perón, to foreign debt under Videla, to simply printing money under Alfonsín. A second conclusion relating to the breakdown of corporatism is the fact that such sources of funds no longer exist. Each of the governments spent resources. By the end of the process, however, all sources of funds were cut off. The gradual impoverishment of the economic groups in conjunction with their abilities to defend their interests blocked direct appropriation from certain sectors. Inflation, used by almost all of the governments, became so exacerbated that individuals first would no longer accept negative interest rates and then would no longer be willing to hold local currency—local capital no longer exists, and any rapid increases in the money supply (using the printing press) will result only in hyperinflation. With all sources of capital, both foreign and domestic, already tapped by 1989, there was no longer the possibility of forming an alliance based on the redistribution of funds (and hence perpetuating the corporatist structure), as the power brokers, who orchestrated the alliances, successively closed themselves off from all such sources.

The Power Brokers

A "power broker" is any individual or organization that is widely accepted as being capable of taking charge of the state apparatus and forming a government. Once in power, the power broker is responsible for mediating between the above corporatist entities, which, in a functioning corporatist structure, it is able to do.

It is difficult to define which groups and individuals can be considered power brokers. There are three considerations that determine a power broker. The first is recent history. Groups that have recently been in power are clearly capable of running a government. The second characteristic of a power broker is public perception. Any government has to have at least initial respect and legitimacy from the corporatist entities and the population as a whole. If a group is perceived by large sectors of the country as being incapable of being in government it is, de facto, incapable. Finally, and most important, a potential power broker must be able to ascend to government through some process—there must be some way for the power broker to be chosen. It is essential to emphasize that the type of process is irrelevant, just so long as there is a process.

In Argentina, there were three processes of ascending to power: the military coup, through limited elections, and through open elections. The fact that no process was considered better than the others, that no process could foster competition and choice rendered all three processes uninstitutionalized. No process of choosing a government was less legitimate or better than any other process. As strange as it may sound, democracy need not be the most legitimate nor even most acceptable (in the population's eyes) form of government. A fundamental aspect of the breakdown of corporatism in the period studied is the elimination of two of these methods and the institutionalization of the last.

There were three power brokers in Argentina during the period studied: the military, the UCR or Radical Party, and Juan Perón (after his death the Peronist or Partido Justicialista Party [PJ]). The methods of gaining office are those listed above: the Peronists through popular mobilizations, the Radicals through circumscribed elections, and the armed forces through the military coup. For each process of taking the reins of government, there was only a single power broker. This is not inevitably the case; many parties can win open electoral contests in advanced democracies, for example. This fact meant that the power broker was implicitly chosen when the decision was made regarding the process of assuming power; the actual coming to power was largely a formality.

The fact that the military now is no longer a contender for power combined with the fact that both the UCR and the PJ compete in open elections (as will be discussed later) has created a whole new set of circumstances. This is one of the most powerful pieces of evidence supporting the theory that the old corporatist structure has broken down. The corporatist entities can no longer, by choosing the rules of ascending to power, ordain the power broker.

Despite these differences, the power brokers shared many traits. The most important was the lack of a stable and secure base of support within society and among the corporatist entities. As the corporatist entities were delinked, the power brokers lost any stable grass-roots power. The Peronist banner ostensibly enveloped both the union movement and the political party as well as several other organizations. This, however, was a mere façade that hid a reality of deep divisions and antagonisms. For example, Perón himself was, as shall be seen, actively opposed by the "Peronist" Montonero terrorist group, and his government (after his death) lost even the support of the CGT. It should become clear in the following pages that the power brokers had no control over the corporatist entities and were able to gain the latter's enduring support only with inducements. Far from establishing any permanent links, the entities freely sought the most advantageous bargain among all of the power brokers.

The consequences of this separation between corporatist entities and power brokers cannot be underestimated. First, it meant that the power broker was always in a relatively weak position as compared to the corporatist entities, even when the government was popular; the power broker in government had no way to mobilize the support it could find in society, which therefore lay latent. This lack of power base resulted in the need to woo the support of the corporatist entities in order both to come to power and to prevent an open political battle—a direct confrontation with the corporatist entities, even when firmly in government, could quite easily cause the regime's downfall. Governments found smooth sailing only so long as there was some concurrence of interests. With the aid of hindsight, it is clear that the concurrence of interests actually was based upon creating stability, albeit temporarily.

A new power broker came to government with, ostensibly, an economic plan, internal cohesion, and popular support. These factors, all fundamentally related to fostering a feeling of stability, were always sufficient to reactivate the economy. The clearest indicator of this was the fact that industry would always work significantly under full capacity during the tumultuous end of each of the governments studied. As demand evaporated, as supplies (particularly imported ones) did not arrive, and as workers struck, both the demand and supply curves shifted significantly inward. With the return of stability, they would shift back outward. The return of stability and the renewed confidence would repeatedly allow for a boom during the first phases of the incoming government's economic plan. In essence, actual GNP was pushed far below its potential during the last phases of the tragic cycle. The most tentative and elementary actions and claims by a new incoming government would allow economic activity to move back towards equilibrium, at a level far closer to the potential GNP. These booms did not require increases in investment as the excess capacity already existed; indeed, the excess installed capacity implied that investment would not be forthcoming during these first years, if other factors remain unchanged.

The initial boom always allowed all of the corporatist entities to profit. As the economy grew rapidly, the bourgeoisie (including the agricultural elite) profited from higher demand, workers from higher real wages and (generally) a decrease in unemployment, and everyone benefited from the abated inflationary spiral. With very little ingenuity, the government was able during this first phase to better the lot of all the corporatist entities and hence to assure its own popularity and legitimacy. The problem inevitably came after the reactivation. The booming economy, in conjunction with limited investment, would bring new inflationary pressures. The lack of structural changes during the first period (when many leaders began to believe wrongly that the economic problems would not be difficult to correct) led to a need for more serious structural changes with the associated social costs. Most important, expectations, so high during the boom, could not be satisfied. With the waning growth and mounting constraints, resistance to the economic plan coalesced.

The effectiveness of the resistance sprung from the interaction between the corporatist entities and the power brokers. During the impasse period, the two actors became delinked, a fact that resulted in persistent contacts between each power broker and all of the corporatist entities. The power brokers hoped to prove their governing capabilities and gain the support necessary to come to or remain in power. The corporatist entities were also eager for these contacts as they were eager to find champions for the policies they wished to see implemented; they wanted the power brokers to offer them inducements for which they would compensate with the desired political support. The communication encouraged the development of factions within each of the power brokers, each of which had privileged relations with and sympathies for a particular corporatist entity. It was through these factions that the corporatist entities and the power brokers communicated.

The coexistence of various factions within each power broker created tremendous problems, however. When the power broker was out of government, economic plans would be drawn up that attempted to satisfy all of the corporatist entities, as each faction was dependent on a different entity for support; promises to redistribute income to all of the entities were a central aspect of trying to return to government and of satisfying all of the internal factional leaders. More important, when the power broker was in government, the plethora of factions caused political struggles and debates within the power broker itself, as each faction fought to defend the interest of its supporters over society at large and the other entities. If and when a rational economic policy was finally implemented (inevitably to the pleasure of some and to the chagrin of other factions), the factional struggle was submerged. The excluded factions developed into something of a semiloyal opposition; as soon as the economic policy faltered, the excluded factions would criticize the policies and encourage the adoption of others that would benefit their supporters.

The pressure on the faction in power was augmented by the continued maneuvering of the other power brokers. Contacts persisted between the power brokers that were out of government and the corporatist entities that, given the traditional political instability, wanted to keep their options open. Upon the first signs of economic difficulties, the other power brokers would voice their opposition in bids to regain control of the government. The governing faction, due to these internal and external pressures, could only with great difficulty (indeed, if at all) completely exclude any particular corporatist entity, as this would imply offering to one of the other power brokers (or internal factions) all of the immense power at the command of the excluded sector. If the corporatist entity saw no possibility of gaining sway with one power broker, the group would have no alternative but to resist the broker wholeheartedly; the group would be forced from semiloyal opposition to actively disloyal opposition.

The need to reform the economy was a central force behind la Revolución Argentina, as it would prove to be for all the following governments. The corporatist breakdown period was also marked by a series of social programs, however. Each government had strong ideas regarding morality and justice, ideas that each government attempted to force upon the society at large. The ideas ranged from religious doctrine to historical interpretation of the nation, from political ideology to personal morals. All the governments here studied, for example, intervened to a greater or lesser extent in university curricula and the judicial system.

The social programs were inevitably implemented with the original economic programs. With regard to this study, which, for the sake of retaining theoretical clarity, relegates these issues to a secondary level, it is important to realize that the social platforms in many ways mirrored the economic programs. As with economic issues, the concept of social policies was accepted and supported by a great many (secondary) corporatist entities, from the church to student unions. As with the economic policies, these programs created a great deal of tension within the governing power broker as well as among the rivalrous corporatist entities. Initially, the social programs, like the economic, would show a fair degree of "success" as popular public actions, if not attitudes, were altered. Inevitably, however, the social aspect would explode—the government's desire to depoliticize society, to encourage a single moral and ideological code, forced such resistance that no degree of coercion could permanently suppress the opposition. This social battle, quite obviously, detracted from the economic reorganization and augmented opposition to the government. Each of the power brokers, when in power, by attempting to force a political outlook on society, further reduced the government's chances of retaining legitimacy and fully implementing an economic policy.

Given all of the above, it is easier to comprehend the failures of Onganía, Perón, Videla, and Alfonsín: The failure of corporatism rests in the inability of the power brokers to intermediate between the corporatist entities while simultaneously implementing a rational program geared toward economic restructuring and political consolidation. This failure results from the skewed power relationship between the brokers and entities, as well as from the internal divisions within the power brokers and the existence of multiple "political currencies" among the corporatist entities. Why were the governments, no matter what they tried, unable to overcome these problems? Were the problems of the period here studied truly inevitable, caused solely by corporatist structural problems? What should be done now? Has the corporatist impasse finally destroyed itself, thus offering the opportunity for the creation of a new consensus in Argentina? To answer these questions, we now turn to the body of the work, analyses of the four governments in question.

Notes

1. The literature is boundless. See the notes for each of the individual chapters as well as the bibliography for an introduction to the sources available.

2. On this point see, for example, Juan Carlos Portantiero, "Political and Economic Crises in Argentina."

3. José Alfredo Martínez de Hoz, personal interview.

4. This term, explained by Samuel Huntington in his book *Political Order in Changing Societies*, refers to periods when various interest groups confront each other "nakedly" with any and all resources they command from strikes to military coups.

5. It must be noted from the outset that although there is agreement among academics regarding the existence of a period of social incorporation and its effects, the period during which it began is subject to great debate. Although most analysts would point to the 1930s, the author is more persuaded by the arguments that incorporation began earlier, certainly by the late teens. Regardless of which decade is chosen, the argument, however, is the same.

6. Gary Wynia, *Argentina: Illusions and Realities*, p. 52.

7. This seems to be a valid conclusion under almost all conditions. For a comparative perspective on Chile, for example, see Henry A. Landsberger and Tim McDaniel, "Hypermobilization in Chile, 1970–1973."

8. Gary Wynia, *Argentina: Illusions and Reality*, p. 61.

9. This dynamic was excellently analyzed and named by Guillermo O'Donnell in his book *Bureaucratic-Authoritarianism*.

10. A more detailed economic explanation of the stop-and-go cycle can be found in "Social Conflict and Populist Policies in Latin America" by Jeffrey Sachs.

11. Gary Wynia, *Argentina: Illusions and Realities*, p. 46.

12. Philippe Schmitter, "Still the Century of Corporatism?" pp. 94–95.

13. The terms "inducements" and "constraints" come from the work by David and Ruth Berrins Collier.

14. David and Ruth Berrins Collier, "Inducements Versus Constraints: Disaggregating Corporatism," p. 979.

15. Eldon Kenworthy, "Argentina: The Politics of Late Industrialization."

16. Samuel Huntington, *Political Order in Changing Societies*, p. 196.

17. This point is well discussed in "Conflicto distributivo y deficit fiscal" by Daniel Heymann and Fernando Navajas, particularly pp. 322–323.

18. See Ricardo Carciofi, *La desarticulación del pacto fiscal.*

19. David and Ruth Berrins Collier, "Inducements Versus Constraints: Disaggregating Corporatism."

20. Juan Carlos de Pablo and Alfonso José Martínez, *Argentina: 30 Years of Economic Policy*, section II, p. 13.

21. Gary Wynia, *Argentina: Illusions and Reality*, p. 160.

22. In order to understand why this is so, it must be realized that upon selling their commodities internationally, the agricultural bourgeoisie has dollars. The return in local currency (the peso and later the austral) depends on how many australs each dollar can purchase, in other words, on the exchange rate.

23. For a full analysis of the beneficial effects of a strong currency for the working classes, please see Jeffrey Sachs, "Social Conflict and Populist Policies in Latin America."

24. Juan Manuel Castillo, personal interview.

25. Jorge Vives, personal interview.

2

Onganía and the Industrial Alliance, 1966–1973

The Onganía Presidency

A military coup in 1966 overthrew President Arturo Illia and brought retired General Juan Carlos Onganía to the presidency. The military had had a long history of interventions into civilian affairs. However, this coup was from the outset different from previous military forays into the political scene. This time the military was eager to hold the reins of power with decision and self-assurance. Onganía's presidency was to be la Revolución Argentina. The reasons for this new-found determination were many.

It had become abundantly clear by 1966 that Argentina had become blocked, that an impasse existed impeding economic development and political stability. The economy was mired in the boom-and-bust cycle that began in the postwar period but showed no signs of abating. The result was relative decline and economic stagnation.

On the political side, Perón remained an awesome force that continued to destabilize all governments and political coalitions. Although these problems already existed in 1955 when Perón was exiled, both the power brokers and the corporatist entities hoped that change could be effected gradually, that time would heal the wounds of Argentine society. It was assumed, for example, that Perón's power would decline over the years, hence leading to greater political stability. All groups, including the Peronist unions that pioneered a movement that called for "Peronism without Perón," believed and hoped that the problems would slowly be outgrown. It was felt that a relationship between the economics and the politics of the country existed, and, it was hoped, an improving economy would lead to greater political stability. Time, instead of alleviating these tensions, however, reinforced them.

The relationship between politics and economics indeed existed, but had the opposite consequences. A dynamic was created whereby the economy stagnated in large part because of the political instability that rendered investments more risky. The reduced investment in the economy, in turn, increased political instability as the more restricted resources gave rise to more fierce and passionate battles regarding the distribution of national income. Each turn of the screw increased the tensions in both the political and economic spheres.

Even given the unfavorable circumstances, President Illia did a poor job of trying to overcome the impasse. His administration would suggest policies, to the acclaim of some corporatist entities and the dismay of others, but the policies would not be implemented; universal disillusionment was the sole consequence. For example, a reform of state enterprises was proposed that centered around the rationalization of the state's railroads. The proposal, which was to save the state $400 million a year,[1] focused on eliminating excess workers and hence was supported by business groups but angered the unions. Illia was unable or unwilling to follow through on the proposal, however. After this fiasco, Illia could never again look toward labor for support. At the same time, the other corporatist entities grew disillusioned with the lack of determination to improve the economic situation. In this fashion, Illia fostered antagonisms between his Radical Party and all of the primary corporatist entities.

Illia also fell into the perennial trap of attempting to reintegrate the Peronist Party. The ban on the Peronist Party was gradually lifted, allowing competition during interim and provincial elections. This act, which was inevitably going to lead to a Peronist victory during the next presidential election, further antagonized large sectors of society. By 1966, all of the primary corporatist entities, as well as society at large, were united in opposition to the government.

Each of the four primary corporatist entities firmly believed by 1966 that fundamental changes had to occur within Argentina; no longer, it was agreed, were mere changes in administration sufficient. The rapid shifts in government (there had been five presidents since Perón's exile) and economic stagnation had adverse effects on all of the entities. Any gains that these entities had made seemed to be ephemeral: Increased wages eaten up by inflation, or the nationalization of oil contracts granted to foreign firms just a few years earlier exemplify the predicaments of the CGT and the international bourgeoisie. The same general conditions also applied, however, to the national bourgeoisie and the agricultural elite. The foundation had been laid for support for la Revolución Argentina.

The choice of the military as the power broker was obvious. The failures of Frondizi and Illia had discredited all factions of the Radical Party. Similarly, the Peronists offered no alternatives. Perón himself was still considered a dangerous character who should not be allowed to return. His followers who remained in Argentina had at various times attempted to form a neo-Peronist party without Perón at its head. It was hoped that such a party could remain cohesive and compete successfully in elections while avoiding the proscription of the old Peronist party. This strategy, however, utterly failed. Perón was unwilling to allow a Peronist party to continue without his de facto leadership; his continued personal popularity and his political manipulations prevented the creation of such a party over his veto. With both the Peronists and the Radicals unacceptable alternatives, all the corporatist entities looked toward the military.

Two factors in the selection of the military are central. First, as is the case with all coups, the military came to power in an uninstitutionalized, indeed, illegal manner—the military toppled Illia and replaced him with Onganía through a coup d'état. Therefore, the widespread support for this change in government was always implicit, the support for the new government assumed but never expressed publicly or officially. This does not at all imply that the military took power without regard to the feelings of society at large and the corporatist entities in particular; quite the contrary, the coup only occurred when the military leaders were certain that there was general support for such action.[2] Indeed, Onganía ascended to the presidency with support from all sectors of society and all of the corporatist entities.

Second, the military from the outset feared internal dissension. Indeed, the choice of Juan Carlos Onganía, a man widely respected in the military and who had fought for internal cohesion, reflected those fears. Onganía had championed the "legalist" group within the military, a group that stressed obedience and internal cohesion. At the same time, his political and economic views were acceptable to, if not favored by, all. He was a moderate nationalist in economic matters, but at the same time believed that the liberals were the experts in this field; in other words, the nationalists thought they had a supporter in Onganía, and the liberals thought they would be able to convince the new president to see the light. On the political side, Onganía had long argued against a coup and military intervention, proving his "democratic" credentials, but had grown convinced of the need for fundamental restructuring before democracy could work. With such views, Onganía gained support from both interventionist and democratic officers. He was the obvious choice for president not only because of his immense authority but also because he represented the best opportunity to avoid internal conflict.[3]

The nearly all-encompassing coalition was of central importance in coming to power. Without this support, the military certainly would have been more hesitant to take power, all the more so considering its intention of remaining in government for such a long period of time—ten years. Similarly, the very idea of effecting elemental change could only arise from widespread and deep concern about the workings of Argentina. In other words, the ability to commence a project akin to la Revolución Argentina was contingent upon support among the primary corporatist entities. This support clearly existed and provided a necessary foundation of stability that allowed a smooth change in governments and that fostered agreement regarding the need for a fundamental restructuring of Argentine politics and economics.

This same widespread support, however, was the Achille's heel of the new regime. The alliance that the military brokered was fundamentally incongruous, as it included all of the primary corporatist entities, each of which had a different agenda.[4] This disparity was not immediately perceived, however. Onganía came to power during a period of stagnation, not crisis as had been the case preceding the military coups in Brazil and Chile. O'Donnell has justly theorized that the relatively smaller problems confronting Argentina at the time of the military takeover translated into less initial concern regarding the economy.[5] The belief that was common during the impasse period—that Argentina's problems were not deeply rooted and could easily be cured—persisted to a large degree within the military during the beginning of la Revolución Argentina. Onganía did not have the stimuli necessary to concentrate all of his efforts on restructuring the economy. At times, indeed, he seemed more concerned with encouraging "appropriate" moral conduct than with solving the structural problems blocking the economy.

The links between the various factions of the military and the corporatist entities further impeded the implementation of a comprehensive and rational economic policy; enormous pressure was brought to bear on Onganía both within the military and from the corporatist entities for widely divergent economic programs. The internal factions within the military would have caused this result under any circumstances. Given the military's willingness to make special commitments to ensure greater support for a coup during the last days of the Illia regime, Onganía operated under especially stringent limitations and acute pressure.

The initial results were reminiscent of the Illia regime. Onganía first offended the unions and then, in a failed attempt at reconciliation, worried the business community. As a part of the first economic phase, the government drew up and began to implement a rationalization program that called for large-scale layoffs at the port of Buenos Aires and for sugar-mill closings in the province of Tucumán. The unions began to feel that they could not look to Onganía for support. In an attempt at reconciliation in August 1966, however, the government intervened in contract negotiations involving the textile workers' and metal workers' unions, which resulted in substantial real wage increases; needless to say, the owners of capital protested the increased costs.[6] The private sector was rendered even more skeptical after a 30 percent wage increase had been offered to government employees, an increase that inevitably served as a guideline for private-sector wage negotiations. Another shift in policy occurred when the government devalued the peso by 6.5 percent in order to satisfy the exporting business community despite the protests of the unions.[7] Eldon Kenworthy summed up the situation well in an article at the time: "[S]ix months after coming to power the junta increasingly resembles its civilian predecessors. Like them, it is dependent on the compliance of various groups for implementing policies, and the price they extract for their cooperation often has the effect of neutralizing these policies."[8] In other words, each of the corporatist entities lobbied for economic rewards. However, given that all of the corporatist entities did the same, the result was contradictory and irrational handling of the economy. None of the corporatist entities was able to consolidate the advantages from any of the favorable policies. This led to demands for more political favors from all sectors, demands that were often implemented but that were not perceived on an economic level by the various groups.

The macroeconomic consequences, however, were obvious to all. Despite the fact that an improved economy was a central, if not the essential, justification for the coup against Illia, the last six months of 1966 showed no improvement in the economic scene. Investment remained stagnant and the economy showed no signs of growing. A restructuring of the economy, which was so desired by the corporatist entities, was not occurring at all. Peronist and Radical leaders began to make calls for new elections. Six months after the coup, the military government was facing the beginnings of a legitimacy problem. This, in turn, was reflected within the military establishment which, it was rumored, set a deadline within which Onganía had to prove his policies successful or face an internal coup.

The Tentative Alliance

Onganía turned to the economic liberals, those he considered experts in this field, for help. Within the military, liberals became more powerful as nationalist-oriented generals were retired. The whole cabinet was reshuffled, reflecting the new direction of the government. Most important, a new economics minister, Adalbert Krieger Vasena, was appointed.

Krieger Vasena was an economic liberal, one associated with and sympathetic towards the UIA. Despite this ideological and professional contact with the UIA, however, his appointment cannot be interpreted as a full-scale alliance between the international bourgeoisie and the government. The shift in course was due to and clearly reflected Onganía's need for economic results instead of faith in or unanimity about the liberal economic program. The military was far from united in the choice of Krieger Vasena, and, of course, the corporatist entities not in agreement with the liberal ideology were in opposition (labor was most distressed, whereas the national bourgeoisie and the agricultural elite were tentatively in favor of the change). In other words, the military chartered only a tentative course regarding economic policy despite its recognition that the first few months of la Revolución Argentina were a total failure.

Several limitations were placed on Krieger Vasena, a so-called "pragmatic liberal" who, Onganía assumed, would be willing to implement less than strictly orthodox policies. Onganía created an office through which all legislation had to pass; the purpose of this office was to accord "a veto over all proposed government policies."[9] It was created, of course, much to the chagrin of the economics team. Further, Krieger Vasena had to agree to certain nationalist goals regarding economic policy: Unemployment was to remain low, a recession was to be avoided, and unions were not to be systematically "atomized" as was advocated by the orthodox liberal groups. Most important, Krieger Vasena had to foster immediate results—legitimacy was already being questioned and Onganía was working under a deadline.

Before Krieger Vasena was even able to announce an economic program, labor balked. Emboldened by its long-time ability to gain concessions through confrontation, the unions brandished their weapons (national strikes and popular mobilizations) against the appointment of a liberal, albeit a "pragmatic" one. In February 1967, just one month after the appointment of Krieger Vasena, the union leadership devised the *Plan de Acción* (Plan of Action). The tactics to be used were quite similar to those used against Illia in 1964 in the *Plan de Lucha* (Plan of Resistance) and from which Illia never completely recovered. The plan was predicated upon exploiting the links between the CGT and the more sympathetic sectors of the military.

> Vandor [head of the CGT] reasoned that the nationalists, then locked in battle with the orthodoxos [the liberals] within the state and lacking support in public opinion, would be forced to either adopt a more conciliatory stance or resort to violent repression, further eroding their already narrow political base. The vandoristas believed [they could] perhaps cement a more favorable *modus vivendi* with Onganía.[10]

In other words, the CGT attempted to take advantage of the legitimacy problems to forge an alliance with the government.

Vandor's line of reasoning was cogent: The sympathetic sectors of the military were eager to avoid a showdown with the labor movement. However, in this instance the liberal sectors had the upper hand. There was a clear need to improve the economic situation. Due to the new appointments within the military, the liberals were at least temporarily in control. Finally, Onganía, whose deadline was not yet approaching, came down this particular time on the liberals' side. In society, the other three corporatist entities still tacitly supported the government and felt that the military offered the best chance for fundamental change. In sum, Onganía's government still had the upper hand in dictating policy at this early point of la Revolución.

Upon the urging of the head of the National Security Council, General Osiris Villegas, and with the support of the economics team and the international business community, the government retaliated against the CGT with determination. Several unions were taken over (the leaders were replaced with government appointees), state employees were warned that adherence to the strike would result in automatic dismissal, and the very legal status and government sanction of several of the unions were openly questioned. Most important, however, was the partial (with threats for complete) elimination of the unions' immense financial resources through the freezing of some of the unions' assets and the elimination of employers' obligatory 1 percent of base salary contributions. The metallurgical and textile unions alone were cut off from approximately $200,000 a month because of this last course of action.[11] The union leadership had no option but to capitulate.

The state's actions against the CGT were not, however, marked with a degree of resolution commensurate with a government that was united about and convinced of the economic plan. The implicit goal of this intervention was not the complete atomization of the labor movement as was desired by the liberal sectors of the military and the liberal corporatist entities. Instead, the actions belied a desire to restrain instead of to dismantle the CGT so as to implement a nominally liberal economic program. Physical repression, for example, was avoided if at all possible, unlike in Brazil and Chile.

Two central points can be gleaned from the government's early experiences with the CGT, however. First, at least toward the beginning of the regime, the state was relatively autonomous in relation to the labor movement. The limited actions taken against the CGT were highly successful, and all indicators suggest that attempts to atomize the unions would also have been. Second, Onganía's policies still reflected attempts to find compromises. Needless to say, the internal divisions within the armed forces and the still awesome power of the corporatist entities determined this "go easy" approach. The result, however, was disastrous—the government expended more resources on attempting not to overly offend any group than on assuring cogent economic policy.

The government was unable (or unwilling) to implement a consistent policy regarding the CGT. Clearly, labor was not a favored entity within the emerging economic alliance. At the same time, the CGT was neither atomized nor well manipulated. For the first years of the economic program, collective bargaining was prohibited, and wage differentials between more and less productive sectors of the economy expanded. Both of these policies could be seen as methods of dividing the working class and encouraging differences among them. At the same time, however, wages within an industry were still generally set for all companies through industrywide labor negotiations. This wage agreement prompted divisions within the business elite along the lines of the national and international bourgeoisies. The latter were far more capable of absorbing labor costs than the former, thus fostering different reactions to wage levels. The uniform regulation reduced the competitiveness of the economy as a whole. More important was the fact that this process of wage settlements promoted camaraderie among the workers in the same industry, if not across industries, and encouraged a united outlook. When labor tensions were to explode, this condition resulted in a coordinated offensive on the part of the workers across companies and industries.

The economics team, due to restrictions imposed by factions of the military, did not fruitfully take advantage of divisions within the labor movement.[12] To better understand the situation, we should look at the various subdivisions within the labor movement. A very small amalgamation of unions, the collaborationists, were, as their name implies, willing to work with the government and support the government's economic and political policies. This group obviously tried to maximize the benefits for their rank and file, but at the same time would offer minimal opposition to the government.

At the other extreme were those union leaders opposing the Onganía regime itself, no matter what policies it implemented. They often hoped for a socialist or communist revolution to replace the whole economic structure and were willing to use almost any means at their disposal to further their goals. This group can be seen as a disloyal opposition.[13] The ideological leader in this group was Amado Olmos until his death in 1968. Despite his passing away, this faction held together under the new leadership of Raimundo Ongaro, who in 1968 forced a split in the CGT.[14] Ongaro was elected to head the new CGT de los Argentinos (CGT of the Argentines), an organization that was in complete opposition to the government. The state, it must be emphasized, could do very little to eliminate this threat directly. Most of the unions and leaders that joined this group had already lost government recognition and their official positions; in other words, these groups and their leaders were outside of the official political organization, and, being highly politicized and ideological, they posed a significant threat to a government that wanted to soften societal divisions. The only way to manipulate and to control this group (short of wholesale violence or jailings, which were not politically feasible) was indirectly.

The third union group, the CGT de Azopardo, led by Augusto Vandor, was the tool that lent itself well to controlling the CGT de los Argentinos. The Vandoristas are best interpreted as a semiloyal opposition. Prior to the 1966 coup, Vandor had been the initiator of an aggressive strategy geared towards extracting the best possible agreements out of the government (one phase of which was the Plan de Lucha during the Illia regime). The basis of this plan was to attack (*golpear*) and then to negotiate (*negociar*). This tack worked very well until the failed strike in February 1967. Reacting to the new firmness and determination on the part of the government, Vandor then believed that tentative support of the government would be more productive in attaining advantages for his rank and file. The government gave no real advantages to the unions that Vandor represented, however. While Vandor argued for restraint among his rank and file and often even explained the need to put off current benefits so as to promote growth and hence a more advantageous economic situation in the future, the government treated the CGT de Azopardo little better than the CGT de los Argentinos.

All of this meant that the union movement was not being reformed at all as the government was unwilling either to atomize or to foster divisions within the CGT. This potent organization that had wrought so many difficulties on previous governments remained unaltered. When it would strike again, the CGT would still be as powerful as it was in 1966. The only way that the government was attempting to control this threat was by ensuring that workers would not suffer too much during the economic reorganization. Unemployment was to remain low, and large wage cuts were not acceptable. Due to the lack of determination in dealing with this threat, the economics team found significant limitations placed on its policymaking capabilities. In the alliance that Onganía was brokering, it can be claimed therefore that labor was only "partially excluded." These factors prevented the creation of a firm alliance with the favored corporatist entities; only a "tentative alliance" was feasible.

At least the policies regarding the favored corporatist entities were far more coherent, however. Despite the limitations placed on the economics team, the fundamental economic reasoning was very sound. Krieger Vasena announced on 13 March 1967 a series of policies geared towards promoting lower inflation and higher growth as well as encouraging investment. The most important aspect of the initial economic plan was a devaluation of the peso by approximately 40 percent, from 255 pesos to the dollar to 350; this was promised to be the last devaluation ever. The devaluation was "fiscally compensated," a technical term that refers to financial regulations and adjustments geared towards eliminating windfall profits and losses due to the devaluation. The major adjustments were a one-time tax on foreign currency holdings and bank accounts, a reduction on import tariffs, and an increase of 16 percent to 25 percent on the export duties levied on traditional (agricultural) products. The reduction in import and increase in export taxes had the double advantage of reducing windfall profits and losses while also limiting the inflationary pressure caused by the devaluation.[15] This was the first time in the history of Argentina's frequent and substantial devaluations that the government also took steps to compensate many of the implicit redistributive effects. Krieger Vasena also announced significant increases in the costs of public services,[16] and several temporary taxes geared toward redressing the budget deficit. For example, a one-time 1 percent tax on real estate was declared.

A series of policies announced shortly after 13 March were aimed at fostering growth, investment, and industrial deepening. Several tax credits were announced, geared toward promoting investment and the purchase of industrial and agricultural machinery. Corporate tax liabilities were reduced, and construction was encouraged through tax subsidies for housing investments. A law that required landowners to renew leases to tenant farmers was repealed in an attempt to foster higher agricultural output. Many changes were made to attract foreign capital and assure the international business community of the seriousness of the economics team; the most important was the complete liberalization of currency markets. Figure 2.1 shows that these actions did not result in significant increases in investment in the immediate term, thus reflecting the defensive outlook of the corporatist entities.

Figure 2.1   Total Investment, 1964–1969

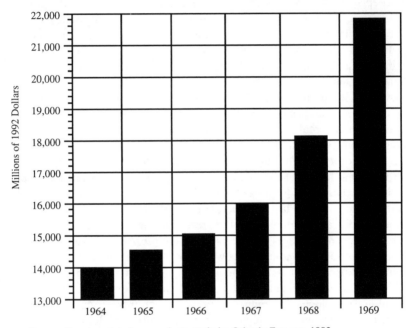

Source: Based on data from a private study by Orlando Ferreres, 1992.

Pivotal among Krieger Vasena's policies were those geared toward arresting the inflationary spiral. Wages were increased by 15 percent across the board but at the same time were frozen for the next twenty-one months. Collective bargaining was also indefinitely suspended. This combination of policies, Krieger Vasena had hoped, would adjust wages for past real-wage depreciation and hence not cause excessive antagonism on the part of the workers while putting long-term and continuous downward pressure on inflation. As inflation continued, real wages would decline, thus lowering total real demand. This gradual decrease in wages implied that many of the costs levied on the working classes were implicitly delayed until a later date as inflation eroded their buying power.

The other major component of the fight against inflation was the creation of a "voluntary" price-freeze agreement with the private sector; it was announced 15 May 1967. In essence, the major industrial companies were invited to agree to a six-month price freeze. Once a company joined, it should be emphasized, it was no longer voluntary—the company was obliged to remain in the structure for the full six months. Companies that joined this anti-inflationary mechanism were promised several advantages. First, government procurement contracts would be made only with these companies. In addition, Krieger Vasena also authorized subsidized credit (at negative real interest rates) to most Argentine households for consumer goods. However, this credit could only be used to buy products from the companies in the price-freeze mechanism. The business community's response was enthusiastic—84 companies joined the mechanism within a week (by 22 May) and another 195 joined shortly thereafter. By November, 1,961 companies had joined.[17] They assumed that this agreement would be renewed at the end of the six-month period. Most important, the government's policy did nothing to control price increases on the part of wholesalers or retailers; this lack of control explains why the consumer price index outpaced inflation (the latter amalgamating wholesale and retail prices to a product's factory costs), a fact important to keep in mind when looking at the future phases of the economic plan. Eventual price adjustments would be granted only for increases in costs due to imported inputs that were above 3 percent, an amount that the government thought the private community could absorb by itself.

In 1968 the economics team decided that the government itself would have to take an active part in the economic restructuring as investment remained stagnant. The plan had two aspects. First, the government wanted to increase its share of direct investment in the economy, particularly in the infrastructure. Second, the economics team hoped and thought that these expansionary policies would foster more private investment. It was hoped that the expansionary policy would push demand beyond industry's capacity to produce. In other words, the economics team tried to ensure that the significant excess capacity present in the economy could be quickly brought on line so as to create a situation in which large-scale investments were necessary to keep pace with growing demand. Clearly, the economic policy relied almost solely on inducements, as contrasted with constraints, to foster investment among the favored corporatist entities.

In order to fund this project, the government increased real receipts by 15 percent and further augmented its financial resources by attracting more international capital and by appropriating the surplus of the National Social Benefits Organization (much as the U.S. government does with Social Security). These resources were used to increase government expenditure on public investment by 30 percent, as can be seen in Table 2.1, to provide the main stimulus to the economy. In conjunction with this, the real money supply was significantly increased with the express aim of reducing the interest rate as a further stimulus to investment.[18]

Table 2.1   The 1967 and 1968 Budgets as Prepared by Krieger Vasena (in billions of pesos)

	1967 (actual)	1968 (budget planned in 1967)
Current Expenditures	427.9	489.4
Operations	273.5	300.0
Transfers	154.4	189.4
Capital Expenditures	156.1	217.0
Other Expenditures	18.0	0
Savings from Increased Efficiency	0	(18.0)
Total	602.0	688.4
Revenues	476.2	574.9
Taxes	419.0	514.2
Other Revenues	57.2	60.7
Inflows of Capital	12.9	65.0
National	7.9	30.0
International	5.0	35.0
Other Revenues	13.7	0
Deficit	99.2	48.5

Source: Juan Carlos de Pablo, *La politica antiinflacionaria en la Argentina, 1967–1990*, Amorrortu, Buenos Aires, 1970, my translation. Reprinted with permission.

A 20 percent tax on the importation of certain capital goods was also implemented with an eye toward promoting development and production of backward-linked economic inputs.[19] At the same time, export taxes on agricultural goods were gradually reduced in order to guarantee the agricultural sector constant real returns.

Implicit in the economic program was an alliance between the national and international bourgeoisies. All of the policies implemented were beneficial to these groups: from the investment credits, to the expansion of the market through consumer credit, to particular tax changes. The central aspect of the economic changes effected was the devaluation, the compensatory aspects of which were beneficial to the industrial sectors at the cost of the agricultural ones; the fact that never before had a devaluation been compensated suggests that this result was expressly desired. Further, an alliance between the industrial sectors made theoretical sense—the industrial sectors were central to promoting backward linkages, expanding the production of capital goods, and reducing technological dependence on the first world. It should be remembered that Krieger Vasena—and Onganía— were almost certainly under pressure to obtain quick results. Given the underutilization of installed industrial capacity, Krieger Vasena could foster an immediate boom period with this industrial coalition, as evidenced in Figure 2.2, without limiting his capacity to fight inflation.

Once again, it is clear that the government had a great deal of relative freedom. Agriculture was largely excluded from the alliance, yet the SRA did not yet oppose the government. "Although Krieger Vasena's economic policy was clearly anti-agriculture, we [the SRA] initially accepted the

Figure 2.2 Annual Growth Rate of GDP, 1966–1970

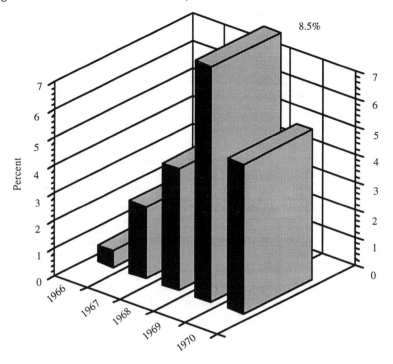

Source: Based on data from William C. Smith, *Authoritarianism and the Crisis of the Argentine Political Economy*, Stanford University Press, Stanford, 1989.

economic costs imposed on us in the hope of some sort of long-term benefits, namely growth and stability. The fact that the policy seemed to us rational and well thought out encouraged us to give the policy some time to work."[20] It is essential to emphasize that the SRA was only partially excluded, however; efforts were made to encourage agribusiness investment through credits, and export duties were gradually reduced in order to offset the effects of the continuing (though declining) inflation.

The results of this first phase of Krieger Vasena's economic program were favorable. Inflation significantly decreased and GNP grew briskly. With the return of stability combined with the calls for rational economic policy, the economy boomed as unused capacity began to be used. The major disappointment was the lack of private investment, which limited the extent to which the economy was being fundamentally modernized. The following was said regarding international capital: "[E]ven with a prestigious economic czar like Krieger Vasena serving as guarantor, international capital had to believe firmly in the future stability of their local allies before investing, and yet investment was needed before future economic expansion could confirm the wisdom of their trust."[21] As far as Argentine capital was concerned, Juan Carlos de Pablo claimed that "the private sector's actions were very conservative and implied a depression-like outlook" despite the brisk economy.[22] The obvious implication of this was that the corporatist entities continued to rely on redistribution of wealth instead of the creation of wealth for higher profits.

Intensification of the Program and Growing Resistance

All indicators were positive at the beginning of 1969, after more than two years of the economic policy: Inflation was down, growth up, and the currency remained stable. Given these achievements, Krieger Vasena entered 1969 with two advantages. First, he could be assured a certain amount of support just because of these favorable conditions. No corporatist entity nor competing power broker could claim that the economy was doing badly or that the policy was unsound. The two power brokers in opposition could not, under these circumstances, rally support in an attempt to return to power, a fact that greatly augmented stability and policy freedom. The second advantage was that industrial capacity was nearly fully utilized. No longer, in other words, could business put off investment by merely increasing output of existing capital; in order to keep up with demand, new productive capacity would have to be built. This was a central advantage in promoting the all-important deepening of industrialization and restructuring of the economy; without such advances, the state of Argentine development would not have progressed, which would merely result in the return of the boom-and-bust cycle.

These advantages could easily become liabilities, however. The excellent economic indicators became baselines: No one could criticize the economic policy so long as they continued, but the deterioration of any one of them would open a Pandora's box. Corporatist entities would complain and some—those that were excluded from the alliance—could be counted on once again to actively oppose the policy. Internal dissension within the military would also be foredoomed. The flames would be fanned by the other power brokers looking for a new opportunity to return to power. Krieger Vasena became, in sum, a slave to continued and unrelenting success, the lack of which would lead to uncertainty, lack of legitimacy, and breakdown of consensus regarding the course of economic policy. All this occurred just as the easy boom phase of the economic policy was rapidly coming to an end.

As if these tensions were not enough, many of the "costs" of the economic policy began straining against the supposed tranquillity. Inflationary pressure returned after two years of expansion of demand and increases in the money supply. A typical economic cycle suggested that a recession was in the making, particularly given the fact that investment had thus far remained low.[23] The continuing, albeit diminished, inflation rate increased the real value of the currency; although in 1967 the exchange rate was highly conducive to exporting and the currency was fundamentally undervalued, by the beginning of 1969 the situation was the opposite.

It is important to emphasize that most of the advantages gained by the industrial corporatist entities came by means of a redistribution, implicit or explicit, from other corporatist entities. Industrialists were clearly in a better position after two years of Krieger Vasena's policies, but this was in no way due to their own merit—they had neither invested nor improved efficiency in any way that might justify their increased profit margins. Obviously, the other groups were growing increasingly disheartened with subsidizing the industrialists. Wages continued to fall in real terms (as can be seen in Figure 2.3), and agriculture suffered from the fixed exchange rate (by 1969, almost all export taxes had already been removed so that compensation for inflation was no longer possible). All of this was more difficult to tolerate because the economy was growing robustly. In short, the goodwill tapped for the short-term sacrifices was wearing thin.

Figure 2.3   Industrial Wages, 1966–1969

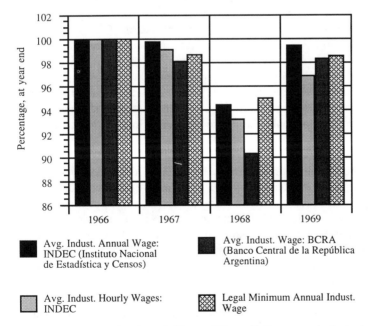

Avg. Indust. Annual Wage: INDEC (Instituto Nacional de Estadística y Censos)

Avg. Indust. Wage: BCRA (Banco Central de la República Argentina)

Avg. Indust. Hourly Wages: INDEC

Legal Minimum Annual Indust. Wage

Source: Based on data from Guillermo O'Donnell, *Bureaucratic-Authoritarianism*, Institute of International Studies, Berkeley, 1979.

Krieger Vasena's range of potential policies that could be used to confront these problems was also becoming limited. As the economy had little to no excess capacity, the trade-off between inflation and growth grew palpable. Moreover, by 1969, he had less ability to use inducements rather than constraints to promote certain economic results. The state, for example, could not further increase spending and investment as this would make the state too central an economic actor for the economic program still to be considered "liberal" and "market oriented."

A further problem related to the implementation of structural changes that were essential to completing the liberal program. Such a program included adjusting relative prices after such a long price freeze and the opening of the economy to foreign competition. The fundamentally liberal economics team was eager to effect this stage of the economic program. Moreover, both the UIA and the SRA were strongly in favor of such changes. Not moving ahead with the more fundamental changes envisioned in the economic plan would cause discord within the economics team as well as with the liberal corporatist entities.

The catch was that implementing these changes would also augment the existing tension. Such structural changes were anathema to the CGE. Increased foreign competition would inevitably reduce the national bourgeoisie's profit margins. Particular companies and even industries feared bankruptcies. New investment to hone efficiency would be necessary, but the returns on these investments could not be assured as bankruptcy, despite any level of investment, was always possible. Of course, the CGT was also very much opposed to any opening of the market. It is important to realize that the structural changes caused a schism among the favored corporatist entities. Moreover, it was impossible for Krieger Vasena to broker a new alliance between the "liberal" SRA and UIA after the former had been asked to sacrifice so much. The necessary orientation of policy and mutual trust simply did not exist. Krieger Vasena's only alternative was to rely increasingly on the international bourgeoisie.

As might be expected under these conditions, Krieger Vasena was determined to take advantage of the full capacity of the economy in order to force investment while holding all the other parts of the plan together; the economic policy became quite consciously a race against time. Krieger Vasena needed to make sure that fundamental restructuring would begin in 1969. Everything would be done to force the industrial sectors, and particularly the UIA, to invest as quickly as possible in the hope that the program could be held together for one more year. After that, if the policies were successful, a general decompression of the tensions could occur as a natural result of growth and new wealth.

An enhanced price freeze was decided upon as the best mechanism to suppress the growing tensions while encouraging growth and investment. The prices of industrial goods were allowed to increase, on average, only a small percentage, one well below the increases in labor costs. In an attempt to correct partially relative prices, however, Krieger Vasena decided that the industrial groups themselves could allocate the price increases. In other words, the weighted average of all industrial prices could only increase by the amount determined by the economics team. Which products within that basket of goods could obtain price increases and by how much were to be determined by the industrialists themselves. In order to control consumer inflation as well as producer's prices, the economics team decided to include wholesalers and retailers within the price control scheme.[24] Having already tapped all the inducements available to them, the policymakers now introduced new constraints in their attempt to spur investment. First, more segments of the economy were included in the price controls (wholesalers and retailers). More important, industrialists were encouraged to invest to counteract the higher labor costs that inevitably reduced profit margins; this can be seen as an implicit constraint of the bourgeoisie. Investments were supposed to counteract decreasing profit margins, compared to just months before when business was supposed to invest so as to profit from recently fattened margins.

Inducements that had already been introduced were kept in place and even reinforced where possible. Government expenditures remained unchanged at their recently increased level to guarantee continued strong demand. In conjunction with this fiscal policy, the monetary base was allowed to expand rapidly; the hope was to reduce real interest rates to spur investment. The inflationary pressures would inevitably mount, given this mixture of fiscal and monetary policy, but, it was hoped, could be controlled through the price freeze.

The economics team also decided that it was essential to improve the lackluster agricultural sector. In view of the fact that the government did not have the resources needed to offer inducements (a devaluation, for example, was impossible given the inflationary pressures), Krieger Vasena opted for a constraint: a new tax ostensibly based on land values. In reality, this tax was to be based on the productive capacity (regardless of previous or current output) of agricultural land as a way to force the agricultural bourgeoisie to improve output and efficiency.[25] This proposal clearly represented a new constraint on the SRA. Consequently, the SRA was more inclined, if not eager, to jump ship upon the first sign of bad news and actively resist the economic policy so as to avoid incurring this new tax. Indeed, the SRA was offered just such an excuse; the land tax was never to be implemented.

It is clear that the completely excluded CGT represented the greatest threat to the economic policy; this corporatist entity was ready to explode at the least of provocations, an occurrence that would jeopardize the whole economic restructuring. With this in mind, Krieger Vasena announced an 8 percent across-the-board wage increase. Despite this, wages continued to decline in real terms. The deterioration of living standards was all the more painful to accept as Onganía's rhetoric stressed the importance of social justice and alluded to the beginning of a second or "social phase" of the Argentine revolution. Further, the wage increases were, once again, denying both the Vandorists and the collaborationists any advantages over the more militant unions. Under these circumstances, all groups were discontented with the labor policy: Industrialists and liberals were unhappy that the unions were not being atomized, and the CGT and economic nationalists were distraught that workers were still being forced to suffer the brunt of the economic policy. The middle road that was being followed was rendered treacherous with the absence of any manipulation of the unions through offering concrete advantages to Vandor.

> The regime's inability to domesticate labor also fueled renewed pressures from big business to dismantle the CGT. This furthered the nationalists' desperation to marshal their dwindling labor support in order to resist the mounting attacks of civilian and military liberals. All came to naught, however, because Onganía could not bring himself to grant his would-be colaboracionista allies real political power.[26]

The final break that forced the Vandoristas into the opposition camp occurred in mid-1968. It was in August of that year that

> [s]hortly after constituting its authorities, the CGT-Azopardo requested an audience with Onganía. Vandorism saw in the government's fragmentation a chance to begin negotiations aimed at saving the unions, with their bureaucratic and ideological limitations, from the quite radical path marked out by the CGT de los Argentinos. Onganía, showing as always admirable evenhandedness but poor political judgement, rejected this request in a public statement declaring that the authorities of the CGT-Azopardo "have not yet been properly recognized [as authentically representative] by the Labor Secretariat." The CGT-Azopardo responded by protesting that the government had no desire for a "dialogue with the workers." But despite Onganía's refusal to talk with the Vandorists, he held secret meetings with participationist leaders. News of these meetings, when leaked to the press, provoked the unanimous disgust of the liberals, upper bourgeoisie, and the Vandorists.[27]

Vandor was offered no advantages over Ongaro of the CGT de los Argentinos while the openly collaborationist unions were at least offered contacts with the government. Under these circumstances, Vandor had no choice but to join the likes of Ongaro in active opposition to the government; if Vandor did not take such steps, he would have risked losing the support of his increasingly restless rank and file to Ongaro, support on which his power and position were contingent. The enmity of the CGT was rendered all the more dangerous as the other corporatist entities grew disenchanted with Onganía and Krieger Vasena. The SRA wanted to avoid the new tax. The CGE was fearful of the structural changes that were to be enforced. Contacts between the CGE and the CGT increased their contacts with the aim of blocking the opening of the economy and of reverting to more populist-oriented policies. These contacts were particularly dangerous as they furthered the schism within the chosen alliance between the UIA and the CGE. These contacts also offered a viable political alternative that had thus far been lacking.

There is currently widespread evidence that the radical unions had, by 1969, long been preparing an affront to the government. The moment for such an action came with the Southern Hemisphere's winter. In May, several social benefits were accidentally annulled for a large sector of the workers in Argentina's second largest and highly industrialized city, Córdoba. At the same time, the trend toward lower unemployment in that particular city was reversed (as shown in Figure 2.4) due to uncontrollable economic factors. These were the sparks that lit the tinder.

Figure 2.4   Unemployment Rate in Argentina, Córdoba, and Buenos Aires, 1966–1969

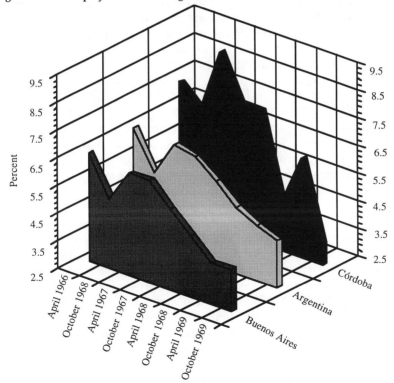

Source: Based on data from Juan Carlos de Pablo and Alfonso José Martínez, *Argentina: Thirty Years of Economic Policy (1958–87)*, unpublished ms., 1988.

On 29 May 1969, a mass uprising erupted in Córdoba, the so-called Cordobazo. The uprising was led by students and union workers, two groups that were closely associated as "many day students worked nightshifts at the factories, and many young car workers were night students; these two groups served as a conduit between affairs in the university and those in the factories."[28] The protest had broad-based support. Almost everyone in the city avoided work and joined in the protest marches. Many, moreover, built barricades, confronted the police with Molotov cocktails and, less frequently, even with sniper attacks. The city was beyond any control. The police could do nothing but retreat and wait for the military to lay siege. After about a week, political order was, for the most part, restored. Onganía's government would never recover.

Onganía's Social Program

Juan Carlos Onganía was a devout Catholic determined to instill a correct moral code to counteract what he interpreted as the moral degeneration typical of the 1960s. This mission was clear from the very beginning of his government when he selected his ministers.[29] The president explicitly avoided anyone who was divorced or who subscribed to any religious faith apart from Catholicism. Individuals known for their piety and sobriety were clearly preferred—several ministers, for example, were teetotalers. Most revealing, however, was his selection in 1966 of Jorge Salimei as his first minister of economics. Salimei, a small-time but successful businessman, had befriended the new president during a religious retreat commonly attended by the most devout. Salimei had had no government experience and no advanced studies in economic policymaking; apart from his upstanding—in Onganía's view—character, Salimei had little to recommend him for this central government post.

Onganía's first policies seemed to portray a greater emphasis on social policy than on economic transformation. While economic policy floundered under Salimei, as described above, Onganía resolutely attacked the social decay he saw around him. The government intervened in the universities in a manner heretofore unparalleled in Argentine history. Student unions were taken over, and Peronist and "morally lax" scholars were threatened and often expelled. Professors were also exposed to similar scrutiny. Needless to say, curricula were altered to stress morality, the valor of the armed services, and degeneracy as aspects of the Peronist movement. Given such forceful and comprehensive intervention, both students and professors could hardly resist.

On a more general level, Onganía attempted to depoliticize Argentine society. The president had a very strong paternalistic instinct; his government was to foster the general good (as interpreted, needless to say, by Onganía and his closest cohorts), and the population was to accept obediently the directions from above. Political debate was quashed: Policies were announced without any social consultation (as compared to consultation with the corporatist entities such as Opus Dei), political parties ceased to exist in everything but name, and censorship grew rampant. Similarly, the church became a far more prominent organization with the express goal of curing the moral ills.

Initially, it seemed as though these policies were successful. No student radicalism was apparent; society seemed accepting of its new role as a passive benefactor of a paternalistic government; and, as far as can be judged, "immoral" behavior—premarital sex and alcohol consumption serve as examples—grew less visible if not less common.

With the Cordobazo returned the explicitly political nature of Argentine society. Student radicalism and heterogeneity returned with a vengeance. As far as can be judged, experimentation typical of the first world in the 1960s became more common.

The social aspect of la Revolución Argentina, in conjunction with the subsequent uprising against it, fundamentally marked the political climate. The country's social tensions were no longer implicit—those with differing points of view now began to actively battle each other in the public arena. Argentine society, long contentious but implicitly and peacefully so, now crossed the fine line that would allow the debates to take on new and palpable importance; turning back would be impossible. It was with the Cordobazo that a Pandora's box was opened that unleashed a cycle of unprecedented violence in Argentina.

> Guerrilla activity, for the most part, emerged after, not before, the Cordobazo. Except in Córdoba itself, the events of May 1969 were less the culmination of an ongoing process than the starting point for new forms of protest and armed struggle that were much more active and violent than those practiced before 1966. This protest and violence would soon become part of the peculiar normality of Argentine politics.[30]

The veritable explosion in violence is well illustrated in Figure 2.5.

The free-for-all war was to destroy any chances of reestablishing stability and legitimacy during the Argentine revolution; this might not have been immediately obvious, however. As will be seen, Krieger Vasena's successors attempted to hold together the fragile economic plan; they were doomed to fail, however. More important still, this internal war would risk not only an economic plan but the very existence and stability of Argentine society. Onganía's successors would all struggle to hold the latter together. They did so in a manner that was always geared toward favoring one ideology, one political group, one interpretation of history over the others. Each of the following governments here studied attempted yet another stabilization plan with an associated social ideology. Stability could

Figure 2.5 Number of Terrorist Actions, 1966–1972

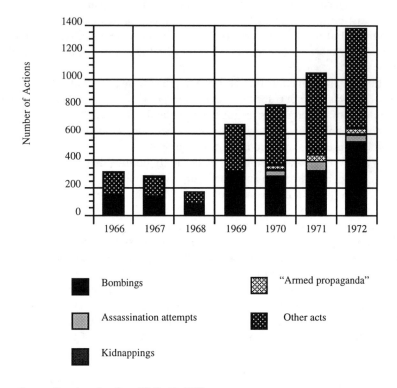

Bombings

Assassination attempts

Kidnappings

"Armed propaganda"

Other acts

Source: Based on data from W. Smith 1989.

be found temporarily, but the process of corporatist breakdown had now begun. These attempts too, it is now clear, were doomed to failure. Instead of offering the promised peace and social harmony, these policies and the reactions against them precipitated a civil war that would cost thousands of lives and would, at a certain point, threaten a Lebanonization of the country. In this cathartic process, all sectors of society would pay dearly, rewarded only with martyrs. Only slowly, after it had become abundantly clear that no group could fully win this struggle, did a process of gradual reconciliation and healing begin, a process that is still under way today.

The Collapse of the Industrial Alliance

To say the least, the Cordobazo was clearly an important and effective challenge to the government. It was questionable whether the government retained any legitimacy. All the same, Onganía attempted to salvage his presidency. He replaced Krieger Vasena, the rest of the economics team, and several other ministers on 11 June 1969. Krieger Vasena became the scapegoat despite the success of his policies. As the underlying tensions were of a largely political nature, however, this ministerial reorganization would not salvage any aspect of la Revolución Argentina, neither the social nor the economic.

Onganía as well as the international bourgeoisie still wanted to profit from the improved economic situation—it seemed senseless to abandon the economic program just as investment surged and the economy began to be fundamentally modernized. It was hoped that the political crisis could be separated from the economic advances. At the time, many representatives of the international bourgeoisie felt such a solution was feasible. For example, John Thompson, an economist of the Federal Reserve Bank of New York, stated in early 1970:

> Undeniably, the government suffered severe setbacks, losing its image as a source of stability and order, as well as its claim that its successes were based on "social consensus." [But] on the whole, the government has weathered the storm well during the last year and the essential gains of the Stabilization Program have been preserved.[31]

To this end, José M. Dagnino Pastore, another "moderate liberal," was appointed to the economics ministry. Pastore was bent on continuing with the economic course charted by Krieger Vasena.

The new economics minister stated on 13 June 1969 that the government would continue the battle against inflation. Monetary policy was tightened. A devaluation was avoided as it was thought that the run on the peso was speculative and could be controlled and slowly reversed. These policies were very successful in and of themselves. For example, the speculative run on the national currency during the second half of 1969 was indeed reversed in 1970, resulting in the recuperation of all of the foreign reserves sold by the Central Bank.[32] Investments, as can be seen in Figure 2.6, began to recover although they still remained weak. Pastore's tremendous success reflects the rationality of the economic policies in themselves—the problem rested in Argentine politics, not in the economic program.

The political tensions quickly resulted in the unraveling of Krieger Vasena's carefully woven economic tapestry as pressure groups successfully lobbied for special concessions. Within the military, the economic nationalists were successful in ensuring the nationalization of the foreign-owned telecommunications companies toward the end of 1969, a move that clearly antagonized the continuing attempt to attract foreign capital, as can be seen in Figure 2.7. Upon the urging of the economics team and the liberal sectors generally, unions were denied the right to bargain collectively as they had been promised. Shortly thereafter, certain sectors of the military, in an effort to regain the unions' tacit support, were successful at lobbying for

Figure 2.6   Change in Investment in Equipment and Machinery During 1969, by Quarter

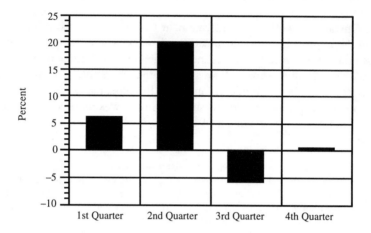

Source: Based on data from O'Donnell 1979.

Figure 2.7   Foreign Investment in Argentina, 1966–1971 (1980 = 100)

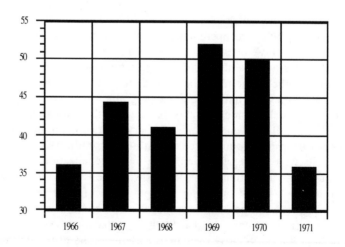

Source: Based on data from de Pablo and Martínez 1988.

large wage increases that resulted in 14 to 17 percent higher costs for wages, an initiative that jeopardized the battle against inflation. Worse, these actions left the unions dissatisfied with the government's policies yet self-assured of their power, an explosive combination.

The five-year National Plan for Development and Security that was developed at this time epitomized the contradictory policies the government was trying to follow.

> One basic thrust of this plan was to leave the state apparatus in charge of investment in infrastructure, while reserving large productive investments for private initiative. But with inconsistency that escaped nobody, the plan asserted that economic growth based largely on transnational capital was leading to rapid economic concentration and denationalization. In view of this, the plan stated a commitment to making this pattern of economic growth "compatible" with the promotion and strengthening of national capital. It also made provisions for important increases in wages and salaries. It did not, however, bother to detail how all these goals would be achieved.[33]

In order to retain the minimal support that it still commanded, the government was forced to offer advantages to all groups. The requisite resources simply did not exist, however. Concretely, this lack of resources manifested itself in a growing budget deficit and the consequent accelerating inflation.

In essence, the internal divisions within the military surfaced as the corporatist entities grew more demanding. Links between various military factions and the corporatist entities strengthened, resulting in policies geared toward avoiding imminent crises instead of promoting growth; inevitably, these policies were irrational and inconsistent. All of the advantages honed during two-and-a-half years of Krieger Vasena's stewardship were rapidly evaporating. The economic agenda of the Argentine revolution, at least under the stewardship of Juan Carlos Onganía, had clearly failed.

The Levingston Presidency and the Shift in Coalitions

Juan Carlos Onganía's government, in obvious shambles, was overthrown by an internal military coup in June 1970. A little-known, lower-level general, Roberto M. Levingston, was chosen to succeed as president. A junta composed of Levingston as well as the head of each military service was created. The junta would, it was hoped, force consensus on the increasingly fragmented military. The result, predictably, was the opposite. Without a single leader able to impose his will on the others, this arrangement "actually contributed to the Balkanization of the state apparatus."[34] Each faction within the military operated with increasing independence, trying to further its own aims while attempting to veto the policies of opposing factions. The policies that resulted were chaotic and incongruous. The ruling junta, instead of giving the government the hoped-for direction and coherence, actually tore it apart.

Pressure was also mounting to change power brokers within society at large and among the corporatist entities. A majority of Argentines called for immediate and unconditional elections. The Peronists and the Radicals, seeing an opportunity to return to power, began to court support more actively among the corporatist entities and heralded the Hora del Pueblo, a manifesto that called for elections. The power brokers' claim that the military was incapable of ruling the country was reinforced with the surge in political violence during the second half of 1970.

Economic policy was jeopardized not only by the factionalization but also by growing instability. The instability resulted in capital flight and defensive actions on the part of all economic actors, as is predicted by the Noah's Ark model.[35] According to this model, individuals sensing a period of crisis do everything possible to protect themselves. Most obviously, this means gathering anything of value that can be sent away safely, including dollars; people prepare themselves for having to go on the ark. Although most rational for the individual, such an outlook clearly augments the social and economic breakdown that is detrimental to the society as a whole. In the midst of this chaos, the new economics minister, Carlos Moyano Llerena, insisted on attempting a long-term economic stabilization program similar to that of Krieger Vasena. Just as had his predecessor, Llerena organized a voluntary price freeze and instituted a new compensated devaluation. He hoped that these two policies would improve the balance of payments situation while keeping a lid on inflation. In reality, however, both goals were jeopardized as inflationary expectations jumped.

> [O]n the one hand, his adjustments broke the 1967 exchange norm by yielding before expectations, which was construed as a show of weakness, and on the other hand, it was not large enough to convince Argentines that this would be the "last" devaluation. The result was that the devaluation, although compensated for, impacted on the price level and gave way to the creation of new inflationary and exchange expectations.[36]

As if the economic policy did not face enough problems, it was further compromised by the military's vetoing a wage freeze for fear of union opposition; even the liberal factions of the military feared that the government could lose control in the face of new labor unrest. Further, Llerena used—almost certainly in response to political pressure—the new funds created through the compensated devaluation (by way of an export tax on agriculture, as had been the case under Krieger Vasena) for social benefits programs. This promotion of consumption contrasted markedly with the increased investment that occurred in the comparable period under Krieger Vasena. Simply put, an economic program similar to that implemented in 1967 was not feasible in the face of political disintegration and economic emergency.

With the continued implementation of an unworkable economic policy, a "defensive alliance" between the CGT and the CGE was coalescing. Levingston believed that he could consolidate his own power by changing to an economic policy more favorable toward these corporatist entities: Levingston was determined to radically shift economic course and create a new alliance between the CGE and the CGT. In October 1970, Llerena was replaced with Aldo Ferrer, a nationalist-oriented economist. Shortly thereafter, Levingston forced the resignation of Francisco Manrique, the last liberal in the cabinet, as well as the liberal governor of Córdoba.

A fundamental aspect of this alliance was—as is common to most Argentine governments—finding resources that could be redistributed to the signatories. Part came from the increased tax receipts from the compensated devaluation described above, although not nearly enough. A desperate attempt was made to augment the supply of credit for the national bourgeoisie. Policies were devised so that all national capital was reserved for Argentine, as opposed to multinational, firms. Due to a series of complex financial regulations and guarantees, however, this policy resulted in the de facto use of foreign loans (see Figure 2.8), which forebode the debt crisis of the 1980s, to subsidize this furtive coalition.[37] Once again, immediate economic benefits were sought at the cost of postponed but significant sacrifices.

Figure 2.8   Foreign Debt, 1966–1973

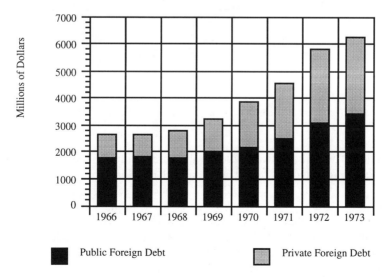

Public Foreign Debt   Private Foreign Debt

Source: Based on data from de Pablo and Martínez 1988.

There was some recovery during the first quarter of 1971, but it was a far cry from the 8 percent real increase that Ferrer was predicting. Moreover, the growth came at the cost of skyrocketing and uncontrollable inflation. In an implicit avowal of his incapacity to control the inflation rate, Ferrer stated that "inflation originated in 'structural problems and sectorial conflicts,' [which] would disappear once development was achieved."[38] Such explanations did not overcome CGE's and CGT's trepidations regarding a military government that had so recently betrayed both groups; despite the shift in policy, a new alliance could not be successfully forged.

Figure 2.9   Annual Inflation Rate, July 1969–April 1973

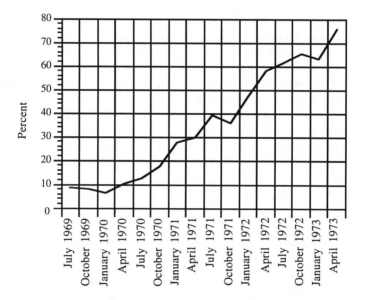

Source: Based on data from de Pablo and Martínez 1988.

All the while, political violence increased and factionalization grew. Levingston resorted to increasingly radical rhetoric in order to mobilize support. Eventually, however, his policies and speeches began to smack of socialism, scaring even factions of his own coalition such as the national bourgeoisie. The attempt at creating a new alliance, so radically different from the one implemented by Krieger Vasena, was impossible. Another internal coup was all but inevitable. In March 1971 General Alejandro Lanusse was appointed the new president.

The Lanusse Presidency and
the Return to Praetorianism

Lanusse's sole goal was to extricate the military from the fiasco that was to have been la Revolución Argentina. The economic policy was geared uniquely toward "postponing the recession that had appeared on the horizon toward the end of 1970 and which threatened to place additional obstacles in the way of Lanusse's project."[39] During this final presidency of la Revolución, which lasted little over two years, there were four ministers of economics. Aldo Ferrer was held over from the Levingston presidency as he refused to resign, and there was not enough political unity within the military to fire him. Lanusse, in order to appoint his own economics minister without overly antagonizing the nationalist sectors of the military, was forced to rearrange the whole cabinet and eliminate the very position of minister of economics.[40]

In June 1971, after the reorganization of the cabinet positions, Juan Quillici was appointed to the position that corresponded to that of minister of economics. His only task was that of fostering economic activity; there was no longer even the rhetoric associated with industrial deepening and economic restructuring. Quillici allowed the public sector deficit to swell, reflecting the mounting demands on government for which no resources were available. Of course, inflation increased. An attempt was made to control the inflationary spiral through wage- and price-freezes; these, however, functioned poorly and resulted in suppressed inflation that would inevitably strike later. Finally, the minister introduced a shadow exchange rate in a desperate attempt to keep the balance of payments situation controllable. This policy, too, had significant future costs.

In October 1971, just six months after Quillici was named minister, Cayetano Licciardo replaced him as the deteriorating economic indicators forced action, or at least the semblance of action, on the part of Lanusse. The new minister attempted a necessary stabilization policy: relatively tight monetary and fiscal policy, negotiations for a standby loan with the IMF, and stop-gap measures to control the mounting current accounts deficits. Under these political conditions, however, such a policy was impossible. Other ministers, under pressure from the corporatist entities and the various factions within the military, implemented policies that clearly negated Licciardo's initiatives. For example, a series of significant wage increases was granted. The minister was also facing pressure from all sectors for expansionary policy. The universal dissatisfaction with the austerity measures forced yet another economics minister to step down.

Finally, in October 1972, Jorge Wehbe took the reins of economic policy. All sectors of the Argentine economy, from the national and international bourgeoisie to the agricultural elite, continued to lobby for an expansionary policy, which reflected less a show of confidence in such an economic policy than a desire to defend oneself in a "praetorian economy." The government's stated goals and rhetoric were contradictory, scaring all the groups. Moreover, government policy had grown too erratic, government legitimacy had plunged too low for any of the corporatist entities to have any faith that their claims would be championed by the new minister. A praetorian economy, in which all of the corporatist entities could openly battle one another with all resources available to them, seemed to be a safer alternative to any attempts at government policy.

Wehbe could do little except try to limit the damage. Again, his efforts were diluted and often negated by policies that were implemented by ministries over which he had no control. As was hoped by the corporatist entities as well as by the military, which was fearful of any further obstacles to its extrication from government, Wehbe was able to prevent a recession. Miraculously, the minister was also able to stabilize the foreign accounts and the exchange rate. On the inflation and government deficit fronts, however, Wehbe could do little except retreat; they both seemed to have a life beyond his control.

In sum, the contradictory policies, each individually implemented to satisfy particular corporatist entities, were a reflection of a struggle regarding income distribution. The creation of wealth, which seemed to have replaced the distribution of wealth as the goal of economic policy for a fleeting moment at the end of Krieger Vasena's stewardship, was now completely forgotten. Moreover, all of his advances were long since lost. The status quo ante la Revolución returned, only with the problems magnified many times over:

> [T]he sharp and frequent fluctuations in real wages and salaries characteristic of the pre-1966 period recurred as workers and employees fought to protect their incomes against rising inflation.
>   Another similarity between the Lanusse period and the era that many believed Krieger Vasena's administration had eliminated for good was that a trend toward lower real wages and salaries accompanied the ever-wider fluctuations in inflation, wages and salaries.[41]

Clearly, the UCR and the Peronists were actively competing for support in order to supplant the military at the reins of power. The hope was that an active economy would strengthen Lanusse's hand in the political struggle with the competing power brokers over the terms of the return to civilian rule. In particular, there was a strong desire to keep Perón from power. The insecurity and the deteriorating situations of the CGT and the CGE resulted, however, in a firm core of support for Perón and a return to his original populistlike policies. He, these corporatist entities believed, would defend their interests.

The political situation reinforced the growing consensus regarding Perón. The central characteristic was growing political violence, violence that took its toll on all social and economic groups from all of the corporatist entities. Many of the terrorist groups were ostensibly fighting for Peronism (the interpretation of which spanned the whole political gambit). Clamping down on such pressures had clearly backfired. This led many to believe that the last possibility for renewed stability and harmony rested on Perón's return.[42]

The Balkanization within the military further weakened Lanusse's bargaining position. In October 1971, a group of ultranationalist, fervently antidemocratic military men staged a coup. The coup was handily put down by Lanusse, but the cost was immense—most important was the fact that the coup rendered worthless Lanusse's threat of not turning the government over to democratic rule, as the factions of the military determined to continue with the transfer of power consolidated their leadership. The military leadership rebuked another of Lanusse's endeavors in February 1973 when he asked all military leaders to sign the Great National Accord, a document that attempted to chart minimally the democratic future of Argentina. Everyone except the highest ranking generals refused.

On the other side, Perón astutely used all the political resources at his disposition to ensure his return to power. This maneuvering was complex and beyond the scope of this book, but included, for example, Perón's refusing to meet with Lanusse after the latter traveled to Spain for just such an encounter. Perón also backed a united platform with other party leaders such as Ricardo Balbín, head of the Radicals, so as to increase pressure for a transfer to civilian rule. After all of these maneuvers, elections were called and Perón decided to sponsor the candidacy of Héctor Cámpora, a long-time Peronist politician best know for his unfaltering loyalty to Perón himself. Despite a last-minute change in the electoral process on the part of the military, Cámpora won the popular election in 1973 with over 49 percent of the vote in the most free and open elections in decades. The Peronist Reconstrucción Nacional was about to begin.

Notes

1. Laura Randall, *An Economic History of Argentina in the Twentieth Century*, p. 91.

2. It is difficult for the observer unfamiliar with Argentine politics to understand how the military can be certain of support among society and the corporatist entities. A useful work in this regard that discusses how the military plays a political role is *Los que Mandan* by J. L. de Imaz. Dr. Martínez de Hoz, who was economic minister under a military regime (1976–1981), explained to the author that the military leaders gain insight into the feelings of the population at large through everyday social contact: "Over dinner, for example, people will begin asking the generals they have over as guests why the military does not take over" (personal interview). Saúl Ubaldini, the leader of the CGT, claims that explicit deals were forged before all coups in the period studied between the military and the corporatist entities (personal interview).

3. See Guillermo O'Donnell, *Bureaucratic Authoritarianism*.

4. Marcelo Cavarozzi, "Political Cycles," p. 34.

5. See, for example, Guillermo O'Donnell, "Reflections on the Patterns of Change in Bureaucratic-Authoritarian States," "State and Alliances in Argentina, 1956–1976," "Tensions in the Bureaucratic-Authoritarian State and the Question of Democracy."

6. Guillermo O'Donnell, *Bureaucratic Authoritarianism*, p. 64.

7. Samuel Baily, "Argentina: Search for Consensus," p. 306.

8. Eldon Kenworthy, "Argentina: The Politics of Late Industrialization," p. 475.

9. Guillermo O'Donnell, *Bureaucratic Authoritarianism*, p. 76.

10. William C. Smith, *Authoritarianism and the Crisis of the Argentine Political Economy*, p. 113.

11. Peter G. Snow, *Political Forces in Argentina*, p. 95.

12. Alberto Grimoldi, personal interview.

13. This term is borrowed from Juan Linz who, in his study *The Breakdown of Democratic Regimes* in which he analyzed groups of political opposition, came to the conclusion that all opposition groups could be labeled loyal, disloyal, and semiloyal. The meanings of these terms should become clear within the text without any further explanations.

14. Ronaldo Munck, *Argentina: From Anarchism to Peronism*, p. 169.

15. Devaluations always increase inflationary pressure as the costs of imported products and of products with international (dollar) prices immediately jump. By reducing import duties, the cost of these products increased to a smaller degree. The increased export duties had the same effect as food prices are determined by international markets—by increasing the wedge between the international price and the price received by the producers, national prices would go up only marginally.

16. Public services refer to the supply of gas, electricity, and sales of gasoline, as examples, and are the source of a large part of the government's revenues.

17. Juan Carlos de Pablo, *Politica antiinflacionaria en la Argentina, 1967–1970*, pp. 32–33, my translation.

18. Although credit was controlled as were official interest rates, Argentina also had a semiofficial financial system, run largely by the notaries, in which the interest rate and the quantity of capital available were largely determined by the money supply.

19. Backward-linked economic inputs refers to the products required to make other products, for example robots for cars or computer chips for computers. As a country develops, it generally tries to "deepen" its industrial base by encouraging backward linkages.

20. Eduardo de Zavalía, president, La Sociedad Rural Argentina, personal interview.

21. William Smith, *Authoritarianism and the Crisis of the Argentine Political Economy*, p. 99.

22. Juan Carlos de Pablo, *Politica antiinflacionaria en la Argentina, 1967–1970*, p. 73, my translation.

23. Gilbert W. Merkx, "Sectoral Clashes and Political Change: The Argentine Experience."

24. Juan Carlos de Pablo, *Politica antiinflacionaria en la Argentina, 1967–1970*, pp. 89-90.

25. This tax can be considered a fixed cost where: Profits = (market price − production costs per unit of output)(total output) − fixed costs. This can be

simplified: Profits = (output)(profit per unit) − fixed costs. As fixed costs are increased, profits are reduced and can turn negative. This can be counterbalanced only by increasing production, as the profit margin per unit of output must be considered an externality as it is determined by market prices.

26. William Smith, *Authoritarianism and the Crisis of the Argentine Political Economy*, p. 123.

27. Guillermo O'Donnell, *Bureaucratic Authoritarianism*, p. 151.

28. David Rock, *Argentina: 1516–1982*, p. 350.

29. This account is based on several of the author's interviews. Most interviewees preferred to remain anonymous regarding these matters.

30. Guillermo O'Donnell, *Bureaucratic Authoritarianism*, p. 163.

31. John Thompson, "Argentine Economic Policy Under the Onganía Regime," pp. 70 and 75.

32. Juan Carlos de Pablo, *Politica antiinflacionaria en la Argentina, 1967–1970*, p. 102. For a more complete analysis of the economics policy, see Chapter 4 in this book.

33. Guillermo O'Donnell, *Bureaucratic Authoritarianism*, p. 181.

34. William Smith, *Authoritarianism and the Crisis of the Argentine Political Economy*, p. 176.

35. The Noah's ark model is a creation of Juan Carlos de Pablo.

36. Mariano Filippini and María Angélica Olcese, "Transitional Economic Policies, 1971–73," p. 195.

37. Guillermo O'Donnell, *Bureaucratic Authoritarianism*, p. 241.

38. Mariano Filippini and María Angélica Olcese, "Transitional Economic Policies, 1971–73," p. 196.

39. Guillermo O'Donnell, *Bureaucratic Authoritarianism*, p. 276; most of the information regarding the economic policy during the Lanusse presidency comes from Filippini and Olcese, where a slightly more detailed analysis can be found.

40. The new position that corresponded to it was the minister of the treasury. For the sake of simplicity, the author will always refer to the ministry in charge of economic policy as the ministry of economics.

41. Guillermo O'Donnell, *Bureaucratic Authoritarianism*, p. 266.

42. See William C. Smith, *Authoritarianism and the Crisis of the Argentine Political Economy*, pp. 216–222.

3

Juan Perón and the Populist Alliance, 1973–1976

The Cámpora Presidency and
the Return to Peronism

Héctor Cámpora was a long-time but completely undistinguished Peronist politician. He was closely associated with the leftist factions of the Peronist party and, as was common with the adherents of these factions, was a strong believer in the mobilization of Peronist supporters. Most important, though, Cámpora was chosen to represent Juan Perón fundamentally because of his unfaltering and unquestioning allegiance to the old general himself. With Cámpora's traits Perón could best broaden his support across all sectors and fringes of the disjoint Peronist movement and society at large. This was to be done in three ways: (1) by discrediting and humiliating the military government, (2) by mobilizing supporters, and (3) by keeping Perón's longer-term policy goals a mystery.

The choice of Cámpora jeopardized the very electoral process. Given Cámpora's leftist tendencies and undistinguished past, many believed that Perón actually hoped that the military would either proscribe his candidate or else postpone the elections. As Perón's return to power was nearly inevitable at this point, such a move by the military government would only have wrought further chaos. The fact that Lanusse could not or would not proscribe Cámpora was justifiably seen as an avowal of weakness of the military government. Perón was hence increasingly seen as the only person, the only power broker, that would be able to return Argentina to some state of stability. It must be noted that this strategy was merely a continuation of the one that Perón implemented throughout his exile, and quite conspicuously since the Cordobazo, a strategy that was not necessarily as good for the Peronist movement as for augmenting Perón's personal power. "Perón's destructive role in part paralleled that . . . of a personalistic, charismatic leader of a populist movement who was unwilling to give up his own power in the larger interest of the movement."[1] And yet these actions brought together a tremendous coalition that would soon sweep Perón to the presidency with at least the tacit support of almost the whole nation.

Clearly, Peronists on the left, including many of the terrorist groups fighting in Perón's name, such as the Montoneros, were jubilant over the choice of Cámpora—the presidential candidate came from these ranks. The campaign slogan ("Cámpora to the presidency, Perón to power"), however, was created so as to unify the diverse and heterogeneous factions within Peronism; each group interpreted "Perón to power" as it so desired. The more conservative facets of Peronism were further encouraged by constant dialogue with the general. The election results revealed that the strategy had worked: Cámpora received just under 50 percent of the popular vote, with support that cut across all sections of society. The new president "represented a transition" during which time "each sector interpreted . . . in its own way the motto 'Perón to power.'"[2]

The attempts to expand the base of support continued even after the electoral victory. On the one hand, Cámpora stepped up his radical leftist rhetoric; indeed, the left felt and seemed to be "on the border of success" during the Cámpora presidency.[3] Unions were actively supported by the government in a growing number of labor disputes, which often involved strikes and factory takeovers.[4] On the other hand, Perón instructed Cámpora to appoint several relatively conservative ministers who were to reassure the capitalist classes. Most important, José Ber Gelbard, the CGE caudillo, was sent to the economics ministry; this clearly calmed the national bourgeoisie as well as owners of capital generally.

As there was a complete lack of a viable liberal political platform, these groups were very receptive to the idea of working with Perón. The SRA and the UIA believed Perón's return to power was inevitable and hence that it was better to try to affect policy from within the movement than to remain completely isolated. In a move geared towards winning over Perón's confidence, the Unión Industrial Argentina dissolved itself and instructed its members to join the traditionally Peronist CGE. Even the SRA, which had historically been the most anti-Peronist of all of the corporatist entities, now "had a collaborationist outlook."[5] Liliana de Riz summed up the situation by explaining that "in 1973 to be 'Argentine' was to be Peronist, to give precedence to national and state reconstruction above any party differences."[6] The Peronists were eager to reinforce this rapprochement with discussions, contacts, and policy commitments.

Within this nearly all-inclusive coalition and despite the chaotic circumstances, the very beginning of an alliance similar in structure to that brokered by Krieger Vasena was discernible. Gelbard, with full support from Perón, formulated a social pact, el Acta de Compromiso Nacional (the Act of National Compromise). This pact was to be the centerpiece of his economic program, and, indeed, of la Reconstrucción Nacional. The CGE, the CGT, and the state were the only signatories; a corporatist alliance between the national bourgeoisie and the unions was being nurtured.[7]

It was becoming clear, however, that the success of any alliance was incompatible with the continued mobilization of all sectors of Peronism. Violence was growing, industry was stalled, and all the various "Peronist" groups called for very different policies. The groups on the extreme left and the extreme right proved to be particularly explosive. The so-called Ezeiza Airport Massacre, in which the extreme left and the extreme right of the Peronist Party clashed violently, leaving scores dead on 20 June 1973, epitomized the growing tensions. In sum, the juxtaposition of such a large coalition with popular mobilization was showing itself to be highly destabilizing.

It seems as though this was part of Perón's overall plan. He simultaneously stoked the fires of discontentment and desires to reinforce his image as the great healer, the savior of Argentina. Certainly, as the crisis grew, many groups, including those such as the SRA that were traditionally vehemently anti-Peronist, were more willing to offer Perón freedom of action and support in a desperate search for a national consensus. The desires that Perón masterfully manipulated within all groups of his coalition, however, were not fulfillable; he did not yet realize the need for trade-offs and clear choices, a fact that was increasingly destroying the chances of success of his presidency. As the social and political situation grew more untenable, all factions began calling for Perón's immediate ascendance to the presidency; each group, of course, still assumed that Perón's true beliefs were similar to its own.

To this end, Héctor Cámpora resigned on 13 July and and called for new elections. The whole democratic process was already somewhat farcical: The country's social fabric was being torn apart by increasingly aggressive and violent terrorists, the economy was in a crisis, and two elections were called within months. To this was added further political chicanery on the part of the Peronists. The president of the Senate, Alejandro Díaz Bialet, was unexpectedly sent abroad so that Raúl Lastiri, president of the lower chamber of the Congress and one of the more supportive of Perón's followers, could be appointed interim president. Perón's second wife, María Estela "Isabel" Martínez de Perón, was chosen to be the vice-presidential candidate so as to solidify further the broad-based support within the movement. Unlike any other Peronist apart from the general himself, she was not associated with any particular faction of Peronism. She also rendered the democratic process even less legitimate in the public's eyes, however; Martínez de Perón had no political expertise and was dependent solely on her husband (and her new family name) for the power that she now wielded.

Given his still awesome popularity, the chaotic situation, and the complete lack of political alternatives, Perón predictably won the election with 65 percent of the vote. He would soon become the fourth Argentine president in fewer than six months and hardly received his mandate in an institutionalized or universally accepted manner.

Perón and the Populist Alliance

General Juan Perón was sworn in as president in October 1973, eighteen years after being overthrown. His popularity resulted in a tremendous amount of freedom of action during the beginning of his short time as president. Perón's first actions, however, did not belie an attempt to create a small and cohesive alliance from the immense coalition that he had assembled. Instead, he obviously offered his support to the economic plan formulated by Gelbard but at the same time tried to satisfy the criticisms of more radical and leftist groups within the movement. At this point, he was not even willing to break with the most dissident of his supporters.

On an economic level, Gelbard worked under many of the same constraints as Krieger Vasena; the "liberal" corporatist entities could not be fully excluded from the economic program. Perón wanted and believed he could lead and help the whole nation, both the traditionally Peronist parts and the anti-Peronist parts. It seems as though the old general really believed that he could foster a national consensus under a Peronist banner that would automatically promote growth and stability. Moreover, given the meltdown of the economy and the corporatist structure, it would have been impossible, regardless of Perón's desires, to exclude completely any groups as powerful as the SRA or UIA.

Many of Gelbard's policies reflected the hesitation of consummating a more intimate partnership between the government and any one or even two corporatist entities. For example, Gelbard made a concerted effort to keep agricultural prices stable and relatively high compared to industrial goods; although the relative prices did shift in a unfavorable manner toward the SRA, agricultural prices declined only slightly and remained well above the levels during the Krieger Vasena period. Despite the explicit goals of limiting and even reversing foreign penetration of the economy, Guido di Tella (a member of the economics team toward the end of the Peronist experiment) claims that the government "was not too strict in applying the law" that was biased against foreign capital, so as to encourage a certain flow of foreign investment.[8]

The alliance the government brokered between the CGE and the CGT was necessarily rendered more tenuous given the compromises made for the benefit of the liberal sectors. La Reconstrucción Nacional could not move beyond a "tentative alliance." The signatories of the National Compromise were clearly the most favored entities in an economic program that was obviously quite populist, but the alliance was forever to remain a tentative one for reasons that should be clear. First, the other two primary corporatist entities were not fully excluded. Second, all factions represented within the power broker, including extremists to the left and even, as will be seen, to the right, had to be satisfied, to the detriment of the core alliance. Finally, the very essence of an alliance between capital and labor implied an unwillingness or an inability to choose one over the other, a condition that necessarily creates certain tensions; these tensions could be controlled during an economic expansion but would prove to be the final downfall during the times of economic recession that would come.

The plan itself, as it related to the favored corporatist entities, had various components. As was mentioned above, the centerpiece of Gelbard's economic plan was a social pact between the state, the CGE, and the CGT. The fundamental goal of the Act of National Compromise, as its name implies, was to create a degree of consensus within Argentine society and particularly between labor and capital; an explicit attempt was made to eliminate the competition among the corporatist entities over the distribution of national income. Implicit in this plan of action was the belief that the creation of wealth through investment would be facilitated by fostering national harmony. The reasoning was certainly sound, which encouraged the tacit support of the excluded corporatist entities.

The social pact called for a greater proportion of national income to go to the working classes through wage increases. The share of wages as a percentage of national income was raised by 4 percent to 46 percent of GNP.[9] It should be noted that the wage increase, although substantial, was far below that called for by the unions. The policy was not to be geared solely towards benefiting the union groups and hence left them somewhat dissatisfied. The wage increase took the form of an across-the-board wage increase of 200 pesos per month (about $20 at the official exchange rate); this plan resulted in a significant flattening of the wage scale. The social pact simultaneously called for a price freeze so as to prevent an inflationary erosion of the increased wages. This meant that these higher costs were to be absorbed by the business groups. In other words, the wage increase was supposed to be a one-time adjustment to increase wages to their "appropriate" levels, after which their real purchasing power would be assured as all prices were to be frozen for two full years.

The social pact had two flaws. First, by decreasing profit margins (increasing costs while freezing prices), the propensity to invest would naturally decline. This decline posed a significant problem as a major goal of the government was once again, as it was under the Onganía regime, an economic restructuring and revitalization. Second, the National Compromise, as it stood alone, was a typical populist economic policy, one that had already been attempted in Argentina (during Perón's first presidency) as well as in other countries, and that had always resulted in failure. Real wages would quickly decline to market levels, a foreign accounts crisis would develop, and inflation would increase.[10] In sum, promoting economic expansion solely through increasing real wages had been proven not to be self-sustaining. A series of measures was therefore simultaneously implemented to ensure a sturdier recovery and significant investment.

The economics team devised two fundamental tools geared towards further increasing demand so as to ensure a self-propelling expansion. The first stimulus was to be greatly increased government investment and spending. Second, industrial exports were to be strongly encouraged through export subsidies and preferential exchange rates. In other words, exports of industrial products were to be an added stimulus to the economy. The most notable push regarding industrial exports was toward socialist countries, particularly Cuba, which proved to be ideal markets for Argentine products. This policy, it should be added, also contented the leftist groups within the Peronist movement. The government also created a new line of highly subsidized credit to the business community; it was designed to help assuage the difficulties of paying higher wages. In reality, however, the negative real interest rates offered a method for the national bourgeoisie to displace a part of the increased labor costs onto the state; the tensions created by an alliance between labor and capital could only be controlled with economic redistribution from the state.

Gelbard also envisioned some structural changes geared toward increasing the efficiency of the economy. A rationalization of state enterprises was planned based on the Italian model offered by IRI (Institutute for Industrial Reconstruction), an organization through which all state holdings were managed. A tax on the productive capacity of land was once again called for (but again, not implemented) as a method to increase agricultural output. It should also be noted that the plan was implemented in an international climate that was highly favorable for Argentina—terms of trade were good and demand for traditional exports was buoyant.

As was the case during the Onganía presidency, immediate results were deemed essential to the economic plan. Inflation was to be arrested in one fell swoop, and growth activated immediately. The need for immediate results resulted not only from the conditional support of the excluded corporatist entities but also from the tension within the chosen alliance. Without growth, the national bourgeoisie could increase profits almost exclusively at the cost of labor and vice versa, a fact that would cause fighting within the alliance. The only hope for a successful alliance was to promote growth so that both capital and labor could profit.

The initial results of Gelbard's plan were excellent. Again, the hope of stability and a rational economic policy caused a boom. With Perón's return to power and the widespread, albeit superficial, consensus he created, reactivation of the economy was easily effected. Inflation declined precipitously (see

Figure 3.1). Unemployment declined markedly over a sustained period of time. The rate of growth declined during the first semester of the economic policy (remaining, however, at a level above the historical mean) but then subsequently rose. Most impressive was the increase in consumption, which, in the second half of 1973, averaged 7 percent over the previous year (7.3 percent for the last quarter), and then jumped to an 11 percent increase for the first nine months of 1974.

Figure 3.1   Monthly Inflation Rate, 1973

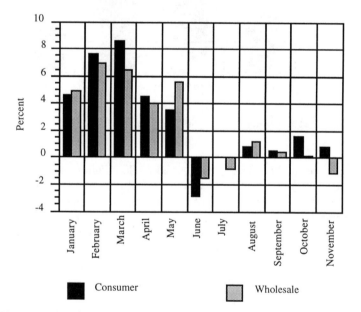

Source: Based on data from de Pablo and Martínez 1988.

Even foreign reserves increased continuously from the beginning of the economic plan, as can be seen in Figure 3.2. The government pointed to these results in order to justify the economic plan as well as Peronism itself. In so doing, however, the legitimacy of Perón's government, like Onganía's, became dependent on favorable economic indicators. This was particularly the case regarding inflation. Perón committed himself to zero inflation, a pronouncement that significantly limited the freedom of the economics team.

Tensions in the plan began to surface quickly. The international sector deteriorated throughout Perón's presidency, as shown in Figure 3.3. This condition was not contemplated during the formation of policy, and hence it

Figure 3.2   Foreign Reserves, 1972–1975

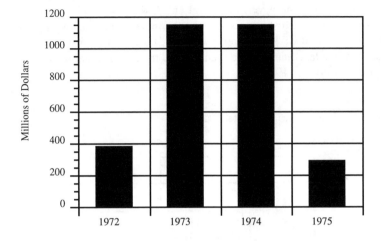

Source: Based on data from de Pablo and Martínez 1988.

caused great difficulties. During this period world inflation increased (largely due to oil prices). This inflation was unavoidably imported into Argentina because the economy was dependent on many foreign intermediate goods. The increase in oil prices also had an adverse effect on the battle against inflation as well as the country's foreign accounts—Argentina's oil bill skyrocketed from $58 million for 1973 to $586 million for the subsequent year.[11] Later on, in July 1974, the European Community prohibited any further importation of Argentine meat, thus closing off one of Argentina's largest markets. All of these international factors further skewed relative prices that were already growing increasingly incongruous with the stringent price freeze.

The other problem was the bulging budget deficit. This deficit reflected the inability of the government to decide upon a distribution of income that the state and the country could afford. The coalition demanded more redistribution than could be extracted from the excluded sectors. The deficit, needless to say, also reflected an inability to unequivocally decide upon a mode of accumulation.

At the same time, the budget deficit was largely and increasingly paid for through monetary emission, that is, the printing of money without assuring sufficient foreign currency and gold reserves. The willingness of the economics team to rapidly increase the money supply seems, according to all economic theory, to contradict the explicit goal of combating inflation. In the short term, such increases in the money supply can be compatible with

Figure 3.3 **Terms of Trade, March 1973–March 1976 (based on 1970 trade mix)**

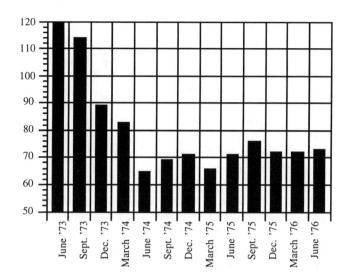

Source: Based on data from Guido di Tella, "Argentina's Economy Under a Labour-based Government, 1973–6," in *The Political Economy of Argentina, 1946–1983*, edited by Guido di Tella and Rudiger Dornbusch, Macmillan, London, 1989.

low inflation as the demand for money increases (that is to say, velocity decreases). An increase in the demand for money is predictable and empirically observed when inflation goes down and political stability returns. To simplify, the greater the economic and political stability in Argentina, the more willing Argentines are to hold pesos instead of buying dollars. This increase in the demand for money during stabilization programs offers the state a temporary source of financing. The state can print and spend an amount of money equal to the increased demand for money without causing inflationary pressures. Indeed, this process was used with success by Krieger Vasena in order to augment state investments. The reliance on monetary emission, however, went far beyond what have been even remotely compatible with zero inflation. Canitrot explained the dynamic at work:

> Gelbard believed he could resolve it as long as the restructuring and the expansion of the economy continued to take place. The expansion, however, was not quite strong enough to resolve the conflicts, so that he needed to foster greater demand the effect of which, besides fully utilizing the excess capacity within the economy, was to promote inflation. In this way inflation once again began its spiral. This reinforced the highly expansionary monetary policy, needed to finance the deficit, by creating increased need for subsidized credit for industry.[12]

This is a clear manifestation of the structural problems caused by corporatism. Peronism, a power broker, was, on the one hand, so enmeshed with both the CGE and the CGT that it had to attempt to redistribute to both, through higher wages, expansionary policy, and state contracts, as examples. At the same time, agriculture could no longer be tapped to the degree that it had been under Perón's first government. It had grown relatively poorer due to decades of stagnation and had developed better defense mechanisms to retain its wealth. The international sector, assuming that property rights would be respected, could offer little to subsidize the economic project but could detract from the country's potential development by refusing to invest. This is to say that the excluded corporatist entities could not be expected to subsidize the chosen alliance.

A further manifestation of the warped corporatist structure was the fact that Perón's government could not even reap the political benefits of the redistribution that it did effect; in other words, the corporatist entities remained capable of far greater mobilization of power than did the government. This imbalance of power resulted from the relatively random recipients of the government's redistribution. The government was incapable of, and probably disinterested in, funneling the redistribution to identifiable and cohesive groups that might then support the government.

In order to understand this, we must attempt to discern the beneficiaries of the government's policies. Overall, they were the labor groups and the industrialists. According to the policies implemented, the greatest beneficiaries within the CGT would have been the lowest wage earners as the increases in wages were mainly across the board; the percentage increases were far higher for low than for high earners.[13] This policy of flattening the wage scale (as can be observed in Figure 3.4) was almost certainly geared towards satisfying the left of the Peronist party. This policy, however, made little sense politically as it has traditionally been the unions of the higher income groups that wielded the most power and that were traditionally Peronist.

Although some of the most important unions, including those representing textile, petroleum, chemical, paper, and steel workers, were able to negotiate "voluntary," but not technically legal, supplementary wages (which do not appear in the figure), the government was seen as the opponent in these negotiations.[14] Clearly, these wage increases eroded the legitimacy of the price and wage freeze and, hence, that of the government itself. A further result was the disenchantment with government enforcement on the part of the weaker unions. Both the powerful and the weak unions found problems with the government's policy and were left to fight for themselves, conditions that limited the ability and desire of union leaders to mobilize the rank and file to support the government.

Figure 3.4   Salary Differentials, May 1973–March 1975

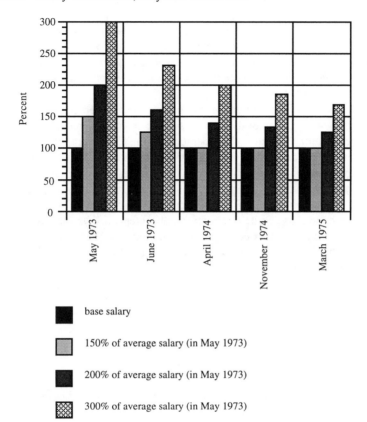

base salary

150% of average salary (in May 1973)

200% of average salary (in May 1973)

300% of average salary (in May 1973)

Source: Based on data from Aldo A. Arnaudo, "El programa antiinflacionaria de 1973," *Desarrollo Económico*, April 1979.

The confused picture regarding the true beneficiaries of the redistribution was mirrored in the industrial sector. On the one hand, the larger, more technologically advanced firms, which were more often than not associated with the UIA rather than the CGE, were far more rigorously policed regarding the price freeze. This directly resulted, other things remaining equal, in lower profits than those of smaller firms. The redistribution between small and large firms was reinforced with increases in demand, both directly through state contracts and indirectly through increased consumer demand, that would mainly benefit the national bourgeoisie. On the other hand, the very structure of the price and wage freeze hurt the CGE more than the UIA. The national bourgeoisie was less technologically advanced and more dependent on manpower for each unit of output. These conditions combined with higher real labor costs resulted in relatively greater pressure on their profit margins as compared to the technologically advanced and less labor-intensive international bourgeoisie. Considering "that the drop in investment was greatest in those sectors where the increase in consumption was most pronounced—especially in nondurable consumer goods,"[15] it seems logical to conclude that firms of the national bourgeoisie were often doing quite poorly despite the populist alliance.

The dearth of investment on the part of the favored corporatist entities also reflected the desire of these groups to profit from the redistribution rather than the creation of wealth. The members of the CGE were, on the whole, in favor of the government's policies. At the same time, however, this group refrained from increasing investment. The policies benefited the members of the CGE through distribution. The desire for redistribution was just as, if not more prominent in the CGT; the increased wages in no way resulted in greater productivity. Quite the contrary, absenteeism skyrocketed during the Peronist government, reflecting the complete lack of desire to help produce more wealth for the country. The reliance on redistribution instead of creation of wealth on the part of the CGE and the CGT represents the inability of the government to mobilize its supposed supporters and to impose efficient constraints on those corporatist entities that were abusing the inducements extended to them.

Cracks in the Alliance

The pressures on Perón and on Gelbard grew on all sides. On the one hand, the Montoneros and other Peronist guerrilla groups began to openly criticize the government. They also refused to lay down the arms with which they would resume their armed struggle after the general's death. Despite the disagreements between the president and the extreme left of his coalition, the bourgeoisie was getting scared that the communist left was getting too powerful. One cannot overemphasize the personal and political fears of this time in Argentina. This group observed that Perón was eager and persistent in his attacks against the owners of capital: Wages were increased and the price freeze was ever more tightly regulated. At the same time, he seemed unable or unwilling to arrest the communist insurgency.[16]

On the economic front, occurrences began to take place that the government could not officially explain. For example, from the signing of the social pact in June 1973 onward, real purchasing power declined significantly despite the low official inflation rate.[17] Matters were made worse for the future as all efforts to restructure and to rationalize the economy were "forgotten as attention was increasingly switched to the stabilization program."[18]

The first major change to the social pact occurred on 27 March 1974, just ten months after the initial signing of the compromise instead of the two years stipulated in the agreement. The changes were geared almost solely towards pacifying the unionized workers. Salaries were increased 13 percent, a move that clearly broke the commitment to two years of frozen prices and wages. Once again the government implemented a wage increase that implicitly flattened wage rates as a minimum increase of 240 pesos was guaranteed to all workers. The minimum wage, in this way, was increased by 30 percent. Welfare transfers were also significantly increased, adding further to the inflationary pressures. To counteract the added pressure on inflation, more stringent monitoring of the price freeze was promised, much to the consternation of business groups. By alienating industry, plans for economic restructuring and renewed investment were becoming increasingly implausible.

The only benefits offered to the CGE related to credit. First, the special subsidized line of credit was extended, the cost of which was, of course, a larger budget deficit and soaring inflationary pressures. Further, regular credit, the interest rate and recipients of which were decided by the state, was offered at a significantly lower rate. This change in financial policy was completely illogical. The real interest rate at the beginning of the stabilization plan skyrocketed as inflation plummeted, but no change in the nominal rate was effected. Now that inflation was clearly and undeniably returning, nominal interest rates were lowered so much that real interest rates would soon be absurdly negative. The change also reflects the growing need of the government to offer inducements to the corporatist entities. Whereas at the beginning of the program, the government could use the implicit constraint of higher wages to try to effect change in the CGE, now all constraints had to be counteracted with inducements. These policies also reflect the growing need to buy some base of support. The popularity and very legitimacy of the government were on the rapid decline, and desperate attempts were made to ensure the legitimacy of the government through popular measures that had economic costs. Perón, therefore, was willing to pay the economic price of higher wages "in order to obtain the support of the CGT."[19]

Perón's choice of favoring the CGT over the CGE with the significant wage increases was largely compromised the next month, however, as "flexible prices" were announced. The goal of zero inflation was necessarily discarded, and the battle over the distribution of income was facilitated through the implicit acceptance of the return of inflation, which jumped to about 50 percent per year (see Figure 3.5). Workers saw their recently won wage increases evaporate into history.

Perón hoped that he would still be able to hold the program together. Certainly, he still had many advantages—he was charismatic and personally popular. More important, many groups, particularly unions, were unwilling or unable to openly attack the president as, after all, these groups and their leaders were "Peronists"; even the Montoneros, although willing to criticize

Figure 3.5   Increase in Inflation Rate over Previous Year, May 1973–May 1976

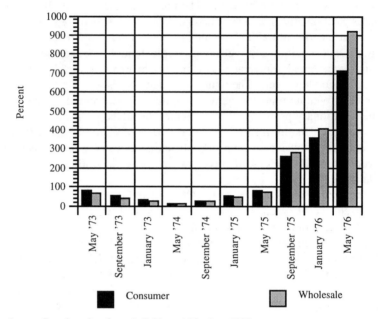

Source: Based on data from de Pablo and Martínez 1988.

the government's policies, would not revert to terrorism in favor of "true Peronism" until after the aging general's death. As of yet, there were no power brokers that offered a viable alternative to the Peronists, thus limiting the pressure on the government: The military had given up power in near disgrace just a year before and the Radicals had, until just about this period, fully collaborated with Perón, hence rendering them almost as guilty as the Justicialist Party for the economic and social tumult.

In June, the president made an all-out attempt to consolidate his power and support the economic plan. He first met with representatives of the CGE in order to reassert his seriousness regarding economic stabilization and restructuring. It was at this time that he also began to buy time by blaming much of the economic team's failure on "speculators" and "enemies of the state." A few days after his meeting with the business leaders, Perón went public with his call for support in the Plaza de Mayo. De Pablo sums up the results of Perón's efforts well: "Perón defended the economic plan in the political arena, giving the former a little bit of oxygen that rendered a readjustment of the economic plan possible. Such a readjustment to the preceding policies might have facilitated more reasonable economic outcomes."[20] Thus it is clear that even had Perón lived, the possibility of economic success was slim. Unfortunately, he died a few weeks later. That slim possibility was buried with the old caudillo.

Perón's Social Program

Juan Perón's social program was diametrically opposed to that of Onganía. The military government wanted to depoliticize Argentine society, to create a paternalistic type of relationship between the government and the governed, and to eliminate all forms of extremism. Finally, one can certainly say that Onganía was conservative. But Perón and his social policy could not be so patly defined as conservative or liberal: It was unclear throughout Perón's exile and even during his whole government in the 1970s whether the aging leader was to the right or to the left, for or against the church, revolutionary or outright conservative. All the same, he quite clearly had a very conscientiously developed social platform that was continuously advocated.

One fundamental trait of la Reconstrucción Nacional was the overt policy to mobilize supporters. The contrast with la Revolución Argentina could not be clearer. Onganía encouraged tacit and quiet agreement on the part of those whom he governed. Their voicing of opinions in any way was not wanted and not heard. Implicitly, Onganía promised Argentines that he would look after their own well-being. Perón, on the other hand, encouraged the mobilization of the Peronist masses from the 1940s onward. Whereas the military government needed public calm to retain legitimacy and stay in power, Perón needed public outcry to be able to return. The energetic actions of Peronist groups served an obvious purpose for Perón—to make him necessary as the great healer and hence to return him to power. The general's ambiguous and vague statements were conscientiously calculated to gain support from all groups. Instead of being grounded in ideology or personal morality, Perón's political actions were determined solely by his calculations to hone support from any and all groups. As the traditional populist alliance between national capital and labor unions had proven itself to be insufficiently strong to keep Perón in power in the 1950s, attempts were multiplied to gain support from anti-Peronist groups in order to enlarge the coalition.

It would be wrong to say, however, that the mobilization of his followers was merely a political maneuver to gain power, as it continued even after the caudillo was once again sworn in as president. Through the vociferous support of his government, Perón believed he could create a "Peronist" state which, by its very nature, would be cohesive and unified. Peronism was to provide an outlet for people's energies, which would be put to productive use and unify various groups under the banner of social justice. Perón was the leader, but he implicitly told his followers it was they who had to seize initiatives and shape the future. Nothing could contrast more with the paternalist viewpoint of la Revolución.

The mobilized "Peronist" state, however, could only be led by the old general himself. Perón always refused to give up his personal power for the greater good of his supporters or of Argentina. His social platform represented what he felt to be an ideal, albeit a very inflammatory and controversial one, but he manipulated this social ideal ruthlessly to defend his personal power. Even in 1973, Perón still felt that he should and could be at the center of Argentina's political stage. His political actions continuously belied his desire to return to power even if such an endeavor sacrificed the welfare of his supposed supporters. For example, he had forcefully and successfully opposed the development of a Peronist movement under the leadership of others, despite the fact that this would have been advantageous for both the populist cause and many of his supporters. He was willing to pander to groups outside his traditional supporters to enlarge his base of support, which was needed not only to return to power but also to retain it. To this end, the general forged alliances with any and all who advocated his leadership regardless of their political and economic outlook. For example, through the more conservative planks of his movement led by José López Rega, Perón sought and largely gained the support of reactionary, economically conservative, and vehemently antiunion groups.

In sum, Perón's social program throughout his exile and during his government was geared toward "Peronizing" Argentine society. Groups that sought their own self-interest, with almost complete disregard as to what that was, under the Peronist banner were praised; those that did so in opposition to him were ostracized. Perón actively encouraged the outlook that "to be 'Argentine' was to be Peronist."[21] This social program, similar to all of those during the corporatist breakdown period, attempted to redefine Argentine society and politics in a manner desired by the power broker. Opposition, as had been the case under Onganía, was not accepted.

The desire to form a united "Peronist" society seemed to be successful in 1973. As described above, the corporatist entities took on a Peronist veneer: The UIA merged with the CGE, and the SRA clearly toned down its traditional anti-Peronist rhetoric. Moreover, Perón was able to foster good relations with the other power brokers, which, as is typical at the beginning of all of the governments studied, seemed incapable or unwilling to challenge the government. Several nationalist factions of the military hoped that Perón could return the country to a more protectionist and populist economic course. The Radical Party, led by Ricardo Balbín, accepted a secondary role in the government that reduced the Radicals to little more than powerless stooges; Balbín thought that attempts to challenge Juan Perón would have been fruitless.

As was typical during the breakdown period, university curricula were altered, this time to stress the justice and importance of the first Peronist government and the tyranny of the coup that overthrew it. The judicial system, as had been the case under Onganía, lost almost all autonomy.

Student unions were encouraged to assume an actively political stance in support of the government. With Gelbard's initial economic results highly positive and with relative social agreement regarding the need for Perón to save the nation, the end of 1973 augured well for the future of la Reconstrucción Nacional.

The sense of control and power that Perón commanded early on was quickly lost, however. The political maneuvering that allowed the creation of such a diverse coalition resulted in the unwitting incorporation of all of Argentina's political, social, and even economic tensions into the very bosom of Peronism. Under the best of circumstances, these tensions were destined to tear the very fabric of Argentine society, but under these circumstances they were destined to pull the Peronist movement asunder as well, and in the process destroy Perón's ability to give any direction to his country. La Reconstrucción Nacional's social policies, as had been typical throughout the corporatist breakdown period, were based on intolerance. Perón demanded that all groups be "Peronist," so much so that even the UIA and the SRA ended up sculpturing alliances with the government. In return, Perón allowed each group to interpret Peronism as it wanted. The fundamental contradictions herein came to the fore because both the political and economic alliances were based on offering privileges to each of the groups, privileges that taken together were clearly contradictory. On a political level, this meant that each group assumed that it would have the ability to influence policy. In the growing chaos, none was able to do so. The result, it was increasingly obvious, was open warfare.

The struggles were becoming evident by the beginning of 1974. Opposition to both the economic and political policies was mounting. Perón began to realize that his social policies had to be rationalized, that all groups could not be included. The Montoneros as well as the other groups on the extreme left were criticized; attempts were made to force them to disarm, all to no avail. At the same time, Perón tried not to fan the growing fire on the right of his movement under López Rega, who led the Argentine Anti-Communist Association (AAA). Perón was trying to counter certain radical sectors with others; this resulted only in further loss of control. The race against time, similar to that conducted by Gelbard on the economic front, was destined to failure. All of these groups had already become too entrenched in certain sectors of the government to be easily weeded out, expectations had grown too much for patience to return, and too many policies had been compromised for there to be renewed faith in the general's calls for support. It was no longer possible to forge a small and cohesive political alliance after having made so many sacrifices to implement a large "tentative" one.

As inflation was repressed and relatively hidden from the public's eye, so too were the growing tensions within Peronism. So long as Juan Perón was alive, it was difficult for the various factions to protest openly and forcefully that his government's policies were not "truly Peronist." Then the general died. Now each group decided that it could best define Peronism and had the responsibility to continue the struggle. The country's problems, and those within the heart of the PJ, exploded into the public's view.

The terrorist groups began violent campaigns. The Montoneros attacked the conservative bastions of the Peronist Party as well as leaders of Argentina's elite society. The AAA countered with bloody repression of the Peronist left as well as of independent socialists and communists. Argentina's legacy of intolerance had finally burst into the open, into an all-out battle in which no one could win and because of which all were to lose.

The general violence augmented the calls for a new government—as Gelbard's economic policy unraveled, so did the very fabric of Argentine society. The generalized violence, akin to nothing less than an open and violent civil war, also set the stage for the harsh repression that was to occur under Videla. By 1976, few saw alternatives to swift and widespread military attacks against all of the armed groups; the so-called Dirty War that Videla was to initiate against all the rebels was actually seen as a necessary step at this juncture. The violence had become so pitched that excesses had become the norm. The impending civil war could be nothing but dirty. The various armed groups, including the military, a nation's theoretical guardian of peace, felt that bloodletting was necessary. Worse, it seems as though everyone involved, the terrorists and the military, were actually eager to do so.

The Shift in Alliances

The relative political stability and cohesion that Perón had been able to foster disintegrated upon his death, even while the eulogies for the deceased general continued to flow. Two of the most important "Peronist" terrorist groups, the Montoneros and La Juventud Peronista, jointly published a manifesto in which the whole concept of a social pact was lambasted and a return to violent resistance was announced. Within the CGT, too, the struggle for control and political outlook intensified.[22] These were only the first groups to break away from the Peronist Party in the battle for "true Peronism."

Perón's wife and vice president, Isabel Martínez de Perón, assumed the presidency. She could do little about the growing political pressures, at least in the short term. Unfortunately, the same cannot be said about economic policy. Martínez de Perón did nothing to take advantage of the small amount of "oxygen" the general had given the program just before his death.

Gelbard remained minister of economics for three more months, during which time no readjustments to the economic policy were made. On 21 October 1974, Alfredo Gómez Morales replaced Gelbard. Gómez Morales was a long-time Peronist who had actually been called upon by Perón to effect an austerity plan in 1952. The plan was successful. The appointment of Gómez Morales to the ministry of economics was widely applauded both within and outside of the Peronist Party. Another small amount of oxygen was given to the economic plan.

The new president gave little importance to the economic plan, however, and the few changes that were implemented were clearly detrimental to the stabilization plan. A second readjustment was deemed necessary to the Act of National Compromise on 1 November, just days after Gómez Morales was appointed minister. This renegotiation dealt almost exclusively with wages, which were increased precipitously (by approximately 45 percent, of which 15 percent was to be effective immediately, the rest within a few months), thus adding more gas to the inflationary fire. Once again, wage increases resulted in the flattening of the pay scale and were also accompanied by large increases in welfare payments. A third readjustment was announced by the president on 1 March 1975, just four months after the previous renegotiation. Again, wages were raised.

The policies implemented were increasingly contradictory. The economics minister attempted to attract foreign capital; simultaneously, however, Martínez de Perón nationalized the oil exploration contracts held by Exxon and Shell and five foreign-owned banks as well as telephone licenses held by Siemens and International Telephone and Telegraph (ITT). Other economic policies were disastrous. The Central Bank no longer even tried to control monetary emission. Foreign currency reserves, which had increased during the Gelbard period, were being rapidly consumed in redistributive ploys. The government was quickly absorbing all the economic resources available in an attempt to prime the economy just when austerity was needed—legitimacy was sought at all costs. The results were dismal, as was typical of these chaotic periods: Growth was arrested and inflation continued to soar (but unemployment was lower).

Although it was unknown when she was chosen as Juan Perón's running mate, Martínez de Perón actually sympathized with the extreme right wing of the Peronist Party that associated with López Rega. Although this fact might not explain why Martínez de Perón failed to resuscitate Gelbard's economic plan, it does go a long way in explaining the shift in alliances that later occurred.

By the middle of June 1975, opposition to the original economic plan (what was left of it) had already jelled. The SRA was increasingly hostile towards the government, as was the UIA. Political crises once again became the norm instead of the exception. Terrorism increased and grew more brutal. Finally, the other power brokers began to distance themselves from the government, hence implicitly offering themselves as alternatives to the Peronists.

Given these circumstances, Martínez de Perón attempted to create a new alliance. Her plan of action contained four main goals: (1) to eliminate leftist terrorism and infiltration of the universities, (2) to bring the military into the political scene as an implicit supporter of the new programs, (3) to break the union leadership and bring it under control, and, related to this last goal, (4) to change economic course, from the nationalist or "populist" policies of Gelbard to traditionally conservative ones.[23] This represented a complete break with all aspects of the originally envisioned Reconstrucción Nacional.

Right-wing paramilitary groups, including the AAA, gained semiofficial status from the government and the military in their battle against left-wing terrorists. Universities, as well as other civic organizations, were taken over and forced to toe the new official political line—simply being a "Peronist" was no longer enough, as one was now asked to actively support the conservative forces in ascendance. The military, in a move that forebode the characteristics of the government that would overthrow the Peronists, was given carte blanche in its war against all those considered subversives.

A few months after having begun her new political policies, Martínez de Perón announced the corresponding economic strategy. She called for freeing prices (which were officially still controlled), devaluating the peso, stimulating private (over public) investment, reducing the budget deficit, and keeping real wages low. On 2 June 1975, Celestino Rodrigo was chosen to implement this new economic strategy. On 4 June, Rodrigo devalued the peso by approximately 100 percent as compared to the dollar. Of and in itself, this change was not sufficient to augment exports as there was insufficient supply for both the still buoyant domestic market as well as the foreign market. To counteract this, Rodrigo's explicit goal was the reduction of real purchasing power through lower real wages. The government declared on 9 June that no wage increases above 38 percent would be authorized, an increase well below the prevailing inflation rate. The CGT voiced its dissatisfaction. In an action that demonstrated the fundamental and growing weakness of the government, Rodrigo increased his offer to 45 percent.

At this point the CGT faced a difficult situation. On the one hand, this organization still used the rhetoric of and defined itself as "Peronist." On the other hand, the "Peronist" government was clearly implementing policies that were harmful to the union rank and file. The labor movement was being forced to cut its ties, however painful, with the Peronist political leadership and assume a new, antagonistic position.

The CGT resolved the conflict by pushing for the resignation of Rodrigo and the rest of López Rega's clan while officially supporting the president herself. On 27 June, the CGT organized a rally ostensibly in support of Martínez de Perón in which opposition to the "treacherous" López Rega and Rodrigo was expressed. The tactic, however, failed. Martínez de Perón continued to offer wage increases that were significantly below the 150 percent that the CGT now demanded.

After a few days of uncertainty, the CGT called a general strike, the first ever during a Peronist government. The unions resigned themselves to out-and-out opposition. After forty-eight hours of complete economic shutdown, Martínez de Perón was forced to declare that any wage increases negotiated between the individual unions and businesses would be approved. The president utterly failed to break the unions. She also failed to garner the support of the armed services. The military, instead of supporting Martínez de Perón, pushed for the resignation of most of the president's cabinet, including López Rega and Rodrigo.[24] The two ministers, as well as several others, duly resigned on 19 July 1975.

The new alliance disastrously failed, and, moreover, failed very quickly. Di Tella concluded that "[i]t may be typical of such turn-arounds that, when the leadership of a party tries to depart sharply from its traditional policies, it loses the support of the faithful without gaining that of the group which would benefit from the new line;"[25] indeed, the Levingston presidency, as well as the Viola presidency to be discussed in the following chapter, further support this hypothesis.

Labor had clearly and decisively won the showdown with Martínez de Perón. However, the CGT as a corporatist entity was more capable of defending its own interests than imposing them on other corporatist entities and more masterly at blocking policy than creating it. The CGT, like all of the primary corporatist entities, had developed into a fundamentally defensive organization incapable of developing a comprehensive policy of its own. In other words, the corporatist entities were incapable of completely bypassing the power brokers. These weaknesses manifested themselves in the months following Martínez de Perón's political defeat.

> Although it had won the battle, the labour movement was not a unified and powerful actor with a clear programme of action and the will to impose it on other important political actors. Faced with the alternative of acting autonomously and attempting to establish its political hegemony, or of negotiating and allying itself with other social forces in the reconstruction of government authority, the CGT opted for the latter.[26]

The CGT too was now ready to support a different power broker in a new alliance designed to recreate some sort of stability.

At this point, the government had lost all legitimacy and popular support. Political warfare grew more and more open and violent. The economy was in crisis. The Radical Party openly admitted that there were no solutions to the problems at hand.[27] Given these circumstances, it was clear that chaos would only grow during the remainder of the government. During this time, the corporatist entities would once again agree on a power broker to attempt fundamental change once again—just as did Perón, the military was to have its second chance.

Praetorianism Revisited

The degree of the problems at hand and the complete lack of legitimacy of Martínez de Perón's government are well illustrated by the actions of the new economics minister, Pedro Bonanni, appointed 22 July 1975. Bonanni legislated a series of measures that bought time, including, for example, wage increases. The minister was unable to come up with a policy that might promote any national reconciliation. Without any policy, Bonanni called for suggestions from representatives of major interest groups, including labor, business, and the military as well as individual political leaders. The result of this effort was a call for a "price peace," the meaning of which was unclear. The lack of initiative and ingenuity brought calls for Bonanni's resignation, especially from the CGT. Just twenty days after his appointment, the minister duly resigned.

Antonio Cafiero became the fifth minister of economics in just over two years. Cafiero was one of the most respected economists within the Peronist party and his appointment was widely applauded. His objectives were to reduce inflation gradually and to promote economic growth as well as employment. The rising unemployment rate was, according to Cafiero, "the most immediate danger."[28] (See Figure 3.6.) Cafiero's policy was based solely on priming the economy to attempt to satisfy all the major corporatist entities. Restructuring or modernizing the economy was no longer discussed nor even given lip-service.

Figure 3.6   Unemployment Rate, April 1973–October 1976

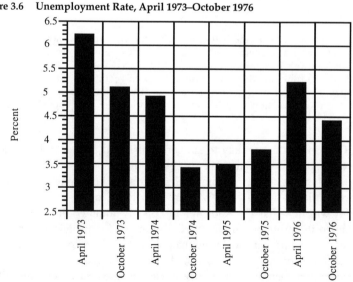

Source : Based on data from de Pablo and Martínez 1988.

In many ways, Cafiero's attempt to promote stability and consensus by returning to a middle-of-the-road economic strategy resembled those of the political impasse period. A reversion to that period was no longer possible, however. Whereas the period between 1955 and 1966 in Argentina corresponded with relative (rather than absolute) economic decline and limited political tensions, Cafiero's program corresponded with a growing economic plight and exploding political crisis. The breakdown of corporatism had begun, and now, one way or another, it had to end.

Cafiero left the ministry of economics on 3 February 1976 with the economy in significantly worse shape. Foreign debt increased substantially (Figure 3.7) without any corresponding increase in investment so as to facilitate paying back loans in the future. The financial situation grew more tenuous as the budget deficit climbed and emission became a more and more important method of financing the government. Needless to say, the inflationary spiral continued.

Figure 3.7   Foreign Debt, 1972–1976

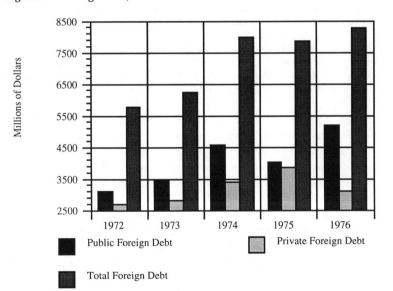

Source: Based on data from de Pablo and Martínez 1988.

The degeneration of the political situation was far more acute. Soon after Cafiero's appointment, Martínez de Perón took a five-week leave of absence from the presidency, during which time Italo Argentino Luder, another prominent Peronist, temporarily took over that position. During the president's absence, a military disagreement surfaced between factions who wanted to return to power and those who did not. This disagreement was resolved with the appointment of Jorge Videla to the top military position. The Radical Party began an investigation into corruption on the part of the president and various members of her inner circle. Clearly, the other power brokers were offering themselves to replace the Peronists. Political violence continued to grow to such proportions that all Argentines felt threatened. Indeed, union members called strikes in order to protest the violence: A full 12 percent of all strikes dealt with complaints about the political instability.[29]

The agricultural sector withheld their products on two occasions, augmenting the precoup atmosphere. The UIA officially broke away from the CGE and then openly attacked the government.[30] Negotiations between the corporatist entities and the military were openly discussed and assumed. Even the corporatist entities who originally formed the populist alliance openly protested the government. Ironically, both the CGT and the CGE called for an austerity plan.

The CGT found itself in a particularly difficult situation.

> Perhaps more than at any other time the internal contradictions of the Peronist labour leadership came out into the open: while it regarded itself, and was regarded by others as part of the government, the labour leadership had to react to rank and file pressure and at least partially satisfy its expectations. This position—of being both judge and interested party—need not be contradictory in times of economic expansion, but becomes impossible to maintain in times of recession when the government cannot respond to working class demands.[31]

Indeed, the crisis during the Peronist government was one, if not the most, fundamental stage in the breakdown of corporatism in Argentina. The CGT was arguably the most powerful of the four primary corporatist entities in 1966; just ten years later, its power was significantly diminished as a result of the failure of its "own" government. The nebulous vertical links between the Peronist Party and the Peronist unions, only partially broken down in 1966 after the attempt at "Peronism without Perón," were now close to nonexistent. Perhaps most important, the man who for two decades purposefully destabilized Argentina and who held the motley Peronist movement together, Juan Perón himself, had died. Gilbert Merkx summed up the changes well:

> The most basic change to have taken place in the Argentina situation is the changed status of Peronism. The Peronist return to power, followed by the subsequent disintegration of the movement, has removed from the center of the political stage the conflict over the reincorporation of Peronism. In a real sense, Peronism has been demystified and is no longer feared by the military nor idealized by the working class. Perón himself is no longer the figure around whom Argentine political debate centers.[32]

Figure 3.8   Annual Growth Rate of GDP, 1972–1976

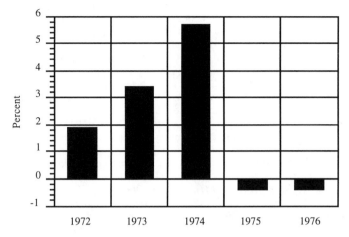

Source: Based on data from de Pablo and Martínez 1988.

Martínez de Perón's final attempt to force some rationality into policy-making was doomed to failure under these circumstances. The president appointed a final economics minister, Emilio Mondelli, on 3 February 1976. The economic situation had grown so precarious (see Figure 3.8) that an austerity program was absolutely necessary: The minister openly advocated a 20 percent reduction in real wages and negotiated a severe austerity plan with the IMF. By this time, however, all legitimacy was lost and, despite the fact that such measures were obviously necessary, Mondelli was unable to implement them. Forty-nine days after his appointment, he and the whole Peronist government were overthrown by a military coup. Jorge Videla was the new Argentine president, and it fell to Dr. José Alfredo Martínez de Hoz to repair the economic situation. Argentina was obviously in the middle of a very fundamental and powerful crisis. The military envisioned el Proceso de Reorganización Nacional (the Process of National Reorganization) to create a reformed and better country.

Notes

1. David and Ruth Berrins Collier, *Shaping the Political Arena*, p. 724.
2. Liliana de Riz, *Retorno y derrumbe: El ultimo gobierno peronista*, p. 55, my translation.
3. Gilbert W. Merkx, "Argentina: Peronism and Power," p. 42.
4. Elizabeth Jelin, "Labour Conflicts Under the Second Peronist Regime, Argentina 1973–76," pp. 236–237.
5. Adolfo Canitrot, *La viabilidad económica de la democracia: un analysis de*

la experiencia peronista 1973–1976, p. 1. Although the CGE and the UIA were officially merged during this period, it is useful to differentiate between the international and national bourgeoisies by separating them in the discussion. This is done by referring to the two original corporatist entities, which can be seen as two factions within one organization.

6. Liliana de Riz, "Política y partidos. Ejercicio de análisis comparado: Argentina, Chile, Brasil y Uruguay," p. 675, my translation.

7. Although the Acta de Compromiso Nacional was signed during the Cámpora presidency on 30 May 1973, its contents will be discussed in the following section on the Perón presidency.

8. Guido di Tella, *Argentina Under Perón, 1973–76*, p. 94.

9. Guido di Tella, "Argentina's Economy Under a Labour-based Government, 1973–6," p. 218.

10. A good description and analysis of populist economic policies can be found in Jeffrey Sachs, "Social Conflict and Populist Policies in Latin America."

11. David Rock, *Argentina: 1516–1982*, p. 364.

12. Adolfo Canitrot, *La viabilidad económica de la democracia: Un analysis de la experiencia peronista 1973–1976*, p. 20, my translation.

13. Aldo A. Arnaudo, "El programa antiinflacionaria de 1973," p. 49.

14. Robert L. Ayres, "The 'Social Pact' as Anti-Inflationary Policy: The Argentine Experience Since 1973," p. 489.

15. Robert L. Ayres, "The 'Social Pact' as Anti-Inflationary Policy: The Argentine Experience Since 1973," p. 486.

16. Adolfo Canitrot, *La viabilidad económica de la democracia: Un analysis de la experiencia peronista 1973–1976*, p. 17.

17. Juan Carlos de Pablo, *Economía Política del Peronismo*, p. 84. By this time, repressed inflation was a central characteristic of the economy in Argentina. It is impossible to estimate with accuracy the amount of inflation that had not yet surfaced, but a few attempts are made by de Pablo (pp. 121–136).

18. Guido di Tella, "Argentina's Economy Under a Labour-based Government, 1973–6," p. 217.

19. Liliana de Riz, *Retorno y derrumbe: El ultimo gobierno peronista*, p. 96, my translation.

20. Juan Carlos de Pablo, *Economía Política del Peronismo*, pp. 87–88.

21. Liliana de Riz, "Política y partidos. Ejercicio de análisis comparado: Argentina, Chile, Brasil y Uruguay," p. 675.

22. Elizabeth Jelin, "Labour Conflicts Under the Second Peronist Regime, Argentina 1973–76," p. 242.

23. This breakdown comes from Guido di Tella, *Argentina Under Perón, 1973–76*, pp. 70–71.

24. Gilbert W. Merkx, "Argentina: Peronism and Power," p. 46.

25. Guido di Tella, *Argentina Under Perón, 1973–76*, p. 72.

26. Elizabeth Jelin, "Labour Conflicts Under the Second Peronist Regime, Argentina 1973–76," p. 246.

27. Guido di Tella, *Argentina Under Perón, 1973–76*, p. 83.

28. As quoted in Juan Carlos de Pablo, *Economía Política del Peronismo*, p. 215.

29. Elizabeth Jelin, "Labour Conflicts Under the Second Peronist Regime, Argentina 1973–76," p. 248.

30. Guido di Tella, *Argentina Under Perón*, 1973–76, p. 79.

31. Elizabeth Jelin, "Labour Conflicts Under the Second Peronist Regime, Argentina 1973–76," p. 247.

32. Gilbert W. Merkx, "Argentina: Peronism and Power," p. 49.

4

Videla and the Liberal Alliance, 1976–1983

The Videla Presidency

By the time General Jorge Videla assumed the Argentine presidency in March 1976 calling for el Proceso de Reorganización Nacional, two attempts at fundamental restructuring in Argentina had already failed—almost half of the period under study, half of the breakdown of corporatism, had already occurred. This recent history weighed heavily on the new president and on the military generally. On the one hand, a military regime had already failed, resulting in the disgrace of the armed services. On the other, the utter chaos of the Peronist government reinforced the military's distrust of civilian politics and particularly of the Peronists. This time, the Proceso, as this regime is commonly called, had to succeed, both to regain the honor of the military and to save the nation. It was less clear who or what might save the military, however, from itself.

The Proceso began during the worst crisis Argentina had ever seen. Terrorism was rampant and took its toll on all social and economic classes. The prior regime had been far more internally unstable than any government that had preceded it. It would not at all be hyperbole to claim that Argentina at this juncture could have continued on the road of national breakdown that occurred in Lebanon during the same period. The economic situation was worse than disastrous—inflation had surpassed 50 percent a month at the end of the Peronist regime, unemployment was rising, and the economy was increasingly paralyzed due to strikes and lack of imported industrial inputs. It should be clear that the situation at the end of the regimes studied was worse than at the beginning. Far from effecting la Revolución Argentina or la Reconstrucción Nacional, these governments were instead destroying the country.

Clearly, coming to power under such inauspicious circumstances renders the job of promoting economic growth and political stability far more difficult. As had been the case for the regimes already analyzed, Videla also suffered from coming to power in an atypical (and in this case, as with all military coups, technically illegal) manner. However, Videla did come to power with several advantages, most of which, ironically, grew out of the crisis itself. There was even more agreement regarding the need for charting a new course than there had been when Onganía or Perón attempted their programs. This initial support for Videla, albeit also reflecting the lack of alternatives, was evident both in society at large and among the corporatist entities. Not even the CGT, the corporatist entity that had exerted so much power over the previous government, protested the military's return to power, and, indeed, many of the individual unions seem to have encouraged the coup. In essence, the greater degree of instability and chaos that preceded the formation of the military government offered greater support for the new government.[1]

Further, as ten years of corporatist breakdown had already occurred, the corporatist entities had grown significantly weaker. This is particularly the case for the CGT and the CGE. The former, as should be clear from the preceding chapter, not only had been a founding signatory of the populist alliance brokered by the Peronist government, but also charted (or at least could have charted) the final stages of Martínez de Perón's government. This close association with a government that had resulted in so much economic and political hardship inevitably weakened this corporatist entity. The fact that the CGT was extremely internally divided by the end of 1975 further weakened its unity, a trait that is essential for the successful operation of any corporatist entity. Similarly, the CGE had been closely associated with the previous regime, particularly regarding economic policy that had, after all, been initially created by a former president of the CGE, Gelbard. The SRA and the UIA, although not overly tarnished by these previous experiments, had deteriorated because of their relative economic decline in a country that was itself in relative economic decline.

Finally, there was an incredible amount of cohesion and unity of opinion within the military. This was the result of two circumstances. First, the level of turbulence in society convinced even the most legalistic of military officials that the military had to intervene. There still existed a wide range of opinions regarding the strategy that should be implemented, however, ranging from the nationalistic call for a form of Peronism without Perón to an ultraconservative call for a complete war of ideological purification. Later, these two groups would be led by men such as Admiral Emilio Massera and General Luciano Menéndez, respectively. The second circumstance that turned to Videla's advantage at the beginning of his tenure was a certain degree of freedom from these groups; the army commander was General Roberto Viola, a personal friend of Videla and one of similar and moderate political views (although, as will be clear later in the chapter, not the same as Videla's). The ideological schism between president and army commander did not exist in 1976 as it had during the Onganía and Levingston governments; Viola could largely protect Videla from attacks originating within the military, hence preventing any internal coups. Videla also maintained his military status, unlike Onganía, who had already retired when asked to assume the presidency. The power broker in government in 1976 was internally relatively united.

Given these conditions, Jorge Videla was able to remain as president for the full five years decreed in his original mandate. In many ways, that can be considered a success in itself. Indeed, for the observer in 1976, this occurrence would have been very difficult to predict—since 1955, governments changed with a frequency that was rivaled only by the changes in economics ministers. During this whole period, Videla was set on implementing a single economic program. Unfortunately, neither the political nor the economic side could be consolidated; all of the advances toward stability made at tremendous costs during the five-year tenure were subsequently to be lost.

Martínez de Hoz and the Economic Plan

President Videla appointed José Alfredo Martínez de Hoz to the ministry of economics. Having already been minister of economics for a brief period in 1963 under President José María Guido, Martínez de Hoz had by 1976 proven in all possible ways his close association with the liberal groups of Argentine business and politics. He was a descendant of a major landowning family and was president of one of Argentina's most important steel mills just before being appointed minister. It was clear from the outset that an implicit alliance between the liberal corporatist entities, the SRA and the UIA, was being created.

From the very beginning of the Martínez de Hoz period, indeed, a great deal of emphasis was placed on structural change. It will be recalled from Chapter 1 that both (and only) the SRA and the UIA were in favor of an open economy. A restructuring of the economy was to be the backbone of the alliance in power. Considering that Argentina had had a closed economy since the 1930s, such a change was to be effected only through significant restructuring; the closed economy had taken such root that a restructuring would inevitably be quite difficult and costly to effect. This change was the basis of the new alliance. Martínez de Hoz outlined his program in the following way: "Our policy was implemented in three directions: (1) redefining the role of the state, (2) liberalization of the economy, and (3) stability. Researchers up until that point had incorrectly concentrated their attention just on stability."[2]

As had been the case with Krieger Vasena, Martínez de Hoz's freedom relating to economic policy was circumscribed in several essential ways. First and most important, the military made it clear that the economic policies were not supposed to increase unemployment;[3] it was felt that increases in unemployment would have a detrimental effect on the battle against subversion. Argentine society was already bordering on anarchy, and social discontent could not be encouraged through personal hardship. The importance of this limitation can be gleaned from the results of the period—there was a general downward trend in unemployment that eventually hit an all-time historical low during the Martínez de Hoz period. This objective was the only explicit limitation on policy, but one with wide-ranging consequences; reorganizations of state companies, for example, could be vetoed if there were any redundancies, as there would inevitably be.

However, there were many other implicit limitations. Clearly, no actions that might impede the antiterrorist campaign were acceptable. In the name of national defense, most policies that in any way limited the military's direct influence and power were blocked; as was typical during the breakdown period, the power broker in government wanted to fully dominate all aspects of society and was intolerant of any competition from other power brokers or social actors. The extent to which this intolerance limited the economics team's freedom cannot be overstated. Public enterprises could not be privatized: Everything from telecommunications to the national airlines to steel mills was considered vital to national defense, regardless of the fact that all of these industries were terribly inefficient and costly. The indirect consequences of this outlook were even greater—for example, it was clear that the military leaders would never allow these firms to go bankrupt, hence offering an implicit government guarantee to all loans made to these firms. No matter what the economics team did or said, the public sector's behavior and power in the marketplace could not be altered. In moving toward a market-based economy, this inability to cut state companies loose would have tremendous repercussions.

Finally and most obviously, military expenditures themselves could not be reduced. Quite the contrary, they were tremendously increased during the period, greatly augmenting the budget deficit (Figure 4.1). As the military knew that the budget of the armed forces would be an ideal area to reduce expenditure, the military leaders tried to portray a regional geopolitical situation in which war was likely. First, the military overemphasized a land dispute with Chile. Then, Argentina claimed that Britain could start a war over territory and ocean rights relating to the Malvinas/Falkland Islands. In retrospect, no conflict would have ever been forced onto Argentina. Unfortunately, the military could get itself into a war. It should also be mentioned that only one minister besides Martínez de Hoz was a civilian. On a practical level, this meant that despite the augmented power of the minister of economics under Videla, the other military ministers still could and did deal directly with the president and the military establishment, not the economics team, regarding policy and expenditures. In theory, Martínez de Hoz was supposed to have a superminister status resembling that of a prime minister; in reality, his powers were greatly circumscribed.

Figure 4.1 Military Spending as a Percentage of Government Expenditure, 1975–1979

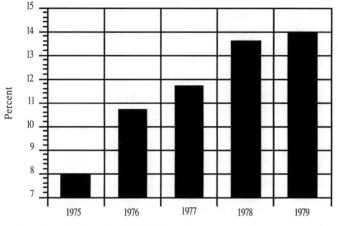

Source: Based on data from W. Smith 1989.

At the same time, however, Martínez de Hoz was given a novel advantage: time. The Proceso was supposed to be, like la Revolución Argentina, a long-term regime. For the reasons enumerated above, this government, however, was under less pressure than Onganía's; unlike Onganía, Videla remained in office for his full mandate. Further, also unlike la Revolución, the economic policy would be allowed to run its course as long as necessary and was of the utmost importance. Finally, whereas Onganía had been a moderate nationalist, Videla was a firm believer in liberalism.

Under these circumstances, the economics team developed three explicit and immediate goals, which were announced on 2 April 1976: (1) monetary and fiscal equilibrium, (2) higher economic growth, and (3) reasonable income distribution.[4] The first measures implemented to attain these goals, announced during the same period, were relatively modest. All price controls were eliminated. The process of the export of agricultural products was completely changed. Under the Peronist regime, it was the state itself that purchased and then exported a large percentage of the country's agricultural product. With this reform, the agricultural producers were free to sell to whomever they wished for whatever price they could obtain. More important, export taxes on agricultural products, which were as high as 40 percent, were eliminated. All the anti–foreign investment laws of the previous government were also revoked. Structural changes were prominent from the very first days of the new economic program.

During the same period, it was announced that wages were to be determined by the government. This policy resulted, as was hoped, in a rapid 30 percent reduction in real wages from the high in 1975. The percentage of national income distributed to wage earners, a variable so important in Perón's government, deteriorated from just under 50 percent at its high to somewhere above 30 percent. The drastic decrease in real wages is evident in Figure 4.2. The reduction in wages was effected for a variety of reasons. One was to reduce manufacturing costs as part of a program to lure new investments. The reduction in real wages was a method of reducing the budget deficit—approximately 50 percent of the government's budget was dedicated to paying state workers. In addition to reducing wages, a series of taxes was also implemented in order to bring the fragile public budget under control.

Figure 4.2   Real Industrial Wages, 1975–1980 (in percentage, 1977=100)

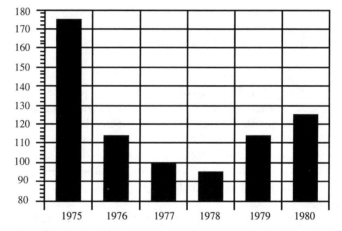

Source: Based on data from Ronaldo Munck with Ricardo Falcon and Bernardo Galitelli, *Argentina: From Anarchism to Peronism*, Zed Books, London, 1987.

Further, public investment, particularly in the infrastructure, was tremendously increased. The higher rate of public investment was continued throughout the Martínez de Hoz period. Monetary policy was fairly loose and remained so throughout the period as well. Both of these factors, other things remaining stable, increased economic activity and kept the economy stimulated throughout the Videla presidency.

The results of this first phase of the economic plan were favorable. The foreign sector improved dramatically and unemployment fell. A good part of this recovery resulted from the new-found political stability (as compared to the end of the Peronist period) and would have resulted no matter what economic policy was implemented. All the same, the policy seemed to have aided the process of stabilization and recovery. Although not immediately perceptible, the structural changes relating to agriculture were a fantastic success: Agricultural production and exports surged the next season as shown in Figure 4.3.

Figure 4.3   Agricultural Production, 1972–1979

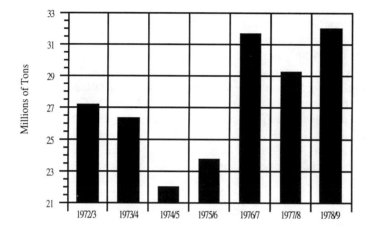

Source: Based on data from de Pablo and Martínez 1988.

The economic alliance was clearly visible. The structural changes all related to and benefited the international sectors and the SRA. It is central to note that the favored corporatist entities were at this point subject to almost no constraints. Martínez de Hoz requested that industrialists and owners of property (such as apartments) not abuse the freeing of prices and act "with responsibility"; some pressure was put on some larger businesses not to fire workers, given the need to keep employment high. In the large scheme of things, however, these were minimal requests and, moreover, requests that did not have to be obeyed. In other words, the favored corporatist entities were offered several new inducements to improve efficiency and to promote growth, but no countervailing constraints were imposed; nothing would force the favored groups to act upon the investment incentives.

At the same time, as had been the case under Perón and Onganía, the excluded corporatist entities were only partially excluded. The CGE was disbanded, after which its members joined the UIA in an odd contrast of circumstances with the Perón's government. Apart from the bourgeoisie's organization, however, they benefited from significantly lower wages and from the removal of the price controls as well as the expansionary aspects of the fiscal and monetary policy. At the same time, the structural changes thus far implemented were in no way detrimental to this group—exports were freed, but not yet imports. This group was clearly not a member of the alliance, but it did not suffer for it. The union groups were in a far worse situation. Wages fell significantly and the military "intervened" in the CGT as well as in forty-five individual unions cumulatively representing over 75 percent of the unionized workers.[5] Even the CGT, however, benefited from the increased employment. Further, the measures were somewhat "'accepted' by the wage earners in the name of 'we have to pay for the mess (our government) created'" at least in the short-term.[6]

The major problem with the results of the first phase of the economic program was the still high inflation rate, although it had fallen significantly from the 50 percent monthly rate at the end of Martínez de Perón's presidency. Complicating matters even more was the fact that inflation dropped from 37.6 percent per month (consumer prices) in March to 2.7 percent in June, only to increase once again to about 7 percent, a level at which it stabilized toward the end of the year, as can be seen in Figure 4.4. Martínez de Hoz had two options, either to ignore inflation and continue exclusively with the structural reforms or else to commit himself to attacking the problem.

Figure 4.4   Monthly Inflation Rate, March 1976–January 1977

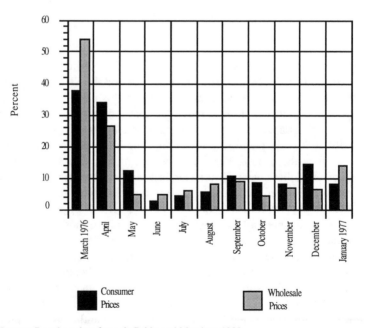

Source: Based on data from de Pablo and Martínez 1988.

The minister chose the latter course of action. From this point on, the government was committed to controlling inflation and the legitimacy of the economics team increasingly rested on this particular economic indicator. The team was relatively successful, but only at the cost of seeing the whole economic program scrapped. The specific restructuring the economics team could and did implement in conjunction with the desire to combat inflation would cause a time-consistency problem that would later explode.

The second phase of the economic policy was created solely to combat inflation; in March 1977, a "price truce" was called by Martínez de Hoz. The major component of this clearly unorthodox instrument was price controls placed on the 700 most important industrial firms. The price freeze was to be in effect for 120 days.[7] Predictably, the rate of inflation fell significantly. Just as predictably, however, the rate of inflation once again mounted during the period immediately following the price truce. Although the operating deficit was fiercely cut, the government's expenditures actually grew, as can be seen in Figure 4.5. Particularly given the fact that monetary and fiscal policy were still strongly expansionary, this attempt at controlling inflation was doomed to failure.

Figure 4.5   Government Budget Deficit, 1975–1982 (as percent of GDP)

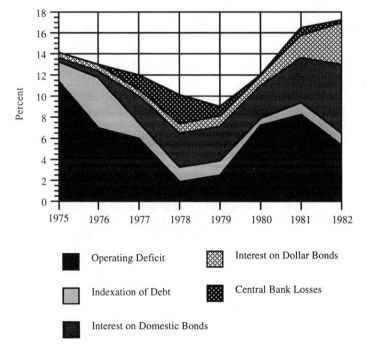

Source: Based on data from Guillermo A. Calvo, "Fractured Liberalism: Argentina Under Martínez de Hoz," *Economic Development and Cultural Change*, April 1986.

The most interesting point about this attempt was the increased reliance on constraints to control the industrial sectors, including the international bourgeoisie. Whereas the first phase of economic policy only requested responsibility regarding price adjustments, the second phase demanded responsibility. A general trend began: A relative shift in the relationship between inducements and constraints began affecting the national and international industrial groups and, to a lesser extent, the agricultural elite.

During this period, a financial reform was formulated by a commission composed of the economics team and leaders of the financial services industry. Fundamentally, it was a structural liberalization of the Argentine banking system encompassing two major changes. First, independent lending authority was restored to the individual banks, revoking the Peronist legislation through which all credit was controlled by the Central Bank—in essence, during the Perón period, it was the government that determined the amount of credit available and that chose the economic groups and actors that were to receive the credit. For example, the government might determine that 20 percent of credit would be extended to agriculture, 50 percent to industry (possibly subdividing this amount even further), and the remaining 30 percent for construction of private homes. Now it was the individual banks that determined, once again, the level of credit and the recipients. In essence, the banking system, nationalized under Perón, was privatized. The second change was novel, however; for the first time in Argentine history, interest rates were freed—banks could offer and charge any interest rate that they wanted, assuming, of course, that lenders and creditors could be found in the market.

Again, one notices the emphasis on structural changes. Another factor is very important, although not immediately perceptible—all deposits were fully guaranteed. This action was not originally planned; deposits were to have been subject to loss if a bank went bankrupt. However, the financial community exerted a great deal of pressure on the government, resulting in the inclusion of this clause.[8] It is worth noting that this pressure bore fruit at the very time that constraints were being imposed on the industrial community, implying, of course, that the economics team and the government generally needed an unflinching ally. This ally was increasingly becoming the financial community, both national and international. Just as it had been the international bourgeoisie that had eventually gained the upper hand under Krieger Vasena and the CGT under Perón, there were already clear signs that this subsector of the international bourgeoisie was the economic team's fundamental partner. Such a conclusion was reinforced by the fact that the budget deficit was increasingly financed through foreign loans. This condition became a central factor later on in the economic program. It also further explains the emphasis on combating inflation, an economic evil that has particularly negative effects on the financial community.

The financial reform was implemented in June 1977, coinciding with the end of the price truce. The period was marked by increasing inflation due to the end of the price truce, and economic recession resulting from the high real interest rates and tight monetary policy.[9] Stagflation was the result: GNP fell at an annualized rate of 10.2 percent between the third quarter of 1977 and the second quarter of 1978. Manufacturing fell by an annualized 22.4 percent rate during the same period, consumption by 12.1 percent, and fixed investment by 21.2 percent. The unemployment rate, too, showed signs of significant increase, from 3.9 percent in April 1977 to 4.2 percent a full year later, a change clearly visible in Figure 4.6.

Figure 4.6   Unemployment Rate, April 1976–April 1982

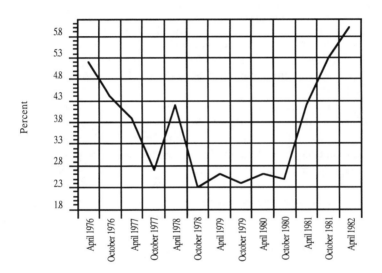

Source: Based on data from de Pablo and Martínez 1988.

As if any recession was not bad enough, this recession coincided with higher inflation. All of the corporatist entities, in other words, were suffering. Further, even the "objective" economic indicators to which Martínez de Hoz had committed himself were deteriorating. A new phase of the economic program was necessary because beneficial results could not be awaited. The simultaneous deterioration of economic indicators and increased pressure on all four of the primary corporatist entities were inevitably resulting in a loss of faith in and legitimacy of the economic program and the government generally. Although the changes already effected in conjunction with the planned opening of the economy would have, in the medium term, resulted in a far more productive economy, this was not enough—results were needed more quickly.

La Tablita and the Growing Resistance

The economics team wanted to lower inflation while priming the economy, something inherently contradictory. The question was how.

> Remarkably, an answer was found for the question. In December of 1978, a new anti-inflationary policy was inaugurated, the advantage of which rested in the fact that it required neither unemployment nor governmental controls on the market. A further advantage, particularly important to the government, was also discerned: that of using the same instruments in an intensified manner in the short term that conformed to the long-term structural changes, to wit, the opening of the economy and the liberalization of the capital markets.[10]

In essence, the economics team wanted to use foreign competition to control domestic inflation.

The new policy had two primary components. The first was the intensification of the opening of the economy to imports through the lowering of import duties. The second component was the reduction in the rate of devaluation of the Argentine currency, the peso. The policy regarding the foreign exchange rate was first referred to as *desindexación*, a phase of the economic program that lasted from May to November 1978. During desindexación, the exchange rate as well as wage rates and public sector prices were readjusted monthly by some amount below the previous month's inflation rate. The "future exchange rate devaluations and changes in public sector prices systematically would be adjusted below the rate of private sector price increases, thus, in theory at least, forcing inflation downward."[11] As the currency was devalued less than the rate of inflation, imports would grow relatively cheaper compared to national products. Local companies would therefore have to control price increases to maintain market share. Smaller increases in prices would result, if all went well, in lower inflation.

The desindexación policy was quickly fortified into what is called a "passive crawling peg" in economic jargon but more commonly referred to in Argentina as *la tablita*. This policy was a good deal more complicated than desindexación—in essence, the economics team announced the changes in the exchange rate (as well as public sector prices and the minimum wage) for the whole upcoming year. During this period, the Argentine currency was to be repeatedly devalued. Each time it was to be devalued by a smaller percentage, however. The exchange rate would be fixed at the end of the year in March

1981, the month Martínez de Hoz was to step down. The theory behind the tablita was quite similar to desindexación in that an inflation rate above the planned devaluations would result in a loss of national competitiveness and, hence, downward pressure on inflation. The belief was that this long-term commitment to reducing inflation at a gradual but determined pace would prove more effective and less costly as the economy adjusted according to rational expectations.

The most notable trend regarding economic policy was the increasing reliance on constraints, particularly relating to the industrial groups and including the UIA, an alliance member. It became increasingly clear that a transformation of the economy would not occur solely by controlling the working class's wage demands.

> The particularity of this process is that in order to discipline the working class it was going to be necessary to discipline the industrial class. This was not perceived until late in the economic program by the industrialists because at the beginning of the economic plan the government implemented classic repressive measures including freezing wages, prohibiting worker protests, and intervening in various unions. Only later was it understood that the objective of economic and financial discipline meant a complete revolution in the functioning of the Argentine economy.[12]

By the end of 1978, the industrial and, to a lesser extent, the agricultural classes began to realize that constraints would be forced upon them, too, albeit through a manipulation of the market mechanism.

The major characteristic of the tablita was the predictable increase in the value of the peso as compared to the dollar; indeed, the cheap dollar was supposed to result in cheaper imports, which would then put pressure on the nation's business groups to reduce costs and hence reduce inflation. The pressure on the economy would increase with the passage of time as the dollar grew cheaper and cheaper. The effects on the corporatist entities were predictable. The CGE suffered tremendously as cheaper imports began to compete with its products that had previously benefited from import protection. Figure 4.7 shows how imported capital goods represented an ever-increasing share of the capital goods market, a good reflection of the effect on Argentine industrial products in general. On 18 October 1980, CONAE (Convocatoria Nacional Empresaria), a mouthpiece of the national bourgeoisie, announced one of many criticisms of the policy by calling for an immediate change in economic policy centering around "consolidation of debts, reduction of tax burden, reduction of public expenditure, increased import duties, and a change in the exchange rate policy."[13]

Even the multinationals were under increasing pressure. General Motors, the sixteenth largest company in Argentina in 1975, closed down its

Figure 4.7   **Spending on Imported and Domestic Capital Goods, 1975–1980 (total spending on capital goods in 1975=100)**

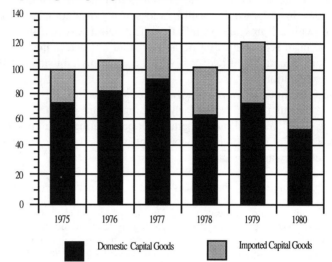

Source: Based on data from W. Smith 1989.

operations in the country during this period. It was becoming cheaper and cheaper to import goods in order to satisfy the local markets, and given the increasing wages in dollar terms, making goods for export was all but impossible. "Ironically, despite new legislation designed to encourage foreign investment, the aperture is making Argentina less attractive to many foreign companies that were previously lured," explained a special report in *Business Week* at the time.[14] In reaction, the UIA called for more stringent efforts regarding monetary and fiscal policy (for reasons that will be discussed below) if the economy was going to continue to be opened. For example, on 18 October 1979, the UIA stated that "import duty reduction should stop until public expenditure is reduced."[15] Even the SRA, the only corporatist entity that would later claim that the Martínez de Hoz period had been successful, complained of the strong peso, which reduced its real returns. On 9 August 1980, the SRA questioned in a press release why everything was being liberalized except the exchange rate. In November 1980, the agricultural producers of Valle del Uco, Mendoza, imposed a lockout in protest of the high exchange rate.[16] Figure 4.8 depicts the rising exchange rate.

Ironically, the CGT's position improved during this period, a fact which placed even greater pressure on the industrial groups. As stated above, at the beginning of the Proceso, collective bargaining was outlawed and wages were determined by the economics team, but this was only a temporary measure as it went against the market ideology as well as those in the military that were

Figure 4.8   Real Exchange Rate, January 1978–September 1980

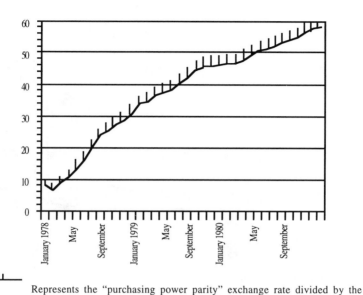

Represents the "purchasing power parity" exchange rate divided by the actual exchange rate in percentage terms. It estimates the overvaluation of the peso in percentage terms.

Source: Based on data from de Pablo and Martínez 1988.

sympathetic toward the unions. The decision was therefore made to free wages (effective August 1979) while keeping collective bargaining illegal—each individual employer bargained with the unions for a specific contract. As a result, real wages rose significantly in 1979 and 1980 as a consequence of liberalized wage negotiations. This increase resulted in part from the tight labor market but also, it would seem, from a desire to assuage increasing CGT resistance that manifested itself in more strike activity and protests. This opposition, it is essential to realize, occurred despite the fact that strikes were illegal. What is particularly interesting is the fact that the beginnings of the defensive alliance between the CGT and the CGE were once again discernible. In particular, strike activity was increasingly linked to economic policies instead of strictly to wage demands. (See Figure 4.9.) Further, strikes occurred with increasing frequency at CGE-type businesses. Although there is no conclusive evidence for this, it would seem plausible, particularly given the illegal nature of strikes, which would have allowed employers to repress the strikers, that these strikes were accepted, if not encouraged, by individual members of the national bourgeoisie.[17]

Figure 4.9   Number of Strikes and Reasons for Them, 1976 –1980

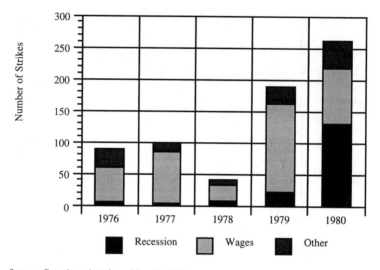

Source: Based on data from Munck 1987.

All in all, however, there was relatively little resistance to the economic plan and the Proceso for most of the time the tablita was implemented; nothing akin to praetorianist comportments of the Martínez de Perón or Lanusse presidencies had yet manifested itself. This tolerance resulted from the fact that a great many advantages were simultaneously being offered to Argentine society and the corporatist entities. Some of these inducements were conscientious, such as priming the economy, while others were unwitting. The common factor among all of them, however, was that they resulted in a time-consistency problem that was to compound the country's economic pressures in the future, ultimately resulting in a change in economic policy. All the sacrifice thus far spent on restructuring the economy would, in other words, be lost for absolutely no reason. Onganía, Perón, and, as we shall see, Alfonsín all postponed structural changes that necessarily required a certain degree of restructuring and sacrifice on the part of all of the corporatist entities; when this sacrifice was imminent, the corporatist entities balked and overthrew the government that they had brought to power only a few years before. This time-consistency problem was mirrored during the Videla presidency despite the fact that Martínez de Hoz began his tenure with fairly widespread structural changes—during the Proceso, market mechanisms, particularly those related to finance, as shall be seen, allowed the greater part of the most painful costs of the structural changes to be delayed. When these debts came due, the pressure to change economic course in order to bail out the private sector grew to irresistible proportions.

The major advantages offered to the corporatist entities that allowed for the postponing of many of the costs of the restructuring were relatively expansionary fiscal and monetary policy. Clearly, fiscal and monetary policy was far more restrictive than it had been under the Peronists or almost any prior Argentine government. However, the policy was expansionary given the anti-inflationary goals and compared to the similar policy implemented in Chile. Then as now, the expansionary policy was most criticized by liberal economists and corporatist entities.

Under these circumstances, the CGT benefited from high employment and hence higher wages than would have otherwise been the case. The industrial groups benefited from the state contracts and from high internal demand, which was not and could not be satisfied only through imports. The results of the priming of the economy, however, were higher inflation and larger adjustment costs. In order to understand why, it is valuable to conceptualize the economy as being made up of those products and services that can be replaced by foreign substitutes and those that cannot. To simplify, the producers of the former could not raise prices due to the international competition whereas the latter could and did raise prices, as is normal during an economic expansion. These sectors included, for example, construction, an industry that benefited from high real-estate prices as well as from significant state investments in the infrastructure. The inflation rate, which depends on changes in prices in both competitive and noncompetitive sectors of the economy, continued despite the international competition. Inflation, of course, also put upward pressure on wage rates in all sectors— workers clearly and justifiably wanted to protect their real purchasing power. The increase in prices was necessarily passed on to the competitive industries, who would still have to buy office space (at the higher prices) and pay the increased wages. The increases could not be passed on to consumers given the fact that comparable goods could be imported for constant prices. With increasing costs and fixed prices, profits were often squeezed into losses. In the short term, the expansionary policy benefited the economic groups; in the long term, however, by increasing demand and causing an expansion, which resulted in continued inflationary pressure in the noncompetitive sectors of the economy, it lengthened the readjustment process and rendered it more costly.

The financial restructuring also resulted in a time-consistency problem, one, however, that was both more dangerous to the economy and economic program and that was also difficult to foresee. In essence, given the traits of the financial restructuring, certain sectors of the banking system ended up resembling a Ponzi scheme, in which new funds, instead of being productively invested, are used to cover private losses. Competition between banks for deposits resulted in tremendous increases in the real interest rate. As all deposits were guaranteed, investors, including many foreigners, looked only to find the highest interest rate regardless of the safety or quality of the bank. At the same time, there was continued demand for loans despite the high interest rates. The budget deficit was partially financed through internal debt (the rest through foreign debt), and state companies, instead of being able to look to the treasury for subsidies as in the past, were forced to borrow in the private sector under Martínez de Hoz. As can be seen in Figure 4.10, the amounts involved in government and paragovernment borrowing were substantial. It was irrelevant to the banks that the companies involved would never earn enough money to pay back the loans; although the economics team explicitly claimed that loans to these companies were not guaranteed (and hence were subject to market forces), in reality an implicit government guarantee existed, particularly for the companies such as Fabricaciones Militares that were linked to the military. "No matter what we said, there was an implicit guarantee regarding the debts of the state's companies, and this created a problem. You can better understand the situation by interpreting the military as a public empire—there are no risks involved."[18]

Figure 4.10   Government Domestic Borrowing, 1975–1980

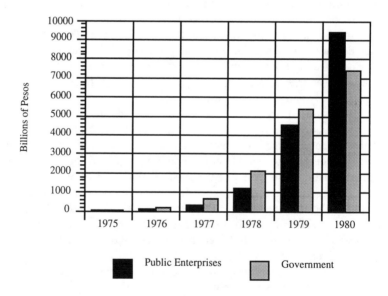

Source: Based on data from Calvo 1986.

The above dynamic in and of itself caused problems in the economy as the vertiginously high interest rates further increased industry's costs. The reaction of the industrial classes to this situation multiplied the problem: They took on debt burdens that could not be paid back. Several companies that were highly in debt continuously had their obligations rolled over by the banks—this was convenient for both parties as it was often the only alternative to bankruptcy, which would have been harmful both to the poorly capitalized banks and, obviously, the owners of the companies. Similarly, companies that would rationally have gone bankrupt with the opening of the economy (large sectors of the CGE, in other words) had nothing to lose by taking out more loans. The eventual bankruptcy might be larger, but this would hardly have negative repercussions on the owner of the business. Indeed, the owner of such a business could actually even profit through these loans by exporting the borrowed capital where the banks could not repossess it; operations such as this largely explain the internationalization of the debt problem and were most probably facilitated with graft. Finally, many individuals and companies took out loans as a bet against the economic program, implicitly assuming that the peso would have to be devalued, thereby resulting in profits for those who exchanged the peso loans for dollars. In sum, the high real interest rates attracted hot money, which was then lent out to Argentine businesses and individuals who then re-exported the capital. In economic terms, the financial system suffered from a moral hazard problem that resulted in a time-consistency dilemma. During the final six months of the Martínez de Hoz period, the growing indebtedness of the country's businesses, both nationally and internationally, took on dizzying proportions. This is shown in Figure 4.11.

Figure 4.11   Private Domestic Debt, 1975–1980

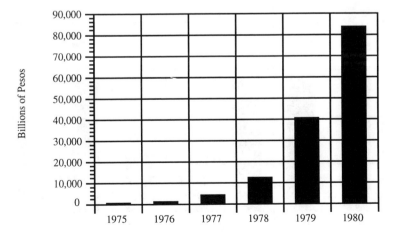

Source: Based on data from Calvo 1986.

The result of this financial Ponzi scheme was two-fold. First, it augmented the eventual total cost of the restructuring by further priming the economy. Second, and more relevant, the increase in debt by almost all groups in the country (from the national bourgeoisie to members of the UIA, such as the Fiat subsidiary in Argentina), multiplied many times over the pressure on the government to change economic policies (and indeed was eventually to result in a de facto nationalization of the debt). International conditions also grew far worse as real dollar interest rates (LIBOR) went from being negative to very positive. This further increases the fiscal burden of the state as can be seen in Figure 4.5.

These stresses resulted in a financial crisis: On Friday, 28 March 1980, Argentina's largest private domestic bank, Banco de Intercambio Regional, was liquidated by the Central Bank. The Banco de Intercambio typified the fast-growing but poorly managed bank, growing during the Proceso from a relatively minor bank into the country's largest. Several other banks also went bankrupt during the same period.

This financial failure caused many short-term economic problems. The increased perceived country risk resulted in tremendous capital flight, which caused problems with the foreign sector. Money supply also grew at an

Figure 4.12   **Budget Deficit as Percentage of GNP, 1975–1981**

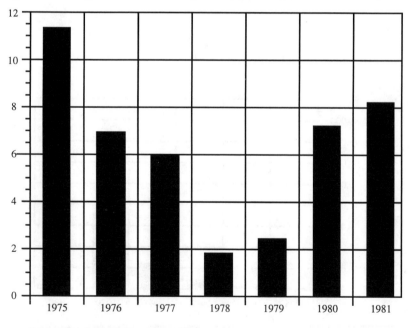

Source: Based on data from Calvo 1986.

increased pace as the government had to pay for the financial bailouts (deposits were guaranteed and hence had to be paid out of the treasury). All of this occurred in a context largely defined by a growing budget deficit that was approximately equal to 7 percent of gross national product (see Figure 4.12). The results were a deepening recession and growing inflationary pressures.

Even more important, however, were the political effects. The very legitimacy of the economic program was jeopardized in one fell swoop—no longer was there a continuous amelioration in economic indicators—which in turn resulted in a problem of legitimacy for the military government itself.

Matters were made worse by the timing of the crisis. It was during this period that Videla's successor was being chosen within the military (Videla was to step down in just under one year). In a very direct way, the corporatist entities, all of which sought economic relief of some sort, gained the upper hand in pressuring the government, which could no longer protect itself by pointing to a controlled and immediately successful restructuring of the economy. Moreover, given the need to limit any further immediate loss of credibility so as to ensure the choice of a sympathetic successor who would continue with similar economic policies, the economics team could not effect certain policies. For example, altering the exchange rate would have been impossible despite the growing overvaluation of the peso. The economics team found itself facing a mounting crisis, but its hands were tied.

In early October 1980, Roberto Viola was chosen to be Videla's successor. This choice represented at least a partial change in policy, but this was not immediately perceptible (it will be discussed in the next section). Instead, it was Viola's silence regarding his planned course that was conspicuous. He stated, "We will have [economic] reactivation without abandoning the struggle against inflation,"[19] which was at the same time vague and economically unviable. A recession was now clearly needed to cool inflationary pressures. Uncertainty was multiplied during the unfolding of a 10 percent devaluation the economics team finally implemented in February. In order to calm the markets, Videla and Viola jointly published a pronouncement that the devaluation resulted from an agreement between the two men regarding the future course of policy, implying, of course, that no other devaluations would occur. Particularly given the fact that the peso was still very overvalued, important economic actors asked for a firmer statement from Viola. The new president declined to speak, however, and it was left up to Martínez de Hoz to reassure financial actors, which was an impossible feat for a lame-duck minister under growing pressure and criticism.

The general insecurity resulted in nothing less than economic disaster. At the end of September 1980, foreign debt stood at $25,193 billion, approximately 50 percent publicly held and 50 percent privately. By the end of 1981, the total foreign debt had jumped to $35,671 billion and continued to increase rapidly (see Figure 4.13). The Central Bank lost one-half of its reserves during the same period. The capital flight continued despite the 100 percent real returns offered in pesos. The economic plan, so meticulously implemented over five years, was being destroyed, in large part because of Viola's silence. After five years, Martínez de Hoz had been able to foster a goodly degree of stability in Argentina, to foster a feeling that finally the economic rules had been set once and for all. Although in September 1980 the economic restructuring still had a long way to go and a tremendous amount of hardship was still ahead, the economy was clearly on better footing. Had the restructuring continued, the economy would have eventually been strengthened, albeit after a violent recession, as was occurring in Chile. The uncertainty was destroying all that had been built up thus far, however. The costs were both immediate and profound—now that Martínez de Hoz's economic policy had been discredited, a change in policy was inevitable.

Figure 4.13   Foreign Debt, 1975–1984

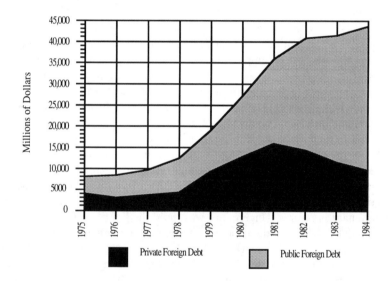

Source: Based on data from de Pablo and Martínez 1988.

The Dirty War

Whereas the military had long been divided regarding economic policy, with very negative effects to be discussed in the next section, by 1976 there was overwhelming agreement that sovereignty was being challenged by an open and violent warfare that the military was losing, that the most elementary glues that held Argentine society together were giving way, and that the defense of the nation and any and all individuals and groups within it was becoming increasingly difficult to ensure. The military was united in its desire to reassert control over society, to eliminate all "enemies of the state," and to disarm all forces besides itself. This desire was the base of the political or social program of Videla's government; it is often referred to as the "Dirty War." An aggressive campaign was devised quite similar to those implemented in neighboring Latin American countries.

The whole judicial system was disregarded as the military thought that the problem had outgrown any potential solutions that the legal system could devise. For example, it was thought that both judges and prosecutors would be subject to threats on their lives or on those of their families by terrorist groups. As the terrorists were quite capable of carrying them out, the military concluded that judges could no longer be the guardians of "justice" or "judicial impartiality." Due process, habeas corpus, and the right to a trial were all forgotten during the Proceso. The military was so fearful of its own inability to control the so-called enemies that it did not even trust its own soldiers, any of whom, it was feared, could be infiltrators or could be subject to blackmail similar to that described above. In response to these preoccupations, the military leadership devised an antiterrorist structure based on cell theory. A large number of crack paramilitary groups were formed from the ranks of the most loyal, most capable, and most vehemently antiterrorist soldiers. Each group, averaging five men, was completely independent, not responsible to anyone. In this way, these groups were isolated from influence peddling from above and from spies within the military. Each cell was responsible for investigating, capturing, and punishing (generally killing) terrorists on their own. It should be noted that these groups were not even responsible for keeping lists of their prey.

Much debate, and, more notably, criticism surrounds these policies of the Proceso. A detailed analysis of the Dirty War is beyond the scope as well as the requisites of this work. It is important to signal, however, that something had to be done to combat the armed threat. The end of the Peronist government was marred by ever-increasing violence that jeopardized all social and economic groups. Indeed, one of the more scary and tragic aspects of the Argentine insurgency and counterinsurgency was the fact that the violence seemed random, that everyone was at risk regardless of political viewpoints. This situation contrasts with the violence in Chile, for example, where the terrible repression was at least focused on certain groups that knew themselves to be at risk. Various of the terrorist groups on both the right and the left had tapped vast economic resources, which included private contributions, funding from other governments, and ransom money from the ever more common kidnappings. These funds allowed each of these armed groups to buy armaments similar to those of the military itself.

It is difficult to comprehend, much less communicate, the magnitude of the problem. One of the best indicators of the need to take swift and decisive action is the fact that the Peronist Party, which was to suffer greatly during the Dirty War, supported the military's initial actions. As far as can be judged, civil society at large also felt that there was a need to find a method, any method, to stem the insurgency.[20]

Unfortunately, however, given both the social and political climate of the time as well as the method chosen to fight the terrorists, the battle against the insurgents quickly took on larger and less justifiable proportions: the military's counterinsurgency measures inevitably went well beyond suppressing armed terrorist groups that were dedicated to overthrowing the state.

From the very beginning of the antiterrorist campaign, the individual cells began to seek out and to kill anyone with a leftist political viewpoint. Whereas the antiterrorist campaigns were originally designed to repress only those who fought to overthrow the state through violent or revolutionary means, all those on the left quickly became targets; socialists, communists, and leftist Peronists were all ruthlessly hunted, whether or not they were involved in terrorist activity. Indeed, many military officials claimed that they saw it as their duty to kill not only all of the terrorists, but also all those that aided or merely even sympathized with the terrorists.

Moreover, the military's campaign quickly degenerated to a level where people were punished and often killed for their morals or because of personal animosities. From the outset, the military claimed, as it had during la Revolución Argentina, that it was going to promote "proper moral values,"[21] which were interpreted in a fashion quite similar to Onganía's. Such considerations clearly played a part in determining the victims of the individual cell groups. In extreme, personal animosities could cause military repression. An example is in order. A senior member of Martínez de Hoz's economics team got into an argument with an air force official regarding some minor, nonpolitical issue. The next day, the economist, who clearly did not even sympathize with the terrorists, was apprehended and held captive. Every day of his captivity he was reminded that his very life depended on the wishes of the particular military official. Given the structure of the cell system, Martínez de Hoz's protests to Videla went unanswered—the president had no method of imposing his will on the individual cells. After several months, the man was finally released.[22]

The Dirty War conducted by the military also continued for several years after the terrorist attacks had clearly abated; after some significant military successes in 1977 and early 1978, it is generally felt that the terrorist groups no longer posed a threat to the sovereignty of the nation and that continuing insurgency actions were primarily desperate publicity stunts.[23] All the same, the antiterrorist activities continued with full force; 1980 was a particularly bloody year. There is still uncertainty regarding the total number of so-called *desaparecidos* or disappeared ones killed during the Dirty War, and even more so regarding how many of those were innocent (that is to say, not at all involved in the terrorist organizations). Most estimates of the total killed, however, range between 20,000 and 30,000. In many ways, these days of darkness can be seen as the nadir of the whole period here studied.

Apart from the immediate goal of subduing the terrorist threat (which was more than accomplished), the suppression campaign was part of a larger program designed to gain support for the government. The military came to power in 1976 promising to restore order to a country that was rapidly disintegrating; a large part of the military government's legitimacy rested on the existence of a terrorist threat and on the military's appearance of being able to eliminate this threat. Given this, it was at first in the government's best interest to magnify the danger of the remaining terrorists and to proceed with swift action to prove its resolve. Similarly, the military used the terrorist threat as a means to quiet opposition from both the corporatist entities as well as the competing power brokers. The existence of a national threat that fostered the need for "sacrifice on the part of all" made complaints against the government more difficult to expound. Given the randomness of the violence, individuals also hesitated to offer opposition to the government due to the palpable fear of reprisals.

By 1980, however, the claim that the terrorists continued to threaten the nation was clearly wearing thin. This change in circumstances allowed for further politicization of policymaking; the very period during which the economic program began to falter coincided with a greater freedom on the part of the corporatist entities to lobby for support. More generally, 1980 was marked with new and growing calls for a return to democracy. The central consequence of these pressures was to be the accession of Viola to the presidency in 1981 and the subsequent appointment of several interest-group representatives to key posts in the economics ministry.

Some politicization was inevitable. The military leaders also seemed, however, to be eager to find other methods of mobilizing support for the Proceso so as to limit calls for democratization and to contain the growing legitimacy crisis. In 1980, Argentina hosted the soccer World Cup for which many public works were commissioned; the economic stimulus and, far more important, the success of the Argentine soccer team (which won) brought the government new support as feelings of patriotism and euphoria swept the country. The above-mentioned border dispute with Chile was emphasized with the implication that war with the neighboring state was all but inevitable, and hence that criticism of the government was inappropriate.

The liberal military leaders grew more and more desperate to find a new and more powerful rallying call as 1981 passed under Viola's stewardship. The corporatist entities were clearly growing increasingly capable of influencing policy. Many of the policies that previously supported the government now boomeranged and ate away at the remaining public trust and legitimacy—unmarked graves of desaparecidos, for example, were found. The deteriorating economy was also blamed on the military.

By the end of 1981, an internal coup brought Leopoldo Galtieri to the presidency. He was determined to recreate the military's base of support, despite the near-continuous protests that were taking place against his government in the Plaza de Mayo (the square in front of the president's office). Under his initiative, plans were well advanced on a new military campaign that was to restore the honor of the military as well as the government's legitimacy: the plans to invade the Malvinas/Falkland Islands, several hundred miles off Argentina's coast.

On 2 April 1982, Galtieri ordered the invasion of the islands. Before it was clear that the British were going to defend the islands, many Argentines applauded the action, although this support was certainly insufficient to allow a new consolidation of the military government. But the British defended the islands, and several thousand more lives were senselessly lost in what was a last-ditch effort to regain legitimacy; the war against the former colonialist power was the final attempt to mobilize popular support for the Proceso. Young Argentine conscripts were not only left on the islands to be handily beaten by the far superior British forces, but also left to die from a lack of supplies. The Argentine military had not even been capable of supplying the necessary clothing to protect the soldiers from the South Atlantic's harsh winter weather conditions. More lives were lost in the chaotic and costly breakdown of corporatism. Far from shoring up the military government, this war was its death blow.

Viola and Economic Breakdown

Within the outgoing economics team, it was well known that Viola was significantly less supportive of the economic program than Videla had been. As soon as Viola was chosen, the economics team realized that it was going to be difficult to ensure the continuation of its policies. "We were all worried about the choice of Viola and asked Videla why someone more supportive of the economic policy had not been chosen. He answered, 'You would be happy if you knew the alternative candidates.'"[24]

As it was, the liberals alone would have been unable to ensure the choice of a candidate "as good as" Viola. The new president was able to shore up the political support needed to win the presidency solely as a result of a defensive alliance he brokered with the corporatist entities. Ironically, Viola, the candidate most favored by the liberal sectors, came to power only with the critical support of the more nationalist groups. "A coalition of industrialists and unions supported Viola and his faction within the military. This military faction was able to gain the upper hand only with the support of this [nationalist] coalition."[25]

The existence of a supporting coalition was clearly visible in the formation of the new cabinet. Instead of having a single economics minister, Viola divided the responsibilities that had been consolidated under Martínez de Hoz. Viola "deliberately selected some of his Cabinet secretaries from the economic sectors that had protested his predecessor's policies. The ministry of Industry went to Eduardo Oxenford, a former president of the Industrial Union, Agriculture to Jorge Aguado of the farmers' CARBAP organization. . . ."[26]

From the very beginning, attempts to help the various corporatist entities were made—the political debts had to be paid. Lorenzo Sigaut, the new finance minister—the most powerful of the many ministers responsible for coordinating policy—further devalued the peso by 29 percent, a move that completely destroyed any remnant of faith in the peso. Moreover, the devaluation was partially compensated; in other words, export taxes were once again imposed on agriculture, the elimination of which had been a central structural reform of the Martínez de Hoz period. Another insightful change related to imports: Sigaut first announced the government's intentions to continue to reduce the import tariffs, but then quickly buckled under the pressure and reversed his position. Several measures were attempted to redress the budget deficit, but without much success.

It became increasingly clear that now that the government had become "politicized." The government had to look to the corporatist entities and society at large for support, and hence it was no longer possible to circumscribe the demands of the various interest groups. The UIA made calls for greater attempts to reactivate the economy. By July 1981, the defensive alliance between the CGE and the CGT was openly announced as a general strike was called by the CGT. The CGE supported the action. The financial crisis, in the meanwhile, constantly grew in proportion as all expected deterioration of the economy and further devaluations.

Indeed, on 2 June 1981, the peso was devalued by a further 20 percent. Twenty days thereafter, Sigaut introduced a two-tier exchange rate, one for commercial transactions and one for financial ones. This was yet another reversion to economic policy typical of the pre–Martínez de Hoz period. In November of the same year, the rest of the financial changes effected by the Videla government were reversed in the Cavallo Plan: Interest rates were regulated and the purchase of foreign exchange controlled. More important, the Cavallo Plan "facilitated a massive liquidation of private debt for which the public sector became responsible."[27] In other words, the questionable loans that so often resulted in capital flight were now to be repaid primarily by the state (and thus the whole population) instead of the contracting parties. The debt was de facto nationalized (note how private foreign debt declines in Figure 4.13). Moreover, the Cavallo Plan effected the largest (and generally most regressive) redistribution of income ever in Argentina as billions of dollars of debts were transferred from elite groups to the society as a whole. The state subsidized many fortunes held overseas. Many firms that had survived so long because of irrational lending, and often corruption, were ultimately saved from bankruptcy while many more honest and moral businessmen had already gone bankrupt.

In the longer term, the debt fiasco forced increased sacrifices on workers who had to endure the inevitable austerity plans, on savers as inflation would repeatedly rob investments, on honest businessmen who did not play financial roulette. Such widespread and random redistribution was hardly a method of promoting stability and political support. Further, as it was effected while Viola was on a leave of absence due to illness, the fact that no one knew who authorized the implementation of the Cavallo Plan was quite damaging to the government; it was and still is unclear how and why these changes were drawn up and implemented, thus promoting popular conceptions that the government was "out of control." The legitimacy of el Proceso was further eroded.

The Viola government was responding to popular pressures regarding political decisions just as much as regarding economic policy. As had occurred toward the end of la Revolución Argentina, the political parties joined together in la Multipartidaria to call for a return to democracy. Viola granted audiences to this group as well as several other important political actors and corporatist entities. This concession caused significant consternation among the hard-line factions of the military. These events occurred during a deteriorating economic situation and growing political upheaval evidenced through strikes, protests, and the like (although terrorism, after the violent and harsh repression of the Videla government, was no longer a central characteristic of Argentina's political panorama). Changes also occurred in the military, which was growing increasingly divided and politicized as all unity was lost. Again, comparisons with the Onganía period are easy to draw. Viola was incapable of controlling the situation either within the military or in society at large, and a palace coup occurred. General Leopoldo Fortunato (ironically) Galtieri assumed the presidency while, as had Lanusse a decade before, retaining direct control of the military.

The End of the Proceso

Leopoldo Galtieri took over power in November 1981. The new president was from the right wing of the military and strongly associated with financial interest groups. He promised the nation to be a man of action as he claimed that "the period of words and promises is over; now is the time for firmness and action."[28] This action, he made clear, referred to the economic sphere; it was quickly to become obvious that he did not refer merely to economic policy, however.

The economic plan he set forth was an explicit attempt to return to a platform similar to that of Martínez de Hoz. Roberto T. Alemann was appointed to the ministry of economics, a position that was once again mighty, with centralized economic policymaking powers. The economic conditions were quite inauspicious, however, for a return to liberal/monetarist economic policy. GNP fell over 11 percent in the last quarter of 1981 (see

Figure 4.14   Annual Growth Rate of GDP, 1975 –1982

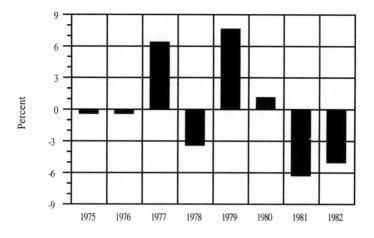

Source: Based on data from de Pablo and Martínez 1988.

Figure 4.14) and industrial production fell well over 20 percent. Real wages declined by a fifth in the same period.

Alemann unified the exchange rate and abolished all changes implemented through the Cavallo Plan except for the nationalization of the debt, which was by now irreversible. In order to counter the growing fiscal deficit, an export tax was instituted and public sector wages were frozen. The minister was also preparing a privatization scheme. Policy, in other words, was increasingly volatile and ad hoc in the public's view; laws such as Cavallo's were reversed within months.

All the economic policies that were anything but immediate in outlook were unexpectedly cut short by Galtieri's invasion of the Malvinas/Falkland Islands. The slim hopes for economic stability under Alemann were completely dashed. In the international sector, Argentina was cut off from the United States and Europe, both of which supported Britain in the ensuing war. Capital flight once again grew precipitously. The war also caused a reversal of the initial implicit goals of Galtieri as industry was once again nurtured; the military action convinced the armed services of the importance of having a domestic industrial base, no matter how inefficient or costly.

After Argentina lost the war, Galtieri's call for action resulted in his and, more notably, the military's complete disgrace. Whereas the invasion of the small islands had initially been geared toward consolidating his support within the military and fostering a new legitimacy for the military government, Galtieri succeeded instead in assuring the swift return to democracy. It also seems as though this final and grandiose military failure further assured a great deal of stability for the impending democracy as the military had so disgraced itself that it was no longer perceived as a viable alternative to run the government.

On 1 July 1982, the last of the military presidents was sworn in; in coming to power, General Reynaldo Bignone promised to return the country to civilian rule. As had been the case with Lanusse, Bignone wanted to ensure that the return to civilian rule would occur in a fashion acceptable to the military. However, the new president was less and less able to dictate the terms as strikes, business lockouts, and political protests once again rocked the country. The situation deteriorated as more and more of the ghosts from the military regime began to escape from the closet—unmarked graves of the desaparecidos came to the public's attention as well as the gravity of the economic crisis caused by shifting economic course midway through Martínez de Hoz's program: shifting course, moreover, without having a clear alternative in mind.

The actual economic (and political) situation grew worse in tandem with the interpretation of the preceding seven years of military rule. The fiscal crisis returned with a vengeance. The inflationary spiral pushed toward historical record levels, creating the by now infamous U-shaped curve seen in Figure 4.15. The foreign sector once again showed itself to be a central problem, for the first time since the beginning of Martínez de Hoz's tenure as economics minister. The IMF was called in for the first time in over six years. Ultimately, a new economic problem began to surface—a foreign debt crisis.

Figure 4.15   Annual Inflation Rate, July 1976 –December 1983

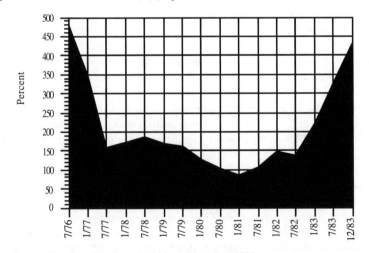

Source: Based on data from de Pablo and Martínez 1988.

All of these results speeded up the election process; initially, elections were to have taken place in 1984. However, the new democratic regime led by Radical Raúl Alfonsín was already in place by December 1983. The political and economic crisis was now his responsibility, and it was his turn to tread where Onganía, Perón, and Videla had all failed. Alfonsín's destiny was similar to that of these predecessors in fostering economic growth and restructuring. But he was to succeed, admittedly due in large part to the breakdown in corporatism that had already occurred, ensuring an incredible degree of political stability. The next chapter will end as it begins: with the democratic and free election of a new president.

Notes

1. This argument, which claims that a greater degree of threat preceding the institutionalization of a military government results in greater initial support for and legitimacy of the government, was first proposed by Guillermo O'Donnell in his book *Bureaucratic Authoritarianism.* The evidence in this study clearly supports this conclusion but also suggests that the same is true for any new government and political system, democratic or military. The increasing crisis offered more initial legitimacy to Perón than to Onganía and more to Videla than Perón.

2. As quoted in Juan Carlos de Pablo and Alfonso José Martínez, *Argentina: 30 Years of Economic Policy (1958–87),* Section III, p. 59.

3. This limitation on policy is widely discussed in new analyses of the Proceso and was confirmed by Martínez de Hoz in an interview with the author.

4. As quoted in Juan Carlos de Pablo and Alfonso José Martínez, *Argentina: 30 Years of Economic Policy (1958–87),* Section III, p. 60.

5. Ronaldo Munck, *Argentina: From Anarchism to Peronism,* p. 210. The government intervened in most of the unions mentioned here very soon after the coup, but the government postponed taking over some unions for a certain period of time.

6. Juan Carlos de Pablo and Alfonso José Martínez, *Argentina: 30 Years of Economic Policy (1958–87),* Section III, p. 67.

7. Aldo Ferrer, "The Argentine Economy, 1976–1979," p. 140.

8. José Alfredo Martínez de Hoz, personal interview. It should also be noted that the former minister now believes that this was the only major error that he and his economics team committed during their stay in power.

9. The high real interest rates are hard to explain given the recessionary pressures and the increased supply of credit that resulted from the liberated markets. Most Argentine economists, however, explain the high demand for credit (resulting in high interest rates) as caused by a combination of ignorance— this was the first time, after all, businessmen had access to limitless credit and had to deal with positive real interest rates—and a belief that the government would inflate on the part of the business community.

10. Adolfo Canitrot, *Teoría y practica del liberalismo,* p. 33.

11. William C. Smith, "Reflections on the Political Economy of Authoritarian Rule and Capitalist Reorganization in Contemporary Argentina," p. 55.

12. Adolfo Canitrot, *Teoría y practica del liberalismo,* p. 7.

13. Juan Carlos de Pablo and Alfonso José Martínez, *Argentina: 30 Years of Economic Policy (1958–87)*, Section III, p. 70.

14. *Business Week*, "Can Argentina's Economic Changes Survive?" p. 81.

15. Juan Carlos de Pablo and Alfonso José Martínez, *Argentina: 30 Years of Economic Policy (1958–87)*, Section III, p. 70.

16. Juan Carlos de Pablo and Alfonso José Martínez, *Argentina: 30 Years of Economic Policy (1958–87)*, Section III, p. 71.

17. Ronaldo Munck, *Argentina: From Anarchism to Peronism*, p. 217.

18. Alfredo Diz, personal interview.

19. As quoted in Juan Carlos de Pablo and Alfonso José Martínez, *Argentina: 30 Years of Economic Policy (1958–87)*, Section III, p. 123.

20. Such conclusions are derived from secondary readings as well as from various discussions about that period of Argentine history. Twenty years clearly blurs and alters one's perceptions of occurrences, particularly controversial ones; the fact that even individuals who are vehement critics of the military and the Dirty War hold this point of view suggest that it is valid, however.

21. David Pion-Berlin, "Military Breakdown and Redemocratization in Argentina," p. 211.

22. This story was relayed to the author by a senior member of Videla's economics team and then confirmed by several others including the economics minister himself.

23. See, for example, *The Ideology of State Terror* by David Pion-Berlin.

24. Alberto Grimoldi, personal interview.

25. Saúl Ubaldini, personal interview.

26. Gary W. Wynia, "The Argentine Revolution Falters," p. 75.

27. Mario Damill and Roberto Frenkel, *Malos tiempos: La economía argentina en la decada de los ochenta*, p. 17.

28. As quoted in William Smith, "Reflections on the Political Economy of Authoritarian Rule and Capitalist Reorganization in Contemporary Argentina," p. 60.

5

Alfonsín and the End of the Breakdown, 1983–1989

The Return to Democracy

Argentines were called to the election booth on 30 October 1983. Once again they were being asked to choose a government after a failed military intervention. Many parallels with 1973 were being drawn: economic crisis, strained relations between civil society and the military, and recent bloodshed. As in 1973, both the Peronists and the Radicals seemed to blame everything on the military, as if the problems the country faced throughout the breakdown period were simple and easily rectified. The situation, however, apart from the simplistic outlook of the PJ and the UCR, was very different, as shall be seen. By 1983, the breakdown of corporatism was almost complete, the period of catharsis almost over. Argentina would have to suffer through another six years of economic deterioration as well as much political uncertainty. However, it was increasingly clear by 1983 that something fundamental had changed.

For the first time during the period here studied, the political crisis at the end of the regime would not be as bad as it had been at the beginning. Certainly, scars of the breakdown period still remain to this day; the violence wrought during the Dirty War, for example, is still the subject of much reflection and analysis. By the end of the Proceso, however, Argentine society was no longer coming apart. Political violence was all but nonexistent, and no one tried to overthrow the government militarily. In sum, the threat of Lebanonization had passed.

The most important change during the period studied, however, was the fact that the Radical Party won open and free elections for the first time in fifty years. Raúl Alfonsín defeated Italo Luder, the Peronist candidate, without having to resort to proscriptions, repression, corruption, or any other political shenanigans. In the past, the Radical Party depended on limitations of the Peronist voice to come to power; now, these two power brokers could, indeed were forced to, compete for power within the same democratic structure. In order to win, the political parties needed to gain the support of individuals, voters, not the leaders of key interest groups; the corporatist entities could no longer choose a power broker by deciding upon the means of ascending to power (coup or open or restricted elections). Argentine elections developed in the 1980s, for the first time ever, into competitive contests between the two major parties. As a consequence, both parties would increasingly have to abide by set rules, those of a democracy, as both brokers were dependent on these same rules to gain power. Any deviation from these rules would not result in being able to assume power in a different manner as in the past, but would result in the public's disillusionment and anger. Attempts by any of the power brokers to once again alter the rules would now result in even greater difficulties in being elected.

The breakdown of corporatism had not yet completely passed, however. Once again, a government came to power under atypical circumstances. Alfonsín's was the first democratically elected government after an extended military rule. The timing of the elections and the transfer of power were frequently changed. When the time finally came for Alfonsín to assume the presidency, he found the country in an economic and political mess that was typical of the periods of regime changes. Despite the Radical government's popular mandate, it lacked the authority and legitimacy that could only result from a stable political structure. Although the process that brought Alfonsín to the presidency was clearly better than those that inaugurated the regimes thus far studied, it still represented an improvised attempt to create some degree of political stability and to extricate the military from this mess. Many in 1983 questioned whether this government would lead to a long-lasting return to democracy or simply represented another vicissitude in Argentina's history. It was not immediately apparent in 1983, and indeed it would not be until a full six years later, that enough had changed to offer the country the stability that it had so long lacked.

Alfonsín had the mixed blessing, also typical of the breakdown period, of coming to power with broad-based support. In comparing the results of the 1973 and of the 1983 elections in Table 5.1, it becomes clear that all parties, from the right to the left, lost ground to Alfonsín's UCR. This set the stage for yet another broad-based alliance that had caused the demise of the governments thus far studied. Given the UCR's successful bid to reach out to all corporatist entities and to seek support from all social and economic classes, it was difficult if not impossible for the new president to support unequivocally certain groups over others; instead, all groups were to be favored. This broad-based coalition was a reflection of the UCR itself which, just as had been the case with the other power brokers, had developed contacts with and sympathies for all of the corporatist entities in Argentina.

Table 5.1   The 1973 (Cámpora) and 1983 (Alfonsín) Election Results (in percent)

Party	1973	1983
Radical	21	50
Peronist	49	39
Center Right	20	4
Left	8	4
Annulled	2	3

Source: Manuel Mora y Araujo, "La naturaleza de la coalición alfonsinista," in *La Argentina Electoral*, edited by Natalio R. Botana et al., Editorial Sudamericana, Buenos Aires, 1985. Reprinted with permission.

In the past, these conditions were to significantly hamper the implementation of a viable economic program. Bernardo Grinspun was the first minister of economics appointed by Raúl Alfonsín. His goals included reducing inflation, increasing growth, raising real wages, promoting industry, augmenting exports, and facilitating the payment of the enormous foreign debt.[1] The most notable feature of the economic program was the complete absence of the concept of economic tradeoffs. "The most important condition we can foster is growth, growth for all sectors. With growth, all of Argentina's problems can be solved including distribution of income, inflation, and industrialization."[2]

Once again, irrational and short-term economic policy was implemented at the beginning of the new regime. The bare outlines of a "tentative alliance" could be discerned between the national bourgeoisie and the wage-earners. The most immediate economic goals of the government were to increase real wages and to foster and to protect national industry that had so suffered during the Martínez de Hoz period. In other words, "the government intended to implement a populist economic plan that was similar to the tradition of the party."[3] At this point in the breakdown of corporatism, it was going to be increasingly difficult to broker even a tentative alliance. There were three principal reasons for this difficulty.

First, the economic resources necessary for the redistribution of income toward the favored corporatist entities implied by a typical corporatist alliance were increasingly difficult to unearth. The country had grown significantly poorer during the period studied. The individual corporatist entities had grown more expert in defending the little that they still controlled. Other founts were similarly closed off: After the debt crisis at the beginning of the 1980s, net new inflows of foreign capital were all but nonexistent. Even personal savings were increasingly held in dollars to protect against the inflationary tax that the government had imposed with increasing frequency and vigor. Export taxes on agriculture would no longer yield enough to subsidize a whole economic program. All in all, there was little surplus in the economy that the government could appropriate.

Second, all of the potential alliances outlined in Chapter 1 had already been attempted: Onganía had brokered the industrial alliance, Perón the populist, and Videla the liberal. All of them had utterly failed. Each failure harmed not only the nation as a whole but even the favored corporatist entities. With these experiences still green, the corporatist entities were reluctant to try a failed coalition again. And yet, no new alliances were feasible.

Third, a new hybrid type of economic group that had developed during the preceding years hindered even the initial implementation of a rational economic plan. This economic group is composed of a series of large holding companies and can cumulatively be referred to as *los capitanes de la industria* or the "captains of industry."[4] Some of these firms are Argentine, while others are the subsidiaries of multinationals. These firms developed as a direct consequence of the vagaries of economic policy during the period thus far studied. Each of the economic policies implemented from 1966 onward fostered conditions that were detrimental to certain economic sectors while highly advantageous to others. The holding companies evolved in reaction to these changing inducements and constraints. On the one hand, firms that were being penalized during certain periods were strongly encouraged to diversify into other fields, assuming they had the economic and financial power to do so. On the other hand, the immense profits that were offered in certain areas opened the potential for incredible economic opportunities. Hence, both a push and a pull were implicitly created for diversification.

The push to diversify was augmented by the near certainty that economic policy would change course again in the future; these firms could buy bankrupt firms at bargain prices and then reap tremendous profits when that industry was once again favored due to a change in policy. For example, these holding companies purchased many money-losing firms that were part of the national bourgeoisie during the Martínez de Hoz period; as soon as policy changed under Viola, however, these firms once again became profitable. Indeed, the more frequently and violently economic policy shifted, the more moneymaking opportunities the capitanes de la industria were offered.

It was the financial might of these holding companies that allowed them to profit by weathering short-term and politically determined economic hardships. The key to the success of these firms was their ability to tap a stable source of funds that gave them a staying power that weaker firms did not have. These resources could only originate from a limited number of advantages. One was to be the subsidiary of a multinational that had privileged access to international capital markets (even through the debt crisis) as well as subsidies from the parent company. Argentine firms, however, needed to find a different source of stable profits. For the most part, this source was found in government contracts—several very large companies were built on the basis of various public works projects. It is essential to remember that all of the economic plans during the breakdown period called for increased government expenditures so as to prime the economy and to invest in key industries and the infrastructure: Public construction and promotion of certain industries (such as the oil and nuclear energy industries) were pillars of all government policies from 1966 onward. At the base of all of the Argentine *capitanes de la industria* were companies involved in one of these areas, often more successful through corruption.

By 1983, most of these holding companies were involved in a wide variety of businesses typical of very different corporatist entities: finance, typical of the international bourgeoisie, internal-market–oriented industries typical of the CGE, and, to a lesser extent, agriculture and export industries. It is essential to realize that these companies profited through the redistribution of wealth, not through investment. In this, los capitanes typified the whole breakdown period; when these economic actors purchased bankrupt companies, for example, they merely maintained (as contrasted with modernized) them until the economic conditions altered. What was important to the capitanes was that funds were constantly being funneled toward at least one of their major operating divisions; more generally, it was imperative that there be a redistribution from society at large (taxpayers and the holders of capital that lost out to inflation) to the corporatist entities (except for the CGT) in general.

The formation of this new group can be seen as the last gasp of the corporatist framework. The capitanes de la industria took their final form during the Martínez de Hoz period when a variety of factors—cheap failing national firms, large financial margins, and significant public contracts—offered very large potential profits. The groups themselves do not really represent a new corporatist entity in and of themselves so much as a superstructure that straddled the various corporatist entities. As such, these holding companies first exacerbated the problems of the corporatist structure by further reducing the total economy's tendency to invest and to modernize as compared to the tendency to speculate on sectors. At the end of the Proceso, these companies actually encouraged rapid changes in policies, almost all of which benefited them: When they could not convince Martínez de Hoz to soften his economic policy, they then supported the rise of Viola; they generally supported the Cavallo financial reform as a way of unloading tremendous debts; they generally supported Galtieri's return to more conservative economics; and finally they supported the return to democracy.

After having perfected a strategy for the economic and political instability of the time, the existence of these groups forced the whole structure's collapse by blocking the implementation of any policy. In essence, the great diversity of these holding groups impeded the selection and implementation of any clear alliance during the Alfonsín government. Each of the corporatist entities (except, of course, for labor) were at least partially controlled by these holding companies. It was unclear, however, whether these powerful economic groups could profit from any of these economic policies more than from any other; Onganía's industrial alliance would have been profitable for them as would Videla's liberal alliance and Perón's populist one. Hence, the Alfonsín government could mobilize support solely for policies geared toward priming the economy and particularly those that did so through public works or state contracts. It would be very difficult for the Radical government ever to move beyond the vague outlines of a tentative populist alliance. Instead, the government was under constant pressure to sign public works contracts, often in return for paybacks.

The nominally populist policy that Grinspun implemented was superficial. Ceilings were set on increases in the exchange and public utility rates as a method both to attempt a reduction in the initial 20 percent monthly inflation rate and to subsidize the populist alliance through manipulation of relative prices. At the same time, the government insisted on keeping its promise for higher real wages by ordering an 8 percent wage increase above the automatic indexation rate.

The economy that Alfonsín had inherited, however, was extremely fragile. The budget deficit was already immense in December 1983 and remained above 12 percent of GNP. Monetary policy was highly expansionary, and inflation continued running at about 20 percent per month. Such circumstances were far from conducive to the implementation of this type of economic policy. In the following months, between January and September 1984, this policy resulted in growing inflationary pressures and increasingly distorted relative prices; far from attempting to confront the significant structural problems in the economy that the government had inherited, the economic policy actively augmented them. Beginning in April, a slight policy shift began to make matters even worse. The economics team was forced by the other ministers and the president to correct the relative price distortions by allowing even greater nominal price increases. This program, in conjunction with no restrictions on monetary and fiscal policy, resulted in ever-increasing inflation.[5]

By the end of September 1984, Alfonsín finally grew aware of the need to adjust the economy. Grinspun's original plan was actually detrimental to the overall situation, and the government's efforts to mobilize support in the CGT (as well as in the CGE) were falling far short of Alfonsín's expectations.

In October 1984, the government found it necessary to implement an IMF-style austerity program. Monetary expansion was curtailed, the peso significantly devalued, and public utility rates increased. Given the tremendous disequilibriums within the economy, this plan resulted in even faster inflation (as a result of the devaluation and higher utility prices), a decline in real salaries, and a sharp contraction in economic activity.[6] Of course, the austerity plan also resulted in near united criticism from all of the corporatist entities (including the capitanes de la industria). All the same, the government was able to continue with this policy through June 1985. By that time, the traditional austerity program, particularly given the lack of structural reforms, had proven itself unviable—there was simply too much opposition to the plan for it to work. Congressional elections were coming up later in the year and Alfonsín's popularity was falling. A solution had to be found. It was time to attempt a more serious economic plan.

The Austral Plan

On 18 February 1985, President Alfonsín replaced Grinspun with Juan Sourrouille. The latter was not a Radical Party member, and his appointment irritated many within the UCR.[7] The appointment of Sourrouille represented something of a shift in alliances. This shift in alliances was also marked by the replacement of several other ministers with members of the very pro-Alfonsín "Coordinadora" faction of the party. Professors Marcelo Cavarozzi and María Grossi termed the first phase of the Radical government, which lasted until February 1985, as "the government of the party." After these changes, the authors suggested interpreting the power shift as one that concentrated decisionmaking in the executive branch, rendering the administration a "government of the president."[8]

No major changes in policy occurred during the first months of Sourrouille's stewardship of the economics ministry, however. During this time, the economic indicators kept deteriorating. By June 1985, inflation was up to 6,900 percent per year, GNP was rapidly declining (the output of the manufacturing sector was 13.2 percent below that of the year before), unemployment had increased by 30 percent, real wages had declined 20 percent, and investment was off 15 percent. It became increasingly clear that something had to be done.

On 14 June 1985, Alfonsín and Sourrouille announced to the public a new economic strategy, a strategy that was quickly to be known as the Austral Plan. The Austral Plan, similar to those implemented in Brazil and Israel during the same period, was a significant break from preceding stabilization plans. This one was to be effected in two stages, the first of which had three fundamental prongs. First, all prices were to be frozen after several readjustments geared towards bringing relative prices into line: a 22 percent increase in wages, a 15 percent decrease in the exchange rate, and a 23.6 percent real increase in public utility rates. Second, a new currency was created to replace the peso. The new currency, the austral, was initially pegged at 0.8 to the dollar. A series of tables of conversion, or *tablitas de desagio*, was created with the goal of facilitating the change between currencies without jeopardizing the everyday working of the economy and previously written contracts. These tables were also designed to limit windfall profits and losses resulting from the precipitous decline in inflation. For example, one of the conversion tables lowered previously negotiated interest rates so that the real rates of return would not be significantly altered.

Regarding fiscal and monetary policy, the government promised to increase revenue to trim the deficit and to cease printing money to finance the remaining deficit. Revenues were to be increased through higher public utility prices, increased export taxes, and increased revenue due to the reduced inflation rate from the Olivera-Tanzi effect.[9] In return for these initiatives, the economics team asked the corporatist entities and society at large to have faith in the Austral Plan and give it a chance to work; if everyone continued to buy dollars and increase prices, the plan would be stillborn. In essence, the government offered an implicit gentlemen's agreement which, if abided by, would be beneficial to all.

This first phase of the plan was extremely successful. The inflation rate fell almost to nil. Over the year that followed the implementation of the Austral Plan, industrial production increased 30 percent, GDP grew tremendously, as can be seen in Figure 5.1, and real wages actually increased by 11 percent. Moreover, unlike the last democratic government's economic plan under Gelbard, there was only a minimal amount of repressed inflation. These spectacular statistics resulted in greatly increased popularity for the government. The UCR won interim elections; hence, Alfonsín was able to renew his mandate and to reinforce his legitimacy.

Figure 5.1   Annual GDP Growth, 1984–1989

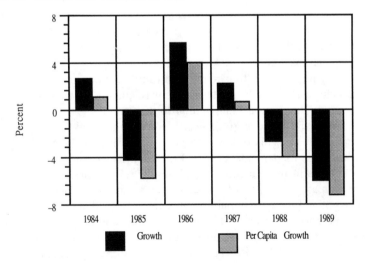

Source: Based on data from *Economist Intelligence Unit, Argentina: A Country Profile*, 1990.

Several other factors were less promising, however. On the political side, Alfonsín was increasingly on the defensive within his own party. The president of the Central Bank, who was a holdover from the Grinspun period at the economics ministry, did not comply with Sourrouille's directives—in essence, the Central Bank continued to increase the money supply. The bank lent immense amounts to the provincial governments, for example. In and of itself, this was incompatible with a permanent reduction in the rate of inflation. Two Radical Party governors, those of Mendoza and Entre Ríos, also disregarded the economic policy as did, more predictably, the Peronist governors.[10]

At the same time, several political and economic weaknesses of the plan began to reveal themselves. A fundamental problem was that the plan did not have an explicit coalition that could be depended upon to mobilize support. In addition, although the reduction in inflation was generally popular and advantageous to all, it benefited no one in particular, and no one supported the plan for ideological reasons either, as this aspect of the plan was very ambiguous and confused—a left-of-center government was implementing a stabilization plan that called for a liberal restructuring of the economy in the longer term. Far from gaining support for the plan, the individual corporatist entities each complained of certain aspects of Sourrouille's work. The CGT criticized the plan as being "a typical IMF-type austerity program that only hurts the workers."[11] The price freeze worried the industrial classes and the increase in export taxes disturbed the SRA. Indeed, it seems that the economics team accepted this popular opposition as inevitable and did little to ensure a more cohesive and positive base of support for the economic policy. Although there was no attempt to drum up defenders of the economic program, none could ever have been found anyway.

> The economic plan was not mine nor even that of the whole economics group—the Austral Plan was the government's economic program. As such it was inevitable that there were to be compromises and even some contradictions. The best we could hope for was to try to mediate the conflicts as best we could. It is not easy to implement policy in a "conflict society."[12]

The government, in other words, believed that resistance to the Austral Plan, indeed any economic policy, was inevitable. This intrinsic belief, juxtaposed with the phenomenal initial results of the Austral Plan, which reduced the political pressure to "fix" the economy, effectively blocked the implementation of the second phase of the plan. It was with the second stage that the state apparatus was supposed to be fundamentally restructured. This phase of the Austral Plan was central to the durable success of the economic policy. Whereas the first phase was merely geared toward stabilization, the second phase was supposed to fundamentally reform the economy. In more technical terms, the economics team had thus far been able to arrest the inertial inflation; now it had to combat the fundamental causes of the country's recurring economic quagmire. These changes were inevitably to include permanently reducing the budget deficit, eliminating the need to print money, and rationalizing state actions. Without such steps, the pressure and distortions that Sourrouille so skillfully eliminated would slowly creep back.

As a first step of the rationalization, the government drew up a bill calling for the privatization of the national airline, Aerolíneas Argentinas. The bill died in Congress, however, where it met with stiff resistance from not only the Peronists but also from many Radicals. As had been the case during the previous governments studied, the power broker in government met great resistance to the economic policy as soon as fundamental reforms were advocated. This resistance came from the other power brokers as well as from "excluded" factions of the power broker itself that were sympathetic to interest groups that would be harmed by the changes. The chances of success were further diminished due to the fact that there was a notable lack of enthusiasm on the part of the government itself. Alfonsín did not realize the importance of restructuring the state and hence did not use his then impressive authority to ramrod legislation through Congress. As had Onganía, Perón, and Viola before him, Alfonsín interpreted the immediate success of the economic stabilization plan to mean that the economy had been miraculously "fixed" somehow.

The economics team, under orders from the president, did not even attempt many of the other structural reforms for which the original plan had called. Plans for new permanent taxes to replace the temporary ones imposed at the beginning of the Austral Plan were shelved; as the old taxes gradually expired, the deficit grew once again. No other privatizations were ever again discussed. No one was fired from the overstaffed ranks of the civil service. Given the tremendous expenditures the government had to keep up under these circumstances, the government could not resist turning once again to the printing press despite its promise in the gentlemen's agreement.

In many ways, the implementation of the Austral Plan returned Alfonsín to the same situation he found upon assuming office. In particular, in both 1983 and 1985 Alfonsín decisively won elections that offered his government a mandate and legitimacy. During the first period, marked by the economic stewardship of Grinspun, the government's relative freedom of action was not utilized; instead, an economic policy geared toward satisfying all groups in the short term was implemented. Although this initial economic phase proved highly costly both politically and economically—resulting in the need for the Austral Plan—Alfonsín did little better in utilizing the second period of relative freedom that came with the immense initial successes of Sourrouille's economic program. It might be added that it was obvious to any economist at the time that fundamental changes had to accompany the price freeze as the latter could only vanquish inertial inflationary pressures. For the benefits to be long lasting, real inflationary pressures had to be beaten as well. Once again, the problem lay not in the initial conceptualization of the plan, which merited special kudos, but rather in the political structure and conceptualizations—the program was not, due to political pressures and miscalculations, fully implemented.

El Tercer Movimiento Histórico

The Alfonsín government, as was typical of the whole period of corporatist breakdown, was eager to effect a political or social program. Indeed, the Radical government was far more eager and convinced of the political side of its platform than of the economic side; the Radicals firmly believed that Argentina's problems were political and not economic in nature. Economic decline was generally considered a side effect of political instability, a point of view quite similar to that of Perón. This point of view largely contrasts with those of the military regimes, where economic policy was generally the more important rallying call. All of the governments are examples of the costs of neglecting the dynamic and reinforcing nature of economic and political problems.

The central aspect of Alfonsín's political agenda was the promotion of democracy, the very implementation of which was to solve all of the nation's problems. "Democracy can heal, teach, and accommodate everybody," claimed Alfonsín in a famous quote that summed up his position well.[13] This social agenda, however, had two fundamental flaws. The first, discussed in the other sections of this chapter, was that democracy in and of itself was no cure for Argentina's economic woes. Indeed, democracy depends on economic stability for its continued survival. As will be seen, democracy still exists in Argentina today because Menem was able to promote a new sense of economic tranquillity.

The second flaw was the fact that democracy implied competition through the electoral process, but this competition did not really exist in Argentina. The Radicals thought of themselves as the only democratic party; hence, the UCR thought that democracy meant that they, the only true democrats, should continuously be in power. If this were the case, there would be no true democratic competition, and hence no democracy. This belief was even more farcical considering that the UCR until 1983 would have lost any free and open election—the Peronist Party was by far the largest throughout the period thus far studied. In sum, democracy remained a warped construct in the Argentina of 1983.

The other power brokers were also not democratically oriented in 1983. The military had always come to power through the coup. Moreover, it was intrinsically impossible for the military to reorient itself as a democratic contender for power; the very concept of democracy excludes the direct control of the state apparatus by the armed forces. The Peronist Party was also not geared towards the democratic process. Peronists in 1983 still thought that it was somehow their natural right to govern the country; their outlook still belied that of a popular movement, as it had while the general had still been alive, rather than that of a cohesive democratic party. The PJ felt no obligation actually to compete for the right to come to government. Some of the leaders of the Peronist organization still had relatively close ties to the CGT (reflecting a desire to mobilize sectors of the population instead of one to win elections through policy suggestions), and many Peronist leaders were closely associated with the former Peronist regimes. All Peronists tried to portray themselves as the true followers of Perón instead of trying to hone support of the party membership. Italo Luder, who had been the presidential candidate in 1983, had been temporarily named president during Martínez de Perón's six-week sick leave. Erminio Iglesias, another leader of the time, talked of renewing the class struggle, of the natural right of the Peronists to rule the country, and the need to radicalize Peronist supporters; all of these ideas were throwbacks to Perón's first stint in government.

Clearly, the circumstances were not fully suitable for promoting democratic competition; the breakdown of corporatism was not yet finished, and all three power brokers were still competing with different political conceptualizations.

At the same time, Alfonsín did not seem eager to foster the competition that would inevitably challenge his leadership. This was the most tragic aspect of the Alfonsín presidency, a trait that was typical of all of the regimes of the period but one that, despite all the talk of democracy, Alfonsín could not overcome. For example, he did not encourage explicit competition within his own party by offering the electorate two clear and distinct sets of policies to choose from. He preferred to pad over differences, which were later to explode into the open, giving the impression that the electorate could not be trusted with policy choices.

More important, Alfonsín did not encourage the development of the more democratic factions of the Peronist Party, the so-called Renovadora faction.[14] To do so would have rendered certain Peronists electable in the public eye, hence creating potential political challengers. Instead, Alfonsín continued to portray the Peronists as antidemocratic and tyrannical. He claimed that because of these tendencies the Peronists were responsible for the chaos of the last Peronist government, particularly under Martínez de Perón. He argued that even the violent repression during the Proceso was their fault as many Peronist unions called for the coup. Certainly, there was some truth in all of this, but the attacks became so pitched that Alfonsín seemed to want the PJ to remain as it had been instead to have it evolve into a more modern party. As a result, he refused to work with any factions of the PJ and refused to admit its potential for developing into a democratic party. These characterizations certainly helped Alfonsín get elected in 1983 and might have even aided the UCR in elections in 1985, but they clearly were detrimental to the development of the Renovadora faction and to the creation of an ingrained democracy. In sum, circumstances were not ideal for fostering a democratic development as the other power brokers had not yet fully evolved, but Alfonsín also seemed eager to avoid promoting the competition so essential to the maturing of the Argentine democracy.

The result of this dichotomy between wild calls for democracy and an implicit desire to limit competition for power was Alfonsín's call for el Tercer Movimiento Histórico (the Third Historical Movement). The first historical movement had been led by the Radical Hipólito Yrigoyen during the incorporation of the middle classes. The second historical movement referred to Perón's incorporation of the working classes. Alfonsín's was to be the institutionalization of democracy. One notes immediately, however, that each of the preceding historical movements coincided with the domination of the political scene by a single power broker, a condition which, it seems clear, Alfonsín also wanted to replicate; this is most clearly evidenced by Alfonsín's attempt to alter the constitution so as to allow the president to be reelected.

A large part of the Tercer Movimiento Histórico was merely rhetorical. Alfonsín used the call for democratization as a method to further his electoral goals and also as a method of heightening the public's awareness of and eagerness for true democracy. The message resonated even more with this society, which was so overwhelmingly disgusted with the military. By supporting "democracy," people hoped and felt they would prevent any possible return to a military government. At first this was quite successful. Slowly, however, the contradiction between the two goals evidenced itself; after several years of the Radical government, the public began to realize just how shallow the calls were.

Several concrete policies were also initiated as a part of the Tercer Movimiento Histórico. These policies were inevitably geared toward mobilizing support for the UCR which, among all of the power brokers, had traditionally had the weakest links with the various corporatist entities. Despite the democratic rhetoric, the Radicals were attempting to level the playing field with the other traditionally stronger power brokers by forging clearer links with some of the corporatist entities. A central example of these policies relates to the attempts to overhaul the CGT, which, although attempted before Alfonsín's announcement of the Third Historical Movement, belied the ideas behind it. The government proposed a new set of laws that would require the "democratization" of the union organization. Three fundamental changes were advanced: (1) the democratic election of all officers (at that point, many of the union leaders had never been elected), (2) minority political representation for all political groups that received more than 20 percent of the vote, and (3) low requirements for running for office (just six months on the job and signatures from just 2 percent of the workers in the organization). Finally, it should be noted that the elections called for in this law would begin with the rank and file electing local union leaders, who would then elect regional leaders, and so on up the ladder. This was the opposite of the top-down approach typical of the CGT thus far and was designed to oust the Peronist leadership concentrated at the top of the power pyramid.[15]

Several lessons must be gleaned from this attempt at reform. First and foremost is the fact that the government lost—the bill was not passed by the upper chamber of the Argentine Congress. This defeat clearly demonstrated that the corporatist entities, or at least the CGT, remained powerful organizations. The CGT could still defend itself against a very popular government, defend itself despite the chaos of the last Peronist government and the relatively harsh exclusion during the Videla government. The return of democracy and the choice of a political party as power broker in and of itself in no way represented the death of corporatism. The corporatist entities, as will be discussed in the following chapter, were weaker, but far from destroyed.

The second important characteristic reflects the outlook of the Radicals. It should be clear from the above outline of the changes proposed that the "new" CGT was to remain a political organization. Political minorities were to be represented within the unions and were to act as a de facto party-affiliated opposition. Further, the very structure of the CGT, a confederation that lends itself well to acting as a politicized corporatist entity, was in no way altered. In other words, instead of attempting to pass legislation that would promote a nonpolitical union movement—for example, by allowing competing unions or by disbanding the apparatus that held the individual unions together in a hierarchical manner—the Radical Party was attempting to utilize the corporatist structure for its own advantage. The appearance and structure would be more democratic, but the initiatives would allow the union movement to retain a traditionally corporatist outlook with clear vertical links. "When we tried to change the union laws in 1984, we were trying to develop popular support for Alfonsín into a more refined and powerful force in the CGT."[16]

These maneuvers fit in well with Alfonsín's call for the Tercer Movimiento Histórico. In essence, despite the years of political instability and economic decline, the corporatist structure including both the power brokers and the corporatist entities continued to exist. Indeed, Alfonsín, despite the democratic jargon, was in many ways trying to reinforce the corporatist structure to his own advantage. The breakdown of corporatism continued despite and not because of the Radical government.

After this important defeat relating to union reform, Alfonsín sought other rallying calls. One was the implementation of the Austral Plan, which tremendously increased the government's popularity, albeit ephemerally. However, as the government's predisposition was not to stress economic policymaking and as the corporatist entities (including the capitanes de la industria) blocked rational economic policymaking, the advantages that could be gained from the Austral Plan were short lived. Under these circumstances, Alfonsín turned increasingly to empty and contradictory rhetoric to mobilize the support that was rapidly evaporating. It should also be noted that attempts to ensure a power base were also made through the amassing of tremendous amounts of money by Alfonsín's Coordinadora faction of the UCR. This money was collected through donations and business dealings, but far more importantly through fairly open corruption.[17] This too belied an outlook common during the heyday of corporatism. It was hoped that these funds would allow the Coordinadora to retain power within the UCR—which has largely been the case—and would allow the UCR to stay in power; instead, this policy precipitated the decline of Alfonsín as the further deleterious consequences on the economy began to be felt.

Once again social policy was contradictory in nature and precipitated greater political and economic crises. Alfonsín's social program had so backfired by the end of his government that it had actually begun to be detrimental for the very continuation of democracy. "The negative impression of vast segments of public opinion regarding Alfonsín's administration damaged not only the governing party but the whole political class [associated with democracy]."[18] Alfonsín's repeated desire to politicize the corporatist entities resulted in the Peronists' reiterating a call for a return to their explicitly corporatist structures of the 1940s. The government's inability to foment controlled competition within the democratic structures brought new calls for a coup.

Indeed, toward the end of the Alfonsín presidency, many believed that the next government would be a military one. Another important prong of the Tercer Movimiento Histórico was the prosecution of the military leaders responsible for the Dirty War, creating some pressures within the military to once again take the reins of power so as to defend their prosecuted colleagues. Investigations were opened and several leading generals were convicted and sent to jail, including former president Videla. This aspect of Alfonsín's platform was also terribly mishandled, as it was difficult for the government as well as society at large to squarely place the blame on a single group. Official rhetoric seemed to vacillate between blaming only the leaders who gave the orders and including the cell units that carried out the policy. The persistent associations made between the PJ and the military government implied at times that it was actually Argentine society as a whole that was cumulatively responsible. Such lack of clarity rendered tenuous the investigation and prosecution of selected individuals. On a pragmatic level, the trials angered the military but did not further weaken the institution—if anything, the Alfonsín government went a long way toward recreating the military's internal cohesion. The various military factions, finding themselves under attack, closed ranks and tried to overcome the wounds and divisions of the past.

Alfonsín's attempt to blame the military for the Dirty War, and, of course, associated economic disaster, was initially quite popular. But this aspect of the Tercer Movimiento Histórico, too, went from being very popular to being very criticized. The Radicals' handling of the military ended up detracting from the stability and legitimacy of the Radical government. Fortunately, by 1989 corporatism had broken down enough so that the democratic institutions survived the humiliation of the government that represented "democracy."

The Unraveling of the Austral Plan

It became increasingly clear by the middle of 1986 that a relaxation of the wage and price freeze was inevitable. Government policy was the direct cause. The government deficit was once again on the rise, due to both higher expenditures and lower receipts. The monetary base was growing at 7 percent a month and showing no signs of slowing as emission was a central method of funding the deficit. Further, as is always the case with price freezes, relative prices became increasingly incongruous.

As a result of these pressures, the Austral II (as it was referred to) was declared on 4 April 1986. The government first adjusted a series of relative prices directly under its control. The austral was devalued by 3.75 percent. In order to increase revenues, public utility rates were increased. These upward readjustments necessarily meant the end of the zero inflation goal implicit in the original Austral Plan. Price increases in the private sector were also once again accepted. Under the Austral II, private sector price increases were to be "administrated" by the government, although the exact meaning of this was unclear. The Radical government was willing to accept a certain level of inflation that would inevitably result from the relaxation of the price freeze.

Unlike the original Austral Plan, the results of this new stage were not at all successful. Relative prices remained skewed. Public utility prices decreased in real terms through September 1987. Despite the impending financial crisis, the government was unwilling or unable to raise these prices in line with inflation for fear of popular opposition; the government was still trying to redistribute resources to the population at large although it was increasingly clear that the state was bankrupt. The cost of this failed attempt at adjustment was predictably high. The most evident consequences were decreasing faith in the government and higher inflation—an average of 4.4 percent monthly for the duration of the Austral II as compared with a 2.7 percent average for the duration of the original Austral program.

There were no signs, moreover, that the increase in the inflation rate would abate; quite the contrary, everything suggested that inflation would go even higher. During the same time, real treasury expenditures increased 8.2 percent (on an annualized basis) while tax receipts declined. With increasing inflation and fiscal laxity, the budget deficit, as shown below, began to bulge once again; as had occurred during the previous three governments, the budget deficit first temporarily decreased only to reach new highs later (Figure 5.2). The money supply also continued to grow quickly, at approximately 6.1 percent per month.[19] The Austral II represented only a series of stop-gap measures that would do little to forestall the return of inflation and economic instability. The Alfonsín government still lacked the political will or ability (due to pressure from within the party or from the corporatist entities) to implement the necessary structural correlates to the stabilization program.

Figure 5.2   Budget Deficit as Percentage of GDP, 1982–1987

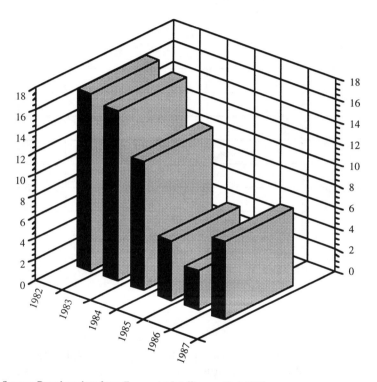

Source: Based on data from *Economist Intelligence Unit* 1990.

Consequently, another series of measures was soon necessary; with each set of policies, inflationary pressures would be forestalled for a shorter period of time. At this point, the government no longer even talked of fundamentally restructuring the economy but instead desperately sought new measures to hold off a financial explosion. Even the foreign debt crisis was ignored by the government because the consequences of the increases would not be felt immediately. This laxity resulted in a ballooning of foreign obligations, as shown in Figure 5.3; new debt was still being taken on to finance the budget deficit, and foreign interest payments that the government could not meet were being capitalized.

The Austral III, yet a new plan, was announced on 29 August 1986. At this point, stop-gap measures were no longer able to check the mounting inflationary pressures; the Austral III was necessarily an orthodox austerity plan, a policy that was anathema to all of the breakdown period governments. Austral III quite simply called for a deactivation of the economy through tighter monetary and fiscal policy. The period can be labeled the "monetarist period." It was hoped that this type of traditional economic medicine would more definitively eliminate inflation.

Figure 5.3   Foreign Debt, 1983–1988

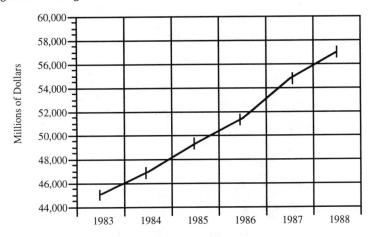

Source: Based on data from Mario Damill and Robert Frenkel, *Hiperinflación y estabilización: La experiencia Argentina reciente*, CEDES, Buenos Aires, 1990.

The government was in fact more serious about fully implementing the Austral III than it had been regarding the preceding Austral plans; the feeling of financial disintegration was growing palpable to all, even to Alfonsín. In order to fully implement the plan, it was first necessary to replace the president of the Central Bank, which had thus far continued to ignore the economics team's directives. Alfonsín appointed as the new president José Luis Machinea, a personal friend and close colleague of both the president and the economics minister Sourrouille. Needless to say, Machinea was assigned the task of controlling increases in credit and money supply.[20] At the same time, the government made a new commitment to limit Central Bank lending: The bank would lend no more than 400 million australs for the rest of the year.

The results of this economic phase were initially typical of austerity measures. Inflation began to fall, but only at the cost of lower real wages (as can be seen in Figure 5.4) and a recession. From a strictly economic point of view, the policy was successful and "necessary" to arrest the inflationary spiral and ensure a more stable future. Just as clear, however, was the fact that the Austral III was politically unpalatable. The government once again buckled under political pressure that called for redistribution and easy answers; the government, having long lost almost all bases of support, had little choice. Monetary policy was once again loosened so that inflation was reignited. Central Bank lending was allowed to reach levels 50 percent greater than the 400-million-australs limit promised. Even confronted with an imminent explosion in the rate of inflation, the government found it impossible to limit redistribution to the various groups. Political direction was completely lacking.

Figure 5.4   Real Wages, 1984–1989 (1983=100)

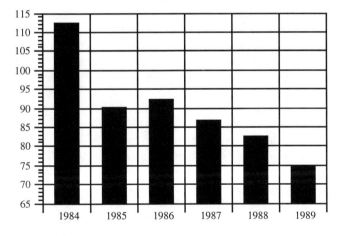

Source: Based on data from *Economist Intelligence Unit* 1990.

By this time, even the government's economic team began to lose all internal consistency. In February 1987, a price freeze was implemented as a last-ditch effort to control inflation. The freeze was greeted with widespread criticism from all of the corporatist groups. The government was seen as so weak that the corporatist entities took it upon themselves to consult one another and devise alternative policies. Even the CGT and the SRA, traditional nemeses, began to hold joint meetings.[21] In a throwback to preceding years, the military became increasingly antagonistic toward the regime. The military was upset about the continuing investigation into the Dirty War. More inauspicious, however, was the fact that the military seemed to grow increasingly concerned about economic affairs.

The military's renewed panache for influencing politics became glaringly clear in March 1987 when Lieutenant Colonel Aldo Ricco led one of a series of uprisings of a nationalist faction of the military, the so called *carapintadas* or painted faces. Alfonsín grew even weaker after he was forced to negotiate a peace personally with the rebels before they would return to the barracks. Apart from rebellions, the military continued to poke its head into civilian and political affairs. For example, it was rumored that this faction of the military had been attempting to broker an agreement with sectors of the CGT.[22] At the same time, the Peronist Party was actively and openly offering itself as an alternative to the Radical Party. The Peronist Party openly criticized the economic program and prepared itself for the upcoming elections in 1987.

Confronted with ever more dissatisfied corporatist entities and with elections later in the year, Alfonsín decided (or felt compelled) to completely politicize the economic program in a desperate attempt to guarantee himself and his government some base of support. In March, he replaced his labor minister with Carlos Alderete, a Peronist union leader associated with the *Grupo de los Quince* faction of the CGT. The reasons for the appointment were numerous. Clearly, Alfonsín hoped to attract the support of workers in the upcoming election, a difficult feat given the increasing unemployment (see Figure 5.5). All the same, Alfonsín hoped that Alderete could pull it off. At least, Alderete should have been able to bring to the government several votes in Congress.

In exchange for his support, the union leader demanded government action regarding certain union laws revoked by the military government, laws that would result in less union democracy, greater union power, and higher real wages. This complete shift in policy regarding the CGT, from head-on confrontation regarding union reforms in 1984 to alliance in 1987, reflects the immense changes in policy and the increasingly ad hoc manner in which policy was formulated. These were direct results of the government's declining popularity and legitimacy. Alfonsín's only hope was that the inclusion of corporatist entities within his government would gird his government for the elections, the remainder of his term in office, and, ideally, for his eventual reelection. Far from gaining any advantages, however, Alfonsín merely facilitated the implanting of social rivalries within his own government.

During the same period, the other corporatist entities were also directly, albeit less conspicuously, involved in policymaking.

> The industrial and agricultural interest groups also lobbied for and eventually obtained representation in the heart of the government, as had the "group of 15" union group with the appointment of minister

Figure 5.5   Unemployment Rate in Buenos Aires, November 1985–April 1989

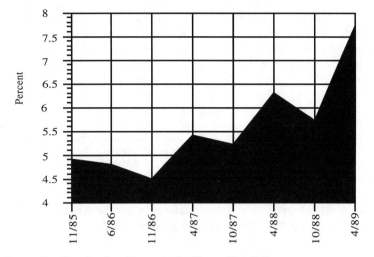

Source: Based on data from *Economist Intelligence Unit* 1990.

Alderete in March 1987. In one way or another, the concessions that were granted to the various interest groups did not have positive political results for the government, however.[23]

Mario Damill and Roberto Frenkel went on to explain that, by including so many groups within the government itself, no group benefited to any degree. Instead, the policies implemented resulted in a contradictory program in which various measures were adopted for the benefit of one entity only to be practically annulled by the measures adopted on behalf of another. Further, the government continued to suffer, as had the governments studied in the previous chapters, from an inability to mobilize support even when policies beneficial to a certain group were implemented.

Worse, this reversion to blatant pandering to the corporatist entities concretely revealed the contradiction implicit in the Tercer Movimiento Histórico and revolted the middle-class electorate that Alfonsín so desperately courted; he sacrificed his democratic ideal in order to attempt to remain in power, a fact that escaped no one. The election booth was seen less and less as the forum for debate and competition between policies. Instead of relying on direct individual involvement, the government tried to mobilize support indirectly, through the corporatist entities. This was interpreted, justifiably, merely as attempts to pander to interest groups in order to stay in power, regardless of the cost; after having so criticized the last Peronist regime, Alfonsín's presidency increasingly resembled the former.

It had become obvious that the politicization of the economic policy backfired when the election results were tallied at the end of 1987. The appointment of Alderete was a clear shift in alliances, one that had the same results as the shifts attempted during the previous governments in the period studied; while no new voters were won over, many of the original voters jumped ship. The Radical Party lost decisively to the Peronists; the former received 37 percent of the vote, the Peronists received 41 percent. At this point all legitimacy of the Alfonsín government was lost.

> The elections had a very strong plebiscitary connotation to them. The results of the elections ended in the complete loss of the legitimacy of the government and its policies. Consequently, the government also lost its capacity, despite a brief moment of relative collaboration on the part of the Peronist party, to administer the crisis.[24]

Under these circumstances, combined with a shaky economic situation and the complete absence of a viable economic plan, the Alfonsín government began down the path that would end in hyperinflation.

The Path Toward Hyperinflation

The Alfonsín government attempted one last stabilization plan toward the end of 1988, the so-called Primavera Plan. The plan was supposed to reduce inflation through a disindexation of prices. Leading Argentine firms were asked to increase prices by less than the inflation rate. The government once again promised to reduce the budget deficit, this time by increasing revenues. As attempts at increasing tax revenue in the past had consistently failed, a new type of attempt to raise funds was made. The government hoped to profit from a dual exchange rate. In essence, the official exchange rate was to be used for imports and most commercial transactions. A "financial" market rate was to be simultaneously used for financial transactions and most (including agricultural) exports. The government hoped to close the budget deficit by profiting from arbitrage—the government would purchase australs at the free market rate and then sell them at the fixed rate.[25]

This plan of action, predictably, met with tremendous resistance and skepticism. The SRA opposed the plan as it construed the dual exchange rate as a method of increasing the export taxes on agricultural products, albeit under a different guise. In order to gain the SRA's support, the government had to lower the existing explicit export taxes. The contradiction in policies escaped no one: In order to gain support for policies geared towards increasing revenue, the government was willing to eliminate taxes (or already existing sources of revenue). It is unclear what the net result on the financial well-being of the state would be, but revenues were clearly not being augmented enough to combat the fiscal deficit.

At the same time, the initial policy also met with stiff resistance from the industrial sectors. These groups were expected to suffer short-term reductions in profit margins as a result of the disindexation aspect of the program. The government attempted to buy support for the Primavera Plan from this group, too. In this case, the industrial groups were offered a reduction in the value-added tax. This reduction had the effect, once again, of decreasing already thin government revenues. The contradictory nature of these policies also escaped no one.

The international financial community, led by the IMF and the World Bank, were especially cognizant of the problems with the Primavera Plan. When Alfonsín had come to power, a great deal of goodwill was extended to him by the democratic world—Alfonsín had been seen as the protector of democracy in a country too long ravaged by coup-happy generals. By 1988, however, this initial goodwill had long been dissipated. Loans would no longer be extended to the Argentine Republic in order to support a stabilization plan. These loans were essential, as they had been for all stabilization plans during the preceding decade, in order to finance the continuing budget deficit in a noninflationary way. This international borrowing allowed a reprieve from the need of turning to the printing presses and the tremendous inflationary pressure thus caused. Now, these international financial institutions were no longer willing to extend credit for makeshift economic plans, so the plan was all but impossible to implement. Argentina had finally and completely lost its international creditworthiness. The next president would not be able to look to the international financial sectors to finance his budget deficit—quite simply, the government could no longer have a deficit. From now on, the difficult and clear-cut policy choices regarding distribution of income and imposing financial constraints through taxation would have to be made early on in the economic plan.

From the beginning, the Primavera Plan worked poorly. Inflation increased from an average of 7.7 percent during the last trimester of 1988, to 9.6 percent in February, and 17.0 percent in March 1989. The plan began to be further undermined by the national political situation that was largely determined during these months by the presidential campaign. On the one hand, the success of Carlos Saúl Menem over Antonio Cafiero in the Peronist Party's primaries had a highly destabilizing effect on the economy. The former candidate, despite the policies he would later implement as president, was associated with the relatively more populist and economically irrational factions of the Peronist Party. At this point most business groups, and particularly the liberal sectors, were fearful of a Menem victory, which, given his success in the primary and growing popularity generally, seemed increasingly probable.

On the other hand, the Radical candidate, Eduardo Angeloz, found it increasingly important to distance himself from Alfonsín's government and its disastrous economic policies in order to protect his dwindling chances of winning the election. Angeloz first demanded that the president dismiss Juan

Sourrouille, who was quickly replaced by Juan Pugliese, an old party hack. The economic situation continued to deteriorate, however, leading to Angeloz's increasingly vitriolic attacks on the government's economic policy. Posters claiming "If Pugliese can't, Angeloz can" covered Buenos Aires and further undermined political and economic confidence in the regime. The virulent and open attacks from all sides, including from within Alfonsín's own party, were similar to the past governments, as was the government's inability to defend itself or chart a viable economic course. The limited maneuvering to topple the government outside of the democratic process, however, marked a distinct break with the past, which is more fully discussed in the next chapter. It seems as though individuals and the corporatist entities increasingly bought dollars and sometimes even made plans to leave the country rather than advocate another coup. This reluctance to overthrow the government may represent the biggest change during the period studied.

The urgency with which people sold their australs to buy dollars fortified the inflationary spiral. Inflation continued its upward stampede: 33 percent in April, and 78.4 percent in May. Finally, on 14 May, Menem won the presidential elections with 49 percent of the vote, whereas Angeloz received 37 percent (the rest was scattered among a plethora of candidates of minor parties). By this time, Alfonsín's government had completely lost all legitimacy. The political plan was in shreds and no economic plan existed. There was a great deal of fear regarding the policies of the future president. In June, the inflation rate reached 114.5 percent per month or just over 2.5 percent a day. Hyperinflation had come to Argentina and was taking on a new meaning.

Figure 5.6   Annual Inflation Rate, 1983–1989

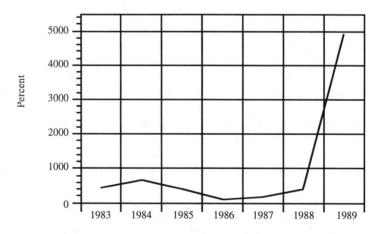

Source: Based on data from Damill and Frenkel 1990.

At first, Alfonsín vowed to finish his term in office. Ultimately realizing his inability to impose any control whatsoever, Alfonsín turned to Menem with the hope of coordinating transitional policies under the guise of a National Unity Government. The incoming president, however, did not want to be associated in any way with Alfonsín's disastrous economic policies. In a move that revealed that at least certain lessons had been learned during the breakdown period, Menem allowed the crisis to grow while keeping his government completely separate so that he would have more freedom to implement policy during his reign. Day by day the country was heading toward anarchy in both the economic and political spheres. The only alternative left to Alfonsín was to resign early and turn over the whole government apparatus to Carlos Menem, the new president.

This transfer of power occurred, as had all the transfers thus far, under abnormal circumstances. Menem took over the presidency several months before planned. As a consequence, policies were not yet fully developed. Further, the new government ascended to power without any clear legal authority to do so in a way that resembled the rise of the previous governments; there were no legal or constitutional provisions that allowed for an early assumption of power by an elected government. The political and economic situation was also comparable to the chaotic periods of the transfers of power during the 1966–1989 period.

Against this inauspicious backdrop, however, there were many important changes. Most obvious, this was the first time in over sixty years of Argentine history that one freely elected democratic president handed power over to another freely elected president. The process of coming to power, the democratic election, was increasingly set. Other factors, too, were very different, and will be analyzed in the following chapter. The corporatist impasse period had finally broken down.

Notes

1. See Bernardo Grinspun, *La evolución de la economía argentina*, Chapter 2, for an outline of the government's initial economic goals.

2. Bernardo Grinspun, personal interview.

3. Mario Damill and Roberto Frenkel, *Malos tiempos*, p. 25.

4. This term is borrowed from the title of a book by Pierre Ostiguy. The development and political and economic consequences of this group of companies is widely debated in Argentina and is discussed in the Ostiguy book as well as in *El nuevo poder económico en la Argentina de los años 80* by Azpiazu et al.

5. Juan Carlos de Pablo and Alfonso José Martínez, *Argentina: 30 Years of Economic Policy*, Section II, p. 182.

6. Mario Damill and Roberto Frenkel, *Malos tiempos*, p. 26.

7. This was my impression from several interviews I conducted despite the fact that no one would be so blunt "on the record." See also Marcelo Cavarozzi and María Grossi, *De la reinvención democratica*, p. 21.

8. Marcelo Cavarozzi and María Grossi, *De la reinvención democratica*, p. 7.

9. The Olivera-Tanzi effect refers to the loss in value of tax receipts during the time between levying and collecting the tax. During periods of high inflation, this loss of revenue can be significant. For example, $100 due in income taxes on January 1 but paid on December 31 during 100 percent inflation is worth only $50 in real terms to the government. Technically, where the inflation accrued between levying and collecting the tax is equal to "x," the percentage of revenue lost is

$$\frac{x}{100 + x} \times 100.$$

10. Edward C. Epstein, "Recent Stabilization Programs in Argentina," p. 1002.

11. Saúl Ubaldini, personal interview

12. Juan Sourrouille, personal interview. The conflict society refers to a book coauthored by Mallon and Sourrouille, *Economic Policymaking in a Conflict Society: The Argentine Case.*

13. Raúl Alfonsín, as quoted in Oscar Camilion, *The Argentine Crisis*, p. 14.

14. See Marcelo Cavarozzi and María Grossi, *De la reinvención democratica.*

15. See, for example, Héctor Palomino, "Les syndicats dans les premières années du gouvernement constitutionnel."

16. Juan Carlos Rua, personal interview.

17. The author heard repeatedly of the so-called 10 percent rule—all business deals, from state contracts to tariff protection, with the state required a contribution to the Coordinadora of 10 percent of the total value of the business. This rule was confirmed by representatives of both large and medium-sized businesses and was even alluded to by a senior member of Alfonsín's government. This "rule" further solidified the implicit alliance between the Capitanes de la Industria and the state and further impeded the implementation of rational policy.

18. Juan Carlos Torre, "Argentina: Il ritorno del Peronismo," p. 111.

19. Juan Carlos de Pablo and Alfonso José Martínez, *Argentina: 30 Years of Economic Policy*, Section II, p. 192.

20. Robert R. Kaufman, "Stabilization and Adjustment in Argentina, Brazil, and Mexico," p. 89.

21. Sofía Villareal et al., "Les organizations patronales," p. 66.

22. Juan Carlos de Pablo and Alfonso José Martínez, *Argentina: 30 Years of Economic Policy*, Section II, p. 196.

23. Mario Damill and Roberto Frenkel, *Malos tiempos*, p. 34.

24. Mario Damill and Roberto Frenkel, *Malos tiempos*, p. 35.

25. Mario Damill and Roberto Frenkel, *Malos tiempos*, pp. 37–41.

6

An Overview of the Breakdown of Corporatism

The Breakdown of Corporatism

The preceding chapters analyzed the Argentine regimes between 1966 and 1989. It is hoped that the reader has been convinced of the similarities of these governments. Despite the very different structures and ideologies embodied in each of the governments, none of them proved able to implement fully a rational economic plan. Side by side with the economic programs, these governments each attempted to effect a social program that eventually augmented the country's problems. The results were disastrous— the economic stagnation and political uncertainty reinforced each other. It was obvious throughout the period as well as in retrospect that the whole period represented one of the most traumatic and destructive in Argentine history.

So far this work had attempted to explain why these failures occurred and why each of the governments, regardless of its policies or structures, seemed unable to break out of the tragic cycle. The answer offered was that each of these governments confronted an immutable (in the short term) corporatist structure that blocked rational policymaking. The various governments had a great deal of difficulty implementing constraints on the corporatist entities that would force greater investment and, hence, economic growth. At the same time, the inducements that were offered would not result in sufficient growth. After a period of time ranging from one to four years, this dearth of new resources caused renewed struggles for a changed distribution of income. The lack of substantial new resources over the whole period studied is obvious in Figure 6.1, which evidences the dearth of income growth (per capita GDP) for the average Argentine. With the resultant struggles, economic policy began to disintegrate and political calm began to erode. First a shift in alliances by the same power broker and then a change in regime type would inevitably follow.

157

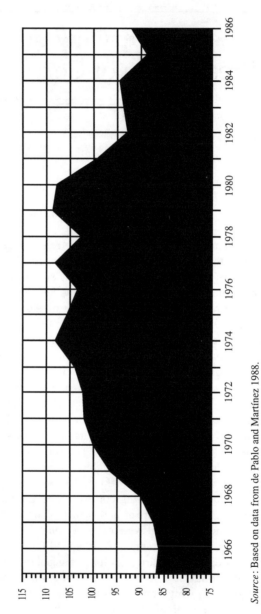

Figure 6.1   Per Capita GDP, 1965–1986 (in percentage, 1970=100)

Source: Based on data from de Pablo and Martínez 1988.

On a more theoretical level, one can associate this recurrent instability with the existence of two separate but interrelated levels of political competition. The first, common to all political systems, relates to the attempts to influence policy on the part of the various corporatist entities, interest groups, and so on. This level can be referred to as the "choice-of-policies game" and was clearly evident throughout the period studied. Each corporatist entity maneuvered to gain government support for its own goals. Sometimes these were successful, as when the financial community lobbied the Martínez de Hoz economic group to guarantee all bank deposits. Other times these maneuvers proved unsuccessful, as when Augusto Vandor announced his Plan de Acción against the appointment of Krieger Vasena. Such competition for support was certainly more vehement than in many other countries, but in and of itself was certainly not abnormal.

The second level, which can be referred to as the "choice-of-regime game," rendered the whole structure much more unstable, however. On this level of political competition, the various power brokers competed for the support of the corporatist entities needed to take control of the government. The very existence of this level limited the policy choices that could be adopted on the first level of political competition. If a corporatist entity were overly excluded in the policymaking process, it would shift the political debate from the first level to the second. The central trait of this second level of competition was the facility with which it could be and was activated. Whereas in more stable countries, change in governments occur over regular intervals, such as at election times, Argentine governments could confront this competition at any moment. The dissatisfaction of any of the corporatist entities could spur renewed debate on the choice-of-regime level as there were necessarily two excluded power brokers eager to find support. By the time two corporatist entities had grown sufficiently dissatisfied with a government's policies, it was only a question of time before the type of regime would shift. As a defense against this, each power broker attempted to gain contacts and sympathies with all of the corporatist entities, a fact that merely further reduced the government's ability to implement rational and comprehensive economic policy in the first place.

The ultimate result was something akin to a Nash suboptimal equilibrium. Each corporatist entity attempted to maximize its own profits. This was done by supporting the redistribution of income over the creation of income. The political instability was a clear deterrent to the long-term investment that is necessary for creating new wealth. Moreover, the profits that could be gained from the redistribution implicit in several economic policies (manipulation of wages, exchange rate, agricultural prices, and so forth) far outstripped any potential economic rewards from investment. Over the longer term, however, these constant battles over income distribution resulted in fewer resources within the economy as a whole to distribute among the various groups. Thus began a dynamic where fewer resources culminated in more pitched competition, which in turn further reduced the available resources. The mounting tensions caused an extended crisis in Argentina.

Despite these continuous threads that spanned the whole period here studied, it has been repeatedly claimed that something changed. The crisis of Argentine political economy and the breakdown of corporatism was tragic, but at least cathartic in nature in that something supposedly changed over the whole period. This chapter is geared towards elucidating just what those changes were. The changes relate to all facets of the old corporatist structure: the power brokers, the corporatist entities, and even the state itself. The changes are all part of the institutionalization of democracy.

Institutionalizing Democracy

The corporatist breakdown period ends with the transfer of power from one democratically elected government to another, the first such transfer in over sixty years of Argentine history. This changeover also reflects the only foreseen or planned transfer of power during the period studied, except for that between Videla and Viola (Viola was duly elected by a group of military leaders as and when it had been planned at the beginning of the military coup). All of the other shifts in governments occurred through a coup against a democracy, coups within the military, harried attempts to extricate the military from the government, or with the death of a president. A central change marking the end of the corporatist breakdown period, according to this study, is the fact that the government changes are now legal and predictable and will continue to be so. The process of selecting a successor and coming to power has become institutionalized.

The absence of an institutionalized process of coming to power caused a plethora of problems. First, the lack of an accepted process of succession meant that no government had the authority that comes from tradition to justify its rule. The type of government, democratic versus military, was always up for debate as both could be supported with rationales, precedents, and theoretical arguments. The lack of an institutionalized process of selecting a government meant that the choice-of-policies game could always be rendered null and void by shifting to the choice-of-regime game.

This tendency during the breakdown period should be abundantly clear at this point. At the end of the Illia, Lanusse, Martínez de Perón, and Bignone presidencies, the game was unexpectedly shifted. The regimes that replaced the preceding ones were always accepted regardless of the type of political structure; this was consistently demonstrated by the overwhelming popularity in society at large and support among the corporatist entities offered to the new governments. As a result, each of the governments in question, assuming each wanted to remain in power and continue to effect policy, had to satisfy the corporatist entities lest the game shift to the second level—once this shift occurred, power would inevitably be lost to another power broker. The shift in regimes became a question of time and explains the persistent time-consistency problems observed in the study of the four governments of the corporatist breakdown period.

This argument can be summarized in another way: All of the governments during the period studied lacked legitimacy, a fact that greatly limited each government's ability to implement policies that would force sacrifice upon any of the primary corporatist entities. This is the central point of this work. To rephrase, the lack of an institutionalized process of choosing a government—implying a process that has a certain degree of tradition and authority—results in the absence of solid legitimacy for the new regime. Without this tradition and authority, legitimacy becomes synonymous with popularity, and as soon as this popularity dips below some critical (although unmeasurable) minimum, the process of choosing a new power broker and type of regime is set into motion.

Why is it that one can say with any assurance that the second level of the political game, that of choosing the type of regime, is effectively closed off and that democracy is finally stable in Argentina? Clearly, the fact that a precedent is already set is advantageous—the Menem regime is the first in decades to come to power in the previously established fashion. The only exception is the brief Viola regime (in other words, Levingston, Lanusse, Galtieri, and Bignone, all of whom came to power through an internal coup, do not count). A tradition, particularly one of such short duration, is hardly enough to justify the claim made above—that legitimacy based on more than mere popularity is now a defining characteristic of the Argentine political system.

The primary political reason for the institutionalization of democracy is the fact that there are no longer any alternatives. The various power brokers operating during the corporatist breakdown period each worked according to very different rules. The UCR was a stereotypical political party that came to power through traditional, although limited elections; Perón led a movement (rather than a party) that depended on elections in conjunction with mass mobilization; and the military took power through the coup d'état. Perón is now dead and his movement has transformed itself into a more typical political party: The Peronist Party has become (for the most part) delinked from the union movement, is firmly in control of the Renovadores (see section below), and relies on electoral primaries to select candidates. These are all novel characteristics for the Partido Justicialista. The military should no longer be considered a power broker and thus no longer offers an alternative to the existent political structure. The UCR remains largely the same but is in the process of narrowing and rationalizing its ideology, resulting in the further consolidation of the political system.

The final year of Alfonsín's presidency confirms this hypothesis. The transfer of power in any structure of government is a central test to that structure's durability. During the final year of the Radical presidency, the democracy was able to resist the tensions caused by primaries within both of the major parties as well as the presidential elections themselves. This was the first time this resistance occurred since Perón's first reelection in 1952. Further, the opposition won, resulting in the need to transfer power from one power broker to another; this transfer occurred for the first time in over sixty years. All of this process occurred, incredibly, during hyperinflation and the associated economic quagmire; never in Argentina's history had the type of regime remained the same in the wake of such intense crisis.

The institutionalization of democracy has many consequences of fundamental import. First and most important, governments no longer face recurring legitimacy problems. The government clearly has the right to implement policies and take initiatives. Related to this is the fact that mandates have more substance—Menem can rest assured that his six-year mandate will not be unexpectedly revoked. Policies geared toward longer-term objectives can be implemented. Constraints have to be borne by the economic actors, who can no longer oppose them by shifting the political debate to the second level of choice of regime.

The Power Brokers

The most fundamental change during the period studied is the effective elimination of the second level of political competition, the choice-of-regime game. In 1966, there were three power brokers, each of which came to power through a different mechanism. This process resulted in a need to change the very structure of the regime in order to change governments and policies. Along with the structure of the political system, the functioning and outlook of the power brokers, which can now be referred to as political parties, has crucially altered.

By the end of the breakdown period, the military had so discredited itself that it was no longer a viable contender for office. At the same time, the Peronists had largely transformed themselves from a movement into a relatively modern party. In other words, by the end of the Alfonsín presidency, there were only two power brokers competing for power in the same arena and with the same weapons, namely, in the electoral booth and with different campaign promises. Democracy had become the sole means of attaining power and has become a stable system of government.

Of course, it would be an overstatement to claim that the new outlook of the power brokers, and, indeed, that democracy itself is well rooted after so short a period of time and after only one transfer of power. However, the changes that have already occurred within the parties are reinforcing themselves as the power brokers have an increasingly vested interest in the system. The Radicals must clearly support the democratic framework as there never was nor ever will be another method for them to ascend to government; the Radicals could never benefit either from coups or from popular movements. At this point, the Peronists as well have a vested interest in democracy. Not only can the Peronists win elections, but they have with Menem. It is far from probable that the PJ would be able to once again gain control of the government through a popular movement. Hence, for this power broker as well, democracy has also developed into the only means of attaining power.

Further, the institutionalization of democracy has allowed a plethora of smaller and generally more extremist parties to develop. These parties allow particular groups to be able to proclaim their political positions and sometimes gain some say in policymaking (this occurs most often when the ruling party does not have an outright majority in Congress). These groups too have a vested interest in the democratic system that grows as these parties become more established. This vested interest in stability on the part of the extremist groups contrasts markedly with their prior behavior geared toward encouraging regime changes and instability. In the past, the lack of viable parties on the left and on the right meant that these groups could only attempt to wield some influence during regime shifts and not within a political framework. For example, the power of the Montoneros, a terrorist group that clearly rested outside the realm of intra- (as compared to inter-) regime politics, could only gain political clout by assisting Perón in returning to power. Similarly, the reactionary anticommunist groups, present under Martínez de Perón and legalized during the Dirty War, could only gain sway by offering support for an internal or external coup. The fact that these extremist groups would inevitably be dissatisfied with the policies eventually implemented (the Montoneros resumed their resistance and the right was unhappy that the Dirty War was not extended into a method of ideological purification) only augmented the political instability—these groups would almost always be willing to support a change in policy and in regime. Now the extremist groups risk losing a great deal in a regime change; even if they currently gain no concrete benefits, at least they have the right and ability to disseminate their ideas and to compete for greater support, advantages that would almost certainly be revoked in a new military coup or a Peronist-like popular movement.

The fact that two of the original three power brokers, as well as the plethora of smaller parties, are united in supporting the democratic structure greatly limits the military's ability to plan a coup. In the past, the competition between the UCR and the PJ regarding the correct structure of government augmented the political chaos typical of the final stages of a regime. This political instability invited military intervention so as "to restore order and stability." Moreover, the competition between the PJ and the UCR often resulted in fostering temporary alliances of one of these power brokers with the military. There were many Peronists who actually called for a coup against Illia, for example. By the end of the Martínez de Perón government, Radicals were divided between accepting the coup as inevitable and actually encouraging it. Even if the military were to attempt to reactivate the second level of political contest by searching for supporters, both the Radicals and Peronists would be united in opposing any such shifts, greatly limiting the military's ability to drum up support.

Another fundamental change that has occurred and continues to occur is the "rationalization" of the Peronist and Radical parties. In the past, these power brokers attempted to forge alliances with all groups and attempted to gain the support of the greatest possible proportion of society. This base of support was essential for coming to power; during the praetorianist periods, the prime asset was having support to form a new government even at the cost of forming a disjoint and incongruous coalition. Increasingly, the political parties are attempting to formulate coherent platforms that will attract a smaller but more cohesive following. During the crisis periods of the past, near unanimity among the corporatist entities was necessary for coming to power; now, parties require only a majority for outright control and a plurality for a leadership position in government. This movement toward more consolidated parties has encouraged the creation of more extremist parties which, in turn, resulted in a further purification of the larger, more moderate parties.

This greater degree of ideological purity has two fundamental consequences. First, policies that are proposed and implemented are more rational and coordinated. This is essential for economic prosperity. It is worth noting as evidence supporting this theory that the Menem government, as will be seen in the next chapter, began effecting a coordinated and rational economic policy from the very first days of taking office; this contrasts with the great vacillation and inconsistency during the first months of the Onganía regime, for example. Second, this internal harmony reduces the possibility of an internal coup, as occurred against Onganía and Viola, or a rapid shift in policy and alliances, as occurred under Martínez de Perón, Levingston, and even, to a certain degree, Alfonsín. Greater stability and legitimacy are the direct consequences.

In order to better understand how and why these changes occurred, it is worth turning to a review of the various political parties.

The Peronist Party

The Peronist or Justicialist Party has changed enormously over the period studied. It was far easier for such a disparate movement to be held together while out of power. During these periods, each faction could assume its own policies represented those of the movement as a whole. The very coming to power in 1973 began the breakdown of Peronism. In coming to power, however, several of the multiple factions would inevitably feel estranged when seeing the policies of another faction implemented. The Ezeiza Airport Massacre during the Cámpora presidency is a clear example of the tensions that inevitably occur when a movement similar to the Peronist one at the beginning of the 1970s comes to power. It should be added that although Perón's ascending to the presidency in reaction to this incident did bring a greater degree of unity to the movement, this unity was ephemeral and short lived. A few weeks before the general's death, the Montoneros marched out of the Plaza de Mayo in protest of the government's policies during a speech by Perón. Not even a masterful politician like Perón could long keep such supporters united behind him.

Perón, however, was far more capable of holding a variegated coalition together than most politicians. For this reason, the general's death itself was an instrumental, if not the single most instrumental, occurrence in the development of the Peronist Party. His personal ability to offer doctrine easily interpreted by completely different groups combined with his capacity to play factions off one another facilitated a superficial unity among the very different Peronist groups. These capacities fostered the peace between López Rega and the Peronist unions, a peace that lasted only until Perón's death. Similarly, despite their open antagonism, the Montoneros only resumed armed struggle after Perón's death.

Isabel Martínez de Perón's presidency further ruptured the Peronist movement. Her attack on unions went far in delinking the Peronist unions and the Peronist Party, a condition without which, for example, the appointment of Alderete would have been impossible. At the same time, the attack on the unions resulted in the resurgence of a non-Peronist labor movement (to be discussed below).

More important, however, the relationship between the Peronist Party and society at large changed during this period. The indescribable chaos of the times resulted in disenchantment, if not disgust, on the part of a huge proportion of society. The chaos was directly associated with the mobilizing and radicalizing traits so central to the Peronist movement. The popular disgust with the very essence of the old PJ caused two changes.

First, it caused the Radical Party to become "electable" and, to even its own surprise, enabled it to win the 1983 (and 1985 congressional) elections. To better realize the link, it must be mentioned that Alfonsín's central attack on Luder (the Peronist candidate) was his association with the preceding Peronist regime. Alfonsín further attacked the links between the Peronist movement and the military as part of his Tercer Movimiento Histórico. In short, Alfonsín's victory can largely be attributed to the terrible results of the last Peronist regime. As the Peronist Party weakened itself, the Radicals grew comparatively stronger.

Second, these circumstances resulted in a greater need within the Peronist Party to reinforce the democratic over movement characteristics. The fact that mobilization and radicalization of the population would no longer be a viable method to come to power meant that the Peronists had to emphasize the other process that seemed available to them—the democratic electoral process.

The Peronist transformation into a democratically oriented party accelerated during the Alfonsín regime.[1] The Peronist loss in 1983 was first and foremost a loss for the traditional sectors of Peronism; most of the candidates in 1983 were still from these factions. This electoral loss led to the replacement of Martínez de Perón as the official leader of the party. The 1985 elections were even more important for the restructuring of the Peronist Party. Again the Peronist Party lost, but, what is more notable, is the fact that the traditional—often referred to even by fellow Peronists as "radical" or "fascist"—candidates fared far more poorly than did the more modern, moderate, and democratic factions often referred to as the Renovadores (Renewers). The Renovadores were able to win some important positions and retain a significant force in the Congress; the traditional sectors were routed except in the more remote and conservative interior provinces. The power structure within the Peronist Party was shifting increasingly in favor of the latter group. "Following the debacle in 1983 and the subsequent shift in 1985, the leaders of the [Peronist] party lost prestige and political control and in their place the leaders of the Renewer faction continued affirming themselves with discourse clearly oriented towards democracy and institutionalization."[2] By the 1987 elections, the Renovadores were firmly in control of the party's apparatus.

One of the most important structural changes effected by the new leadership was the creation of primaries within the party. In the past, the candidates were chosen by the party and union leadership. The new primary system resembles that common in the United States and that used by the UCR. This change has many ramifications. It proves the Renovadores' commitment to democratic reform. The primary system also subverts the old corporatist structure in which the PJ had to pander to the corporatist entities for the support needed to gain power; now, the PJ's leadership depends on an electorate both within their own ranks and in society at large for support. The dependence on the Peronist Party members circumscribes the leadership's ability to disregard the rank-and-file's concerns about forging alliances with an entity.

Menem's policies thus far, to be reviewed in the next chapter, confirm the changes in the party and also encourage a further narrowing of the Peronist movement. For example, a faction of the Peronist Party in Congress, the so-called *Grupo de los Ocho*, is currently in opposition to the government. A further faction of the party, Peronismo de las Bases, also with representatives in the Congress, has plans of forming a separate party unless Menem changes course.[3] As Menem gains more support from outside of his party from groups that agree with his policies and as he continues to lose support from within his party from groups that do not, policymaking will grow increasingly rational. The Peronist Party, as the others, will grow more ideologically coherent, ensuring greater facility of rational policymaking well into the future.

In sum, the character of the Peronist Party has completely altered and continues to do so. It is impossible to rule out a return to traditional policies, but such a reaction would be very difficult and becomes ever more so with the passing of time. The Peronist Party is now a far more united, democratic (in other words, less personalistic), cohesive, and coherent power broker.

> After years of building up corporatistlike links between the party and various interest groups, the Peronist Party under Menem is now actively breaking down these links. Argentine political society used to look like this [drawing a picture similar to Wiarda's model in Figure 1.1]. Now Menem is destroying everything in the middle and the result can be interpreted as the integration of the formerly incorporated groups.[4]

The effect of this on Argentine politics cannot be underestimated.

The Radical Party

Throughout the period studied, the Radical Party has been a democratically oriented power broker. Internal primaries have long been prominent in the Radical ranks. Moreover, among all of the power brokers the Radical Party had the weakest contacts with the corporatist entities. It was therefore easier for the UCR to split itself from the direct contacts with the CGT, the UIA, and so on. In these ways, the UCR has long been well beyond the development of the PJ. Whereas the structure of the UCR has long been apt for democracy, the party has been less well organized for formulating and implementing rational policy. The fundamental problem of representing too many disjoint and contradictory interests and ideological viewpoints has long afflicted the Radicals. Indeed, this was a fundamental weakness of the Alfonsín presidency. Grinspun's economic policies, and to a slightly lesser extent Sourrouille's, belied a desire to benefit all groups, something that is just not possible in the short term.

On this level, the UCR has fallen behind the developments of the PJ; the Radical leadership is still attempting to veil the internal dissensions instead of trying to forge a more cohesive political union. All the same, the tensions within the party have been growing ever more apparent.[5] The first phase of the Alfonsín presidency was aptly called "the government of the party" by Professors Marcelo Cavarozzi and María Grossi. Alfonsín made all political appointments from within the party in an attempt to satisfy all groups. Such an attempt was doomed to be futile, however. The second phase of the government, the so-called "government of the president," was marked by political appointments from outside the party (most notably, that of Sourrouille) and from the Coordinadora faction of the UCR, a faction controlled by Alfonsín. This shift in alliances caused significant tensions within the UCR.[6] The tensions grew to outright antagonism during the 1989 presidential campaign when Angeloz did everything possible to distance himself from the president, by demanding the resignation of Sourrouille, by attacking the economic policy, and by promising something different.

The tensions continue to grow in the UCR today. Alfonsín strongly criticizes Menem's policies, and Angeloz is a relatively strong supporter (indeed, Menem's economic policies are almost identical to those proposed by Angeloz during the election campaign). Angeloz and others within the UCR have created a new internal faction[7] that could eventually develop into a separate party. The continued weakness of the UCR at the polls reinforces the need to reorganize the party into a more cohesive group with specific and viable policy alternatives. It is worth noting that the 1991 election results were very unfavorable for the Radicals—the party lost in all but two electoral regions. Interestingly, the lists in the two areas where the UCR won were headed by individuals most vociferous about the need to implement rational economic policy and to create a more cohesive political party: Eduardo Angeloz won the governorship of Córdoba and Fernando de la Rúa won the governorship of the city of Buenos Aires. The clearest losers were those individuals most associated with Alfonsín and the Coordinadora, in other words those individuals associated with the attempts to hold the party together at any cost, associated with corruption, and associated with the Tercer Movimiento Histórico. After this victory, Angeloz announced his hopes of gaining support for another presidential bid in 1995, a campaign that has kept and will continue to keep the pressure on the other Radical leaders to renovate the party.

In other words, the UCR is still largely in the process of reorganizing. However, the tensions within the party have grown to such a pitch that rationalization of the party ideology is all but inevitable. Moreover, the poor election results make such a change in outlook unavoidable if the UCR is to remain a force in Argentine politics. The attempts to gain support among all groups has become a clear weakness for the UCR. As the regime choice game has passed, it is now more important to hone a bare majority that is more cohesively constituted. Currently, all the groups that could potentially support the UCR are increasingly looking elsewhere. The more leftist UCR supporters are voting increasingly for the Socialist Party; the more economically liberal sectors are voting for Menem. People are no longer willing to support a party without clear policies for fear of what policies might eventually be implemented. Hence, the reorganization of the UCR is imperative. The internal divisions provide the necessary fault lines. It now is only a question of time before the UCR develops more rational policies; the odds are that they will be in place in time for the next presidential elections.

Parties on the Left and on the Right

Since the return to democracy in 1983, parties on the left and right of the political spectrum have found a new atmosphere of freedom in which to operate. This situation is quite atypical of recent Argentine history. They are able to compete freely and uninhibitedly for public support. They are allowed to disseminate their views. Rallies and public meetings are not prohibited as they were during much of the period studied. In sum, these groups have grown in prominence and power during these past few years. Due to this, they all have a vested interest in the continuation of the democratic system.

At the same time, these political parties have remained weak compared to the more mainstream political groups. This weakness minimizes fears of these groups coming to power and radically shifting policy. This intermediary level of power and involvement in the political system largely eliminates any destabilizing effects these groups could have on the political system. These extremes no longer act as destabilizing factors as they are well integrated into the political system. Their own vested interests are now in the system.

As an example of a stable party on the left, the Socialist Party has become an important voice. The party has developed a national organization but retains its power base in industrialized Rosario, Argentina's third largest city.

> Given the base we now have, we are working on creating a cohesive political and economic program to offer as an alternative to that of Menem. We are now powerful enough to do that, although, I must admit, we are far from being able to even think about implementing our own program by ourselves.[8]

In offering a democratic alternative, the left will not have to resort to violence or subversion to promote its views. Moreover, the existence of a cohesive and rational left will also inhibit the PJ and the UCR from attempting to expand their influence to the left, which would result in more disjoint and tentative coalitions.

On the right, the Unión Centro Democrático (UCD), led by the preeminent liberal Alvaro Alsogaray, has become an important force. The party is currently in a coalition with the Menem government and has been given much responsibility for reforming the state. Alsogaray and his representatives have been responsible for such important matters as privatizations and debt negotiations. Clearly, this group has national stature and offers a means through which true economic libertarians can voice their opinions. At the same time, the party is in no position to set the political agenda, much less to govern alone. The party's electoral results are minute and its base of support is exclusively in the Buenos Aires area.

> For us, being part of the government is an ideological triumph and a
> position from which we can demonstrate our dedication, honesty, and
> seriousness. At the same time, it is a great risk for the UCD as we risk
> being absorbed ideologically by the Peronists and disappearing as a
> political party.[9]

Thus far, the UCD remains neither more nor less than a party with moderate
power. As such, it will be able to continue to stabilize the democracy that is
still taking root.

The Military

A fundamental change wrought during the period studied is the elimination of
the military as a power broker. This change was gradual and has many
discernible components. The most important aspects of the destruction of the
military as power broker can be enumerated as follows: (1) greater and more
established internal dissension that prohibits the military from functioning as
an arbitrator in control of the government, (2) mistrust and unpopularity of
the military in society at large and among the corporatist entities, (3) the
gradual destruction of contacts between the military and the corporatist
entities, a process that can be termed the "delinking" of the military, and (4)
increasing relative emphasis within the military on conditions directly related
to its status as a corporatist entity over those conditions related to the
military's status as a power broker. All of these individual transformations
point to the fact that the military should increasingly be interpreted as a
corporatist entity or, more aptly, an interest group rather than a power
broker. This is an essential change in the breakdown of corporatism.

Internal dissensions have had a prominent place in military politics
throughout Argentine history. In the period preceding that here studied, two
factions of the military actually engaged in open battle. The resolution of
this internal crisis in favor of the so-called *azules* faction, however, was a
central prerequisite for the 1966 coup, as the military was cognizant of the
need for unity in order to lead a successful Revolución Argentina. All the
same, this first long-term military government proceeded to break down
because of growing and uncontrollable tensions within the armed services.
First these tensions resulted in two internal coups (against Onganía and
Levingston). Then the military had to return to civil rule. The fact that the
process itself occurred during a period of growing political instability and
economic stagnation further disgraced this institution. As if to add insult to
injury, it was Perón, a figure still loathed within the military, who came to
power. During the whole slide towards redemocratization, the various
military factions took to blaming one another.

As a result of this first failure, the military was more cautious in taking
power a second time—it was not until Martínez de Perón's government had
been completely discredited that a coup finally occurred. As if the military

had been privy to O'Donnell's work before it was published, the military wanted to see the crisis level hit new highs before taking power. It was commonly believed that the greater degree of crisis before the coup, the more freedom, support, and legitimacy the military government would command within society upon assuming power. Similarly, it was felt that the more society broke down, the more the military officers would be forced to unite in a desperate attempt to save the country. For example, regarding the timing of the coup, one military leader was quoted as saying that it would be "better a minute too late than a minute too soon."[10] Despite the very conscientious attempts to foster cohesion among the military ranks, in the end the Proceso de Reorganización proved to be even more divisive than the Revolución.

During the first years of the Proceso, Videla was able to keep control over the military. As a result, relatively consistent polices were implemented. Videla himself, however, began to have doubts of continued cohesion when a new president had to be appointed, as evidenced by his discussions with his economics team ("You would be happy if you knew the alternative candidates"[11]). Indeed, his trepidations proved well founded as Viola was quickly overthrown by an internal coup due to the growing rifts within the military. When Galtieri assumed the presidency, the Proceso and the military were already well along the road of breakdown.

The new president's "get things done image" was geared not only toward regaining popular support for the military government but also toward forcing a greater degree of unity within the military itself. Realizing that renewed fervency regarding the economy was not sufficient to effect these goals, the Malvinas/Falkland War was initiated. It must be emphasized that this war, it is now clear, was geared as much toward promoting unity within the military as towards fostering popularity;[12] in other words, the war, supported in all quarters of the military, was a means toward remolding the unity that had gradually been lost since 1976. The consequent military defeat completely polarized the various factions.

The Bignone regime was supported only by the army; both the navy and air force refused any continued responsibility for the government. This stand clearly reveals the growing disagreements among the armed services. The weak bargaining position of this last military president vis-à-vis the democratic parties resulted in the constant advancement of the election date. In large part, Bignone could not resist the civilian groups' pressure because of the internal dissension within the military. This situation was quite comparable to that of Lanusse.

The divisions have only grown since the return of democratic rule despite Alfonsín's poorly handled investigation into the Dirty War. Most of the rebellions since the return to democracy (four under Alfonsín and one under Menem) were led by lower ranking officers, a fact that reflects insubordination and disagreement with superiors. The issues involved, moreover, were often military in nature and not political in the broader sense:

"[M]any of the younger officers were unhappy with the generals and admirals who refused to reorganize and modernize their services in the wake of the Falkland (Malvinas) War," stated Gary Wynia in referring to the 1987 mutiny against Alfonsín.[13]

In the most recent uprising (December 1990), the small rebel factions were violently and swiftly put down by the loyal officers, which might reflect growing support for democratic rule of law on the latter's part. More certainly, however, this action against fellow soldiers reflects a complete lack of unity among the various military factions. This evident lack of unity, which has grown over the period studied, prohibits the efficient functioning of the power broker in government. More important, leading military officials have long realized this and hence could not easily be convinced to retake power. "I cannot imagine the military attempting to take power again anytime soon. There would have to be a crisis beyond the scope of any in Argentina's history in order to convince the leadership of the lack of any other alternatives."[14]

Mistrust and unpopularity of the military in society at large and among the corporatist entities has been an important change as well. To a large degree, the distrust is a direct consequence of the obvious dissension within the military—how can an institution divided in itself that has already failed twice in attempting political and economic reform ever be trusted to lead a government again? Further, the corporatist entities that have supported military coups have all suffered at some point during the military regime. Having been betrayed by the military, the corporatist entities have inevitably grown more mistrustful of this power broker.

In the past, the unpopularity of the military has been ephemeral. However, the disfavor coinciding with the Proceso's decline seems far more ingrained in the Argentine psyche. For example, many of Perón's supporters who jeered the military in 1973—"Se van, se van, y nunca vuelveran" (They're going, they're going, and never again will they be returning)— supported the 1976 coup. This switch contrasts markedly with the near unanimous disgust with the military uprising in 1987, almost four full years after the military extrication from government, during a worsening economic situation. This aversion for the military was once again demonstrated at the end of 1990 when over 80 percent of Argentine society was against the impending amnesty for jailed military officers.

Considering that in both 1966 and in 1976 the military only took power when there was clear and widespread support for its doing so, the enduring lack of support for and trust in the military are important changes that have manifested themselves during the period studied. These new societal tendencies are yet another reason for the elimination of the military as a potential power broker.

The delinking of the military can be seen as another component of the lack of popularity of and trust in this institution; given these feelings, corporatist entities would, theoretically at least, be less interested in cultivating contacts with the armed services. The roots of the delinking are far more profound and concrete, however, and result from the antiterrorist structure during the Proceso. The key characteristic of the cell structure was the complete elimination of a line of command as each group was completely independent. On a practical level, this resulted (as was hoped and planned) in the inability of using influence to protect a *desaparecido* no matter how important, rich, or socially connected; the head of the CGT, for example, despite the close relationship he had traditionally been afforded with the military, could not protect an individual suspected by any of the individual cell groups. This was not just the case for those on the left. The apprehended member of Videla's economics team, as discussed in Chapter 4, is an example of just such an individual on the right. When this man was finally released, it was made clear to him that his freedom had come solely as a result of the particular whims of the cell commander.

Although the formulation of economic and other policies was never nearly so insulated, there was a conscientious attempt to limit the input of the various corporatist entities regarding these polices, too. One analyst of the Proceso claims that Videla attempted to implement

a political strategy that insulated state leaders from societal demands. By coercively demobilizing popular classes and denying the dominant classes their traditional "entrance ways" into state policy-making circles (i.e., by limiting personal contacts with military elites), Videla created a pressure-free environment that allowed the government to function as if special interests did not matter.[15]

As David Pion-Berlin's study claims, these contacts clearly continued, however. Under Videla, instead of there being contacts between the economics team and the corporatist entities, as was typical, there were contacts between the corporatist entities and the factions of the military that were excluded from the policymaking process, those that disagreed with the economic plan. This eventually resulted in Viola's election and the associated change in policies. All the same, the result of Videla's attempt to insulate the policymaking elite resulted in a breakdown of contacts between the corporatist entities and the military. As contacts with corporatist groups are an essential defining characteristic of a power broker, the severing of these links went far in transforming the military.

The shift towards acting like a corporatist entity instead of a power broker both reflects and augments the above changes. It should be clear that there has constantly been a tension within the military in Argentina (as, indeed, in every country where the military has political aspirations) between acting as a corporatist entity and as a power broker. Theoretically, there need not be a contradiction in simultaneously being both. Certainly, the military continued to be a corporatist entity during the period here studied (for the purposes of this study, the military was considered a "secondary" corporatist entity and hence was not analyzed). However, it should be just as clear that such a dual role creates a tension. On the one hand, a corporatist entity by nature tries to get as much as possible for the interest group it represents. On the other, the power broker in government not only has the power to allocate the desired resources (creating a conflict of interest) but also is supposed to be able to objectively mediate between the various corporatist entities. As long as the military can mediate fairly objectively, thus, by definition acts like a power broker, the policies can be relatively rational and successful. The mediation becomes difficult if not impossible when the military begins to take on the exclusive outlook of a corporatist entity. In other words, it is here proposed that although the military simultaneously plays both roles, one necessarily predominates to a greater or lesser degree over the other.

During the Onganía regime, the military acted a great deal more like a power broker than a corporatist group. For example, military spending under Onganía was not greatly increased, reflecting the military's conscientious desire to attempt to mediate interests as objectively as possible. It might be noted, however, that the Argentine military was never as much of a power broker (as compared to corporatist entity) as had been the Brazilian military at the beginning of its bureaucratic authoritarian regime when military expenditures actually decreased as a part of the economic plan. This at least partially explains why the Brazilian military remains so much more of a political force under democracy than the Argentine.[16] By the time of the Videla government, the military acted relatively more like a corporatist entity. Military expenditures were greatly increased. The restructuring of the state, a central aspect of Martínez de Hoz's original plan, including privatizations, was effectively blocked by the military as corporatist entity.

Since the return to democratic rule, most of the military's complaints regarding policy (voiced, among other ways, through rebellions) centered around military as opposed to national affairs. Prominent issues have included the legal actions taken against the former military leaders, soldiers' and officers' wages, and military "honor." These contrast markedly with those issues that have traditionally interested the military including, for example, economic policy and the status of the Peronists. The military continues to develop more and more into a corporatist entity rather than a power broker.

The relative and growing ascendance of the corporatist entity—over the power broker—aspects of the military is probably simultaneously a cause and an effect of the changes outlined above. Discerning the cause and effect is less important in this study, however, than is the observation that a return to military rule grows less likely as that institution increasingly develops into a corporatist entity instead of a power broker.

The State

The breakdown of the old corporatist structure in Argentina also manifested itself by imposing implicit but evident limitations on the operation of the state. On the economic side, the state has no longer been capable of redistributing income to any of the corporatist entities. This ability was a central characteristic of all of the tentative alliances during the corporatist breakdown period—no longer can a power broker promote an alliance based on economic redistribution.

As a consequence, there is a greater degree of consensus regarding policy among the major political parties. The economic limitations have grown increasingly entrenched in the parties' very outlook. Many of the platforms attempted during the breakdown period could no longer be attempted—Gelbard's priming of the economy without monetary constraint would result almost immediately in hyperinflation today. These limitations, both economic and ideological, further buttress stability, particularly relating to economic policy.

The greater stability should, and, indeed, is resulting in higher investments as Argentina's political risk decreases. The economic fruits will aid the political consolidation. Whereas a destabilizing dynamic was in operation during the breakdown period, a new one is now in place, one that has thus far promoted democratic consolidation and the economic rejuvenation. The dynamic should continue, almost certainly with growing vigor, in the years to come.

The Economics of the Public Sector

Throughout the breakdown period, the government offered inducements to the various corporatist entities. These inducements were in actuality little different from an outright distribution of income. The nature of the tentative alliances required economic favors to be distributed to almost all of the corporatist entities at almost all times—exclusion from the alliance more often meant receiving no benefits than it meant actually suffering with constraints. Of course, sometimes these benefits were merely a secondary consequence of other economic policies, such as the benefits workers gained from the subsidized loans under Krieger Vasena or lower unemployment under Martínez de Hoz, but they were inducements all the same.

All of these benefits came at a cost. Finding the resources to redistribute was a pivotal problem for all of the governments analyzed. At the very beginning of each of the governments, constraints that directly or indirectly provided revenues, which could then be distributed to other corporatist entities, could often be imposed—Onganía's compensated devaluation, Gelbard's lowering profit margins, and Martínez de Hoz's lower wages are all examples. The constraints were never really commensurate with the inducements, however—the government always offered more in economic inducements than they ever raised in economic constraints, even at the beginning of each of the governments. This manifested itself in the ever-present budget deficit. Moreover, the situation grew worse with time during each government. As the governments began their slides into the praetorianist abyss, inducements were used with greater flamboyance while constraints were rendered inoperable; the budget deficits swelled. When the regime was finally replaced by another, the incoming government was forced to find additional resources to tap.

These sources of funding have changed over the years but have included agricultural taxes, foreign borrowing, monetary expansion, and controlled (negative) domestic interest rates. Others of secondary importance were not mentioned in this work. Each of these has been closed off to the government. The agricultural sector is no longer willing to subsidize the other corporatist entities (any attempt to do so could result in an immediate and prolonged lockout, as almost happened during the Alfonsín presidency). Moreover, as will be discussed below, the agricultural sector is no longer rich enough, does not export enough, to fund significant government expenditures. The foreign debt crisis has closed off sources of foreign credit. The years of economic tumult have resulted in savvy financial actors who are no longer willing to see their savings eaten up through negative real interest rates or through unexpected bursts of inflation; monetary expansion is no longer an option. Even common workers learned of the need to buy dollars during the Alfonsín presidency: Men in overalls buying dollars became a common sight in the financial district of Buenos Aires in 1989.

The hyperinflation in which the Alfonsín presidency ended represented the exhaustion of the final source of funds for redistribution that the Argentine state could appropriate, that of prolonged and excessive printing of money. When no one is any longer willing to hold on to a nation's currency that nation has lost all creditworthiness. As many Argentine economists affirmed, "Hyperinflation represented the complete bankruptcy of the state." For this reason, no power broker that could gain control of the state would be able to redistribute income to an amalgamation of corporatist entities.[17] All of this is a consequence of Argentina's relative economic stagnation, clearly visible in Figure 6.2.

The fact that economic resources can no longer be tapped and distributed to the corporatist entities means that there is no longer any stimulus to try to broker an alliance similar to those of the breakdown period. Power brokers command no resources with which to buy support, and corporatist entities can receive no special payment for aiding the ascent of a power broker. This is clear to the power brokers and corporatist entities alike. Clearly, without such potential alliances, there is a far weaker incentive to topple the regime in order to effect new policies. The benefits of shifting the political competition to the second level are greatly diminished.

Figure 6.2   Argentina's Per Capita GNP Compared to Other Countries, 1960–1983 (expressed in terms of other countries' per capita GNP)

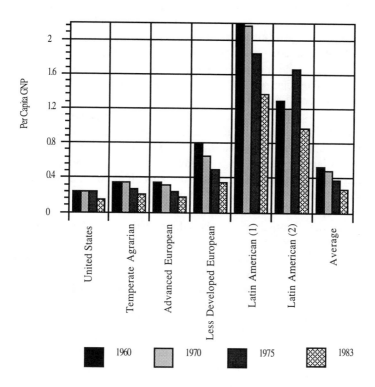

Source: Based on data from W. Smith 1989.

Note: The bars in this figure show Argentina's GNP as a proportion of other countries' per capita GNP. For example, if Argentina's GNP were $100 and the United States's GNP were $200, then the bar for the United States would be .5, i.e., Argentina's per capita GNP would be half that of the United States's. *Temperate Agrarian*: Canada, New Zealand. *Advanced European*: Germany, Belgium, France, UK, Holland, Norway, Sweden, Switzerland. *Less Developed European*: Austria, Spain, Finland, Greece, Ireland, Italy, Portugal. *Latin American (1)*: Brazil, Colombia, Mexico, Peru. *Latin American (2)*: Chile and Uruguay.

At the same time, the costs of shifting the level of the political game have grown. The uncertainty engendered by such a shift would render investments, which are growing in Argentina, more risky. Instability would result without any possibility of gain. Under these conditions, many claim that Menem has no alternative but to break with the past regarding both policies and government structure.

The Growth of Consensus Among Power Brokers

A general consensus has been developing among the most important parties (and even, as far as can be judged, within the military) regarding economic and even social policy. The important parties that could in the near future lead an Argentine government have increasingly similar platforms and would most probably implement similar policies. The creation of a political center in Argentina and the movement toward this center by the major political forces render the country increasingly stable and cohesive. There are many causes for this recent change.

One certainly relates to the development of more extremist parties that are accepted within the political system. The smaller, more extremist parties have stolen supporters from both the PJ and the UCR. As the extremes have left the two largest parties, their policy initiatives have moved toward the middle ground. As democracy consolidates, both of these parties will increasingly realize that election-winning support will always lie toward the center of the political spectrum.

Indeed, the corporatist entities, which at this point are no more than loose interest groups with varying degrees of power, are increasingly demanding centrist policies. On the economic side, there is a growing cognizance that the redistributive battles might have resulted in ephemeral gains. Over decades, however, the destructive economic polices have led to the impoverishment of all. Even regarding the social agenda there is growing agreement that the extremism of the past fostered only more extremism. Onganía's desire to foster a moral Catholic society resulted concretely in just the opposite—a rebellious, revolutionary, and relatively amoral society. As fewer individuals and groups try to impose their moral views on society, Argentina has grown more tolerant. In an odd twist, many of the more extreme outlooks have simultaneously died out—anarchists are few and far between in modern-day Argentina. The tolerance has also grown to encompass greater tolerance for interpretations of the past; it is less relevant to blame the Dirty War on a certain group than to simply ensure that it does not happen again.

The costs of the economic policy, even if it does not call for redistribution between economic sectors, can no longer be postponed through budget deficits, through the postponement of structural changes, and the like. All of these maneuvers can be seen as attempts to redistribute funds intertemporally, augmenting the current resources and standard of living at the cost of those in the future; this is the very essence of government deficit spending wasted on consumption instead of investment. These policies rely on the creditworthiness of the state so that the government can "borrow" from the future. The bankruptcy of the state means that the Argentine Republic has no credit left—no one, no institution will waste its resources on policies that cannot be paid for.

As a result, certain policies are no longer feasible, and, more importantly, everyone knows it. Unbacked printing of currency is the clearest example of a policy, often used during the breakdown period, that is no longer feasible; resorting to the printing presses would almost immediately result in skyrocketing inflation. The state's lack of creditworthiness also prevents budget deficits; as no one is willing to sponsor deficit spending by lending to the government, the deficit would soon lead to resorting to the printing presses. Unbacked monetary expansion and budget deficits are now intimately related, and neither is a viable course of action. Indeed, none of the economic policies implemented during the breakdown period would be effective today.

In sum, new structural constraints confront the making of government policy. Within this new structure, certain goals must be attained, the most obvious being a balanced budget. It should be remembered that the Argentine state had a very large structural deficit in 1989 and continues to have one if one considers unpaid pensions and the like. This gap has to be closed, but the methods of doing so are fairly limited. To close a deficit, the government can either reduce expenditure or increase revenues. As will be seen, both measures were needed under Menem. However, both goals are relatively long-term goals that had to be furthered from day one but that would not reap benefits for several months. Meanwhile, several stopgap measures were needed and would have been no matter what party came to power. These measures can be summarized under three headings.

First, expenditures had to be slashed even if this meant that previously assumed obligations could not be met; the state could simply not pay for all of the responsibilities that previous governments had assumed. As will be seen in the next chapter, Menem was forced to temporarily freeze payment of public contracts and to avoid fully paying the state sector's wage and pension bill. Second, revenues had to be increased. Menem implemented, as had sometimes occurred during the breakdown period, several temporary emergency taxes. Third, all structural changes that could result in immediate funds, most notably privatizations, had to be effected as swiftly as possible. This all was to occur with the realization that structural changes geared toward fundamentally eliminating the structural deficit had to occur simultaneously; if the structural changes were not to be effected, inflationary pressures and the like would return, as they had throughout the breakdown period, as the temporary measures expired. The fact that both economic actors and the political leaders increasingly realize the need for such a course of events fosters stability; everyone increasingly expects a similar development of policies.

Just as important as the structural limitations that force the implementation of certain strategies is the ideological context in which these policies are developed. Liberal economic ideas have a long history in Argentina. Indeed, these ideas imported from England at the end of the last century were dominant until the incorporation period of Argentine history. The tenets of the liberal ideology were, as evidenced, much debated during the breakdown period, a fact that fueled the repeated crises of the breakdown period; without the lack of agreement regarding the type of economic policy to implement, the breakdown period would not have been so mercurial.

In hindsight, however, it seems as though the breakdown period also represented the gradual development of a consensus regarding the importance of the free market. A liberal program was first proposed by Krieger Vasena, albeit in a tentative manner. Martínez de Hoz's program was heavily imbued with the rhetoric of limiting the state's role through privatizations and such—although advances were made, the rhetoric of the government certainly outstripped the actions, due in large part to the resistance of the military. Even the Austral Plan discussed at length the need for reducing the state sector as a method of reducing the fiscal deficit and monetary expansion, prime causes of inflation. By 1989, it became clear that the best formulated economic programs of the preceding years all contained free-market ideas and that the failure of the programs lay not so much in poorly conceptualized programs as in the fact that none of the economic plans was fully implemented. Almost no one noticed it at the time, but by 1989 there was a widespread consensus that seemed to be very deep rooted regarding economic policy; the positive side of the slow and painful convergence of ideas during the breakdown period is the fact that these ideas now seem to be fairly well ingrained among the political and economic elite, even among those that formerly held other viewpoints.[18]

The best representation of this consensus is the fact that the three main presidential candidates in 1989 (Menem, Angeloz, and, a distant third, Alsogaray) all had similar economic plans, although, it must be admitted, Menem's was not clear until after he assumed office. In other words, the breakdown of corporatism has mirrored the growth of a relatively free market or capitalist ideology. This transformation is certainly reinforced by the events in Eastern Europe as well as the rest of Latin America generally, and particularly the recent economic advances in Chile and Mexico. These trends are further exemplified in the occurrences during the Menem government thus far (see next chapter).

The effect of this convergence of policies is to promote stability, to limit "play" on the second political plane, and to increase legitimacy. More concretely, by reducing the variety of politically viable (as compared to those represented by the extreme left and right) ideologies, there is less temptation to undermine a regime. At the same time, investment becomes less risky as the possibility of radical shifts in policy, as experienced during the last period of each of the regimes studied, is less probable; even political opponents no longer pose the same level of economic threat.

The Corporatist Entities

The breakdown period fundamentally changed the corporatist entities. Each of the corporatist entities at some juncture suffered direct attacks from the government; Videla, for example, intervened in several unions and forced the closure of the CGE. At the same time, the constant economic crisis during the breakdown period had tremendous effects on the entities and individual economic actors that formed the memberships. The fundamental result was the softening, if not the total elimination, of the economic fault lines between the various types of economic actors.

It is no longer so easy to divide all economic actors into a limited number of groups in which the members all have very similar concerns and characteristics. In essence, the differences between economic actors, even those operating in the same sectors of the economy, have grown far more significant in comparison to the similarities. To the extent that similarities still do exist, it is questionable to what degree these interests can be mobilized to affect policy. The primary corporatist entities of the breakdown period, with the possible exception of the SRA, to be discussed below, have slowly been transformed into, at worst, weak organizations that group together economic actors with some similar objectives and concerns; the corporatist entities have degenerated into loose interest groups. As interest groups, the modern-day associations, which include the CGE, CGT, SRA, and UIA, have far less power and are consequently less capable of destabilizing governments and economic policies.

There were several changes that were wrought on the corporatist entities that have, in my opinion, forever changed the destabilizing aspects of these groups. First, the member companies themselves have changed tremendously. The economic actors that exist today are, by and large, far more viable in a competitive economy than was the pool of economic actors in 1966. The weakest companies were, quite simply, weeded out during the past decades of crisis. Many went bankrupt. Others were bought out by the capitanes de la industria. The period that most exemplifies this restructuring of individual companies is that led by Martínez de Hoz. The opening of the economy in conjunction with the rising value of the peso caused the economic failure of many companies, primarily of the national but even of the international bourgeoisie (such as General Motors). Most of those that resisted the pressure of the time invested heavily. The nationalization of the foreign debt further strengthened the position of these companies as this act cleared their balance sheets.

Although less evident, the crises through the period studied eliminated many of the less viable companies. For this reason, the capitaled classes today are relatively more capable of competing and more willing to compete in the market, for they have better odds of winning than did the pool of companies in the past. Few companies and industries need active government support to survive. Without such dire circumstances, it is far harder to mobilize support among the corporatist entities. In the equation offered in Chapter 1, *Power of Corporatist Entity = Power of Members × Mobilizing Capabilities*, the mobilizing capabilities have decreased significantly. The resultant pool of economic actors has a different set of priorities than the preceding pools. Greater market competition does not necessarily spell disaster for whole sectors of the economy as it once did: "I don't think any firms or industries are doomed. Each company's future will depend mainly on its ability and willingness to invest and on the government's keeping a level playing field."[19] Indeed, as this quote suggests, the trend has moved away from fostering redistribution to any particular group by keeping a "level playing field."

Associated with the restructuring of individual companies is the formation of the capitanes de la industria. These firms are a direct consequence of conscientious attempts to render individual companies more viable regardless of the political considerations. As a result, these companies can survive without active support from the government. Certainly, as will be discussed below, the limits on state contracts have and will continue to have a deleterious effect on these companies, but these state subsidies do not represent a grave threat to the mammoth holding companies.

The captains of industry best epitomize the fact that the fault lines between various economic sectors are less clearly defined and important in Argentina today than in the Argentina of 1966. As was stated in the first chapter, these fault lines in the economy forced a corporatist structure regardless of whether clear corporatist representative institutions existed. As long as clear economic segmentation persisted, one company or individual from a particular sector could and often did represent all those economic actors working under similar conditions; the landowner, in talking with a general over dinner, represented necessarily the whole SRA in the general's mind, for he could be sure during the breakdown period that all landowners faced a similar economic panorama. If this one individual were to support a military coup for economic reasons, odds were very good that others in this economic category would as well. As these clear fault lines no longer exist, the only individuals that can persuasively speak for a interest group now are representative of individual pressure groups, including those that had been corporatist entities—the CGT, CGE, SRA, and UIA.

The structures that supported the corporatist entities are collapsing. The individual groups are far more internally divided and less capable of mobilizing support. In part this is a consequence of the microeconomic changes outlined above. Other causes merely relate to the difficult and complex histories of the individual structures, however. The vagaries of the political scene forced the individual corporatist entities to change appearances and structure so as to better encounter the political situation. The clearest example of this was the merger between the UIA and the CGE during the

Perón and the Videla governments. Under Perón, the UIA voluntarily dissolved itself in order to merge with the politically more powerful CGE, whereas the CGE was forcibly closed down by the military in 1976, forcing the members to join the UIA. Over the long term, these maneuvers fundamentally weakened these pressure groups. In the past, the CGE and UIA could regroup because of the ever-present fault lines in the economy that forced a similar outlook among certain companies. This is no longer the case. A similar history can be recounted regarding the CGT. The union group has become more politically factionalized since the times of Vandor; the Peronist government, the military government, and even Alfonsín's fostered more and deeper schisms. These changes prevented the individual groups from developing policy suggestions that were highly favorable to all of the members, which in turn limited the mobilizing capacities of the corporatist entities.

Indeed, all of the corporatist entities had at one point or another protested Alfonsín's policies, but never were the results as explosive as they had been in the past. The hyperinflation was caused more by poor management of the economy than by destabilizing actions on the part of the corporatist entities, and the political situation remained stronger as evidenced by the ability to transfer power to another democratic regime.

This trend is reinforced by the more limited ability to foster large-scale transfers of income. The progressive impoverishment of the state discussed above represents the diminishing ability to redistribute resources on the scale typical of the breakdown period. It would no longer be possible for any government to benefit workers as did Perón's or to benefit the international financial community as did Videla's. The inability of government policy to foster such increases in profit margins also limits the ability and value of political lobbying on the part of the corporatist entities for three reasons. First and most obvious, it is more difficult to mobilize the significant support necessary to affect government policymaking. Second, without such large-scale transfers internal divisions within the individual groups cannot be papered over; for example, Perón had to raise wages significantly in order to gain the support of all labor groups despite the flattening of wages among unions which, other things being equal, should cause internal union haggling. Finally and most importantly, there are significantly reduced political returns (redistribution) as contrasted to economic (investment) returns. Given the smaller advantages that could be gained from an agricultural lockout, for example, such actions no longer justify the costs of reduced sales and cash flow. At the same time, given the greater stability, returns on investment have gone up as the political risks have gone down.

As a consequence, there is a greater emphasis on competing in the market as opposed to in the political sphere.

The so-called capitanes de la industria have been criticized for the political influence we wielded. To be perfectly honest, our actions and outlooks were well represented by our critics. What they do not realize was how central political influence was to our very survival— government policy was not the difference between slightly higher or lower profits, but between profiting and going bust. The biggest change is that now the rules seem to be set, and we are looking to maximize our profits within the market as compared to the political sphere. In the past, seventy percent of our time was spent trying to influence policy, now seventy percent is spent running the business side and looking for new investments. What no one seemed to realize is that the policy process determined where we were forced to go for profits. We never chose the political arena as the correct one for business to be conducted in.[20]

Overall, then, the former corporatist entities have grown into more motley and variegated organizations. This impedes the concentration of power and mobilizing capabilities characteristic of the breakdown period. These changes mirror the changes within the workings of the average individual firms; Argentine firms today are, on the whole, more able and more willing to compete within the market. Certainly, the national bourgeoisie, dependent on the internal market, still exists, but its ability to compete with new imports and to attempt to export is greatly enhanced. Even those firms that cannot have less of an incentive to look to the state for aid as there are very few resources that can be redistributed. All of this has resulted in a greater desire to allow economic benefit to accrue to those successful in the market place instead of to those in the political arena. This feeling began under Alfonsín but has really started taking root with Menem.

The shift to the market place is self-reinforcing. Successful companies have vested interests in keeping the rules of the game fixed. As other companies go bankrupt, they can no longer lobby for a return to the old ways. Moreover, the very corporatist structures so common during the breakdown period are now disabled by lack of use.

We used to have constant meetings, meeting with the US Chamber of Commerce, the Embassy, the UIA, every group possible. Now they are a waste of time for us and almost everyone else who was involved in them. The rules are increasingly set by the market, which is fine by us as we can now worry about running our business instead of about protecting ourselves from daily attacks.[21]

Of course, the development and changes within each of the individual corporatist entities is very different. Although the CGE, CGT, SRA, and UIA were not the exclusive representatives of the four major sectors of the economy, they were the major and traditional representatives. We now turn to a brief look at the development of each of these organizations to exemplify the changes wrought by the breakdown period on the corporatist structures.

La Confederación General de Trabajo

La Confederación General de Trabajo was quite probably the most powerful of the primary corporatist entities at the beginning of the corporatist breakdown period. Since then, however, it has grown significantly weaker. Each government attacked the influence, explicitly or unwittingly, of this group. During the Onganía regime, the split of the CGT into two factions, combined with the further diversification of the economy with the influx of foreign investment, was the precursor to more fundamental rifts in this corporatist entity. These divisions were significantly expanded during Martínez de Perón's government; some unions supported the Peronist government to the very end while others encouraged the coup.

Once the new military regime was in power, a policy of active repression of the labor movement ensued. Many unions were actively repressed, a fact that certainly weakened the CGT. Further, the Martínez de Hoz period was marked by a significant shift in the composition of GNP away from manufacturing and toward services, a sector noteworthy for its lower-paying jobs and more docile unions. The entire period under study was marked by the growth of self-employment and of the unofficial economy, which, according to one estimate made in 1989, accounted for up to 60 percent of total GNP in that year.[22] Indeed, the growth of the informal sector has harmed the CGT as well as the other corporatist entities as something that officially does not exist is only with difficulty represented politically. The black market represents an attempt to move away from the effects of politics, to ignore the political dictates, not an attempt to become further embroiled with politics in order to influence policy.

During the last years of the Proceso, there had been much discussion in Argentina regarding the supposed destruction of the union organization. The unions had been harshly repressed, and Argentine industry had radically changed. It was clear in the subsequent years, however, that the CGT was not yet dead. The resistance it could muster against Alfonsín's overhaul of the organization was the clearest manifestation of the resurgence of union power. In other ways that were less obvious, however, the old structure continued to fall apart.

Alfonsín was unable to win over the labor organization, but significant advances were made in creating a grass-roots Radical CGT organization. One Radical unionist estimated in 1990 that approximately 20 percent of the labor movement was Radical.[23] This Radical support solidified the divisions between the Peronist and non-Peronist union factions. At the same time, the divisions within the Peronist camp, clear since the Martínez de Perón presidency, continued to expand. Some Peronists supported Alfonsín. Others became increasingly apolitical, searching only for pragmatic methods of improving their rank-and-file's conditions. Others remained militant. The appointment of Alderete, one of the more corrupt, militant, and "Peronist" of the union leaders, to minister of labor merely demonstrated the complexities and divisions of the union movement under the relatively simple veneer. It was no longer possible for the union movement to support unanimously and forcefully a particular power broker.

All the same, the CGT remained the most powerful of all of the corporatist entities at the end of the breakdown period. However, from Menem's assumption of power in 1989 until the current day, union power has rapidly dissipated. In large part, this was a direct result of the new democratic structure, which necessarily rendered the old corporatist organizations weaker. Menem won on widespread support that was particularly strong in the lower and working classes. His support from these classes has been confirmed in interim elections. Even though his policies are not prounion, union leaders can no longer claim that they represent the workers—Menem is now able to mobilize their support directly through the ballot box. No longer can corporatist leaders claim that only they know what is best for their members.

Finally, it must also be noted that Menem has a great advantage because he is a "Peronist," despite the fact that his policies are far from typical of Peronism. Empty rhetoric is not as damaging to him as it would be to a non-Peronist. His claims that Juan Perón himself would have implemented such policies if he were alive today certainly cannot be proven, but neither can they be disproven. It is far easier for someone of a particular organization to dismantle what that organization built than for an outsider to do it. As one analyst at the U.S. Embassy in Buenos Aires claimed, "Menem has an advantage with the unions similar to that Nixon had in opening up China."[24]

The union representing the railroad workers made a proposal in August 1992 that exemplified the change in outlook on the part of many unions. Argentine railroads have long been overstaffed, as a method of buying political patronage and reducing unemployment figures, and tremendous loss makers. The Menem government has made clear that it refuses to contemplate forever subsidizing the Argentine railroads and has transferred most of the financial costs of running individual railroads to the provinces through which they run. With this political drive, the union realized that sooner or later, all railroad subsidies, from the national government as well as the provinces, would end. In reaction, the union leaders did not call for a strike, as would have been the case in the past. Instead, in conjunction with the provinces, the leaders worked on a rationalization strategy that included firing redundant workers and in some cases reducing wages in order to make the railroad services economically viable.

La Sociedad Rural Argentina

La Sociedad Rural Argentina was under almost constant attack during the corporatist breakdown period. The compensated devaluation utilized by Krieger Vasena was a method of forcing the agricultural elite to pay for the industrial development of the country, a method that was attempted with less success (due to the greater instability) under various subsequent ministers of economics. Other attacks included the dreaded land tax attempted by both Krieger Vasena and Gelbard. During the same period, international conditions turned worse for the SRA, particularly relating to the closing of the European market to Argentine beef. The overvalued currency toward the end of the Social Pact also had very negative effects. The Martínez de Hoz period, in contrast, was marked by the flourishing of agricultural sectors. By 1979, however, the increasingly overvalued peso was clearly cutting into the SRA's net profits. The return to more nationalist policies under Viola was a clear disappointment for the SRA, as must have been Galtieri's war, which effectively closed off the economy. Alfonsín's moderately populist government, and particularly the attempts to tax agricultural exports through a two-tier exchange rate, also had negative consequences on this sector.

Whereas the SRA is typical for its relative impoverishment and economic sacrifice, the continued cohesion within the SRA contrasts with all of the other original corporatist groups. In part, this results from the near constant attack it faced during the breakdown period; its members did not become divided nor did the organization become discredited in the public eye. "As a family confronting problems, the SRA has grown closer and more cohesive over the past decades."[25] This tendency is reinforced by a series of peculiarities of the agribusiness. In the short term, profits are almost solely contingent on market prices, an extraneous factor for the individual farmer. Moreover, small investments must be planned many months in advance (due to crop cycles) and large ones planned even years ahead. For these reasons, agricultural producers face similar conditions regardless of different management techniques or investment levels. The divisions that can occur within and between manufacturing industries are far deeper and more numerous than in the agricultural business.

The divisions that have occurred in the SRA generally resulted in individual members either leaving the association or else becoming inactive. The organization has gotten smaller but has remained relatively ideologically pure. For example, a significant amount of land is now controlled by industrial groups who have vertically integrated the agricultural production with later products. Benetton has begun to raise sheep for wool, for example, yet the company does not suffer with lower wool prices as these merely signify lower input costs for their final products. Further, several companies, including subsidiaries of the Argentine multinational Bunge y Born, have started packaging and processing foods, markets in which lower prices for inputs also result in higher profits. These companies operate largely without interaction with the SRA, although they are officially members.

The economic hardship and the disengagement of much land from the SRA structure has allowed the SRA to remain quite cohesive despite the breakdown period. At the same time, these same factors have weakened the group tremendously. This is the only organization that is very much of a corporatist entity and not merely an interest group, but the desires of the members can no longer be so easily promoted; in the entities' power equation, the brute resources of the individual members of the SRA are greatly diminished. On an aggregate level, this can be discerned by the declining importance of agriculture in Argentina's total GNP and in Argentina's exports.

The limited power of the SRA certainly buttresses the hypothesis that the Menem presidency can represent a fundamental change with the past. The SRA is certainly no longer capable of destroying an economic program. Just as important, however, is the fact that the SRA realizes the need for a change, a fact that will limit this group's desire to use the power it still wields. The SRA is still a fairly cohesive corporatist entity, but at least it is a relatively more enlightened one than it once was.

> The agricultural sector more than most realizes the need for stability. The land cannot be exported as can capital, and investment decisions are made many months in advance. When Menem came in during a period of true economic crisis, we had little choice but to support him tentatively. Now that it is obvious that his plan is rational and that we will not be asked to pay for industrialization, we actively support him, even if there are some unavoidable short-term costs.[26]

La Confederación General Económica

La Confederación General Económica, the national bourgeoisie, also came under particular duress during the period studied. The Krieger Vasena period led to the increased penetration of the economy by multinational corporations, many of which simply bought out national firms. The chaos at the end of the Peronist government also wreaked havoc on the CGE; the foreign accounts problem, for example, led to great difficulty in importing essential intermediate goods, and the labor mobilizations and wage hikes induced high costs on the home front. During the Videla presidency, bankruptcies in this sector skyrocketed as cheaper and more competitive imports began to flood the market. Particularly hard hit were industries such as domestic electronics, textiles, and capital goods where some combination of cheap unskilled labor and high technology result in competitive advantages.

The same indicators that represent the decline of the CGT also apply for this corporatist entity. The growth of services occurred almost completely at the cost of the manufacturing sectors. The unofficial economy, preponderantly made up of self-employed individuals and composed only marginally of manufacturing, has also grown at the cost of the CGE.

The CGE, however, is not weaker only because of the duress suffered by the national bourgeoisie during the breakdown period. The CGE also suffers from major internal divisions as well as the loss of many of its former members. It is a complex organization composed of three branches, one representing industry, another merchants, and the last, small marginal farmers. Moreover, the CGE has affiliated chambers in almost all of the country's provinces. Despite these divisions and the different issues confronting the various members, the CGE remained a cohesive organization until well into the breakdown period. Under Gelbard, who led the CGE before assuming the position of minister, the CGE was able to mobilize strong support and find common ground that bridged the divisions.

The CGE's success waned during the last stage of the Peronist government and during the Proceso. Gelbard's plan was largely seen, correctly, as that of the CGE; its failure therefore largely discredited the organization. In the public's eye, the CGE lost significant legitimacy during the chaos under Martínez de Perón. As soon as Videla became president, the CGE was taken over and disbanded. As a result, many of the CGE's industrial members, traditionally the most important within the organization, for lack of an alternative joined the UIA. At the same time, the CGE's old caudillo, Gelbard, who did a great deal to hold the organization together, went into exile. The lack of a center to the CGE opened up divisions that could no longer be bridged even when the CGE was officially reconstituted under Alfonsín.

As a result, many of the members who joined the UIA, those around whom the basis of consensus was really formed, never returned to the CGE. The members from the interior provinces began to fight against those who remained from the highly industrialized Buenos Aires region. The different economic groups also began to find greater difficulties in finding common ground regarding what type of economic policy should be implemented.

On a purely political level, the CGE, traditionally Peronist, had grown politically motley. This diversity limited the potential for preferential contacts with any of the power brokers; there are currently not only Peronist and Radicals within the CGE, but also communists, socialists, and supporters of the rightist UCD. The context, moreover, was one in which all of these actors were significantly weaker than they had been in the past and where many of the old companies had either gone bankrupt or had been purchased by the capitanes de la industria. In the power equation, both the brute resources and the mobilizing potential were greatly diminished. The net result was that the CGE, both as an individual institution and as an amalgamation of the national bourgeoisie, "has absolutely no power today."[27]

What does remain of this organization has changed greatly in character. No longer does the CGE hope to effect income redistribution as there is a recognition of the state's limited ability to do so. "Subsidies might even be appropriate for some small companies, but I realize that there are no such funds available."[28] Instead the CGE is trying to help its members adjust to the rigors of growing competition. A major project, for example, is to better understand the success of small and medium-sized companies in Italy with the hope that some lessons could be learned for Argentine counterparts. This project includes studies, seminars, and even a CGE-sponsored trip to Italy.[29]

La Unión Industrial Argentina

La Unión Industrial Argentina and the international bourgeoisie have also suffered from the vagaries of Argentine political economy. After prosperous years under Krieger Vasena, the rest of the Revolución Argentina proved to be far more treacherous. Levingston implemented nationalist economic policies, and Lanusse oversaw a period of praetorianism. The Peronist government was far worse: Bank deposits were regulated by the government (with a negative effect on the financial industry), laws explicitly antagonistic to foreign firms were implemented, and, of course, the political and economic conditions hurt this group as much as they had the CGE. The growing pressures at the end of the tablita squeezed this group too, only to be followed by the tragic political and economic policies effected during Galtieri's reign. The debt crisis completely cut off the international financial community from the Argentine market. Clearly, the loose amalgamation referred to under the heading of the international bourgeoisie has not only been weakened but also divided.

The UIA itself has also grown into more of an interest group than a corporatist entity. The UIA grew immensely, as measured by number of members and percentage of GNP the members produced, during the breakdown period; for example, in 1990, 91.4 percent of the value of manufactured goods produced in Argentina was produced by members of the UIA.[30] This in part reflects the loss of brute resources commanded by the CGE. However, the result has been the creation of an amorphous and largely undefinable representative organization. Whereas the UIA once represented exclusively large and powerful companies, now 23.2 percent and 69.9 percent of the member companies are medium and small, respectively.[31] As a reaction to this ratio, there are two distinct think tanks run by the UIA, one doing studies for the larger firms, the other for the smaller. Clearly, this leads to controversies as to which policies should be favored. The UIA's secretary offered an example: "Many within the UIA believe that there should be low tariffs even for industries such as textiles and electronics that would have a great deal of difficulty competing with imports. I personally agree with these industries that such policies are incorrect."[32]

Again, the recognition of the fact that there are no longer the resources that would be required to implement an industrial policy, such as Krieger Vasena's, beneficial to all industries (which would assuage the tensions within the organization) further limits the UIA's mobilizing capabilities. "I would like to see more of an industrial policy, but I realize there are no resources for this, that right now there are no alternatives to the current policies."[33]

The result has been the deactivation of the UIA. "The Unión has become so big and diversified that they really are unable to influence policy at all. If we have to get something done, it is far more efficient to do it by ourselves."[34] Indeed, the UIA, as all of the other secondary representatives of the international bourgeoisie, is no longer seen as a forum through which the international bourgeoisie can increase profits. That bourgeoisie in particular, moreover, is eager to compete in the market, given its natural advantages, a fact that limits attempts to resuscitate the old and largely hollow structure. "Everyone is now forced to look to an open and competitive market for profits because the sugar-daddy state is bankrupt. And I'm sure that we and the companies we invested in and represent [generally associated with the international bourgeoisie] can do quite well under these circumstances."[35]

Los Capitanes de la Industria

Los Capitanes de la Industria as a group never really represented a corporatist entity. Indeed, there is little to no direct communication between these mammoth holding companies apart from the limited interaction within the increasingly weak organizations such as the UIA. The capitanes, however, both individually and as an amalgamation, are powerful interest groups. For this reason, it is essential to gain some understanding of their outlook in order to predict the country's future. The restructuring offers these groups new opportunities from which to profit. Indeed, it is just such groups that are ideally situated to take advantage of privatizations and greater integration with the international sectors.

It must be kept in mind, however, that these groups will suffer on some levels as well. State contracts are not and will not flow as freely as in the past. Industries such as the steel industry that were protected for the benefit of these groups will no longer be so, a change that will result in, at the very least, lower profit margins. The reduction and rationalization of public works contracts will hit some of the companies particularly hard. Overall, however, this group seems very much in favor of the economic changes that will be discussed in the following chapter. In essence, the capitanes realize more clearly than many other groups the costs of redistribution instead of investment. As redistribution can only be marginally advantageous to such diversified groups, growth and investment are more attractive. It is just such companies that should have a vested interest in promoting the long-term health of the country.

Moreover, there is a realization that some sacrifice will have to be accepted in some divisions. Jorge Donoso, an executive at Techint, a large and diversified holding group, openly admitted that the contracting companies, which had been largely dependent on public works, would shrink significantly in importance. At the same time, the company is excited about many new investments, in railroads and oil, that are possible only through the privatizations. The most important political goal for the company is merely making sure that no other company gets subsidies to tilt the relatively level playing field that now exists. It does not seem likely that such subsidies are going to be implemented, however:

> We, as I think most companies, are not asking for subsidies because as soon as one starts asking for, and, worse, getting subsidies everyone will be forced to jump on the bandwagon. That would be the end of all hopes of stability and growth. And more important, the government knows that it would be the end.[36]

Notes

1. This part of the analysis is based largely on the work of Marcelo Cavarozzi and María Grossi in their work *De la reinvención democratica al reflujo politico y la hyperinflación*. The author was able to discuss the ideas therein in personal interviews with Prof. Cavarozzi.

2. Juan Carlos Torre, "Argentina: Il ritorno del Peronismo," p. 105, author's translation.

3. Ugo Garnero, personal interview.

4. Juan Carlos Herrera, personal interview.

5. This section relies heavily upon an interview conducted with Eduardo Molina.

6. Bernardo Grinspun, in an interview with the author, for example, still criticized Alfonsín's decision "to go outside of the party."

7. This implies offering electors two groups or "lists" from the same party in the general elections. It is similar to creating an official and publicly recognized faction within a party.

8. Guillermo Boero, personal interview.

9. Federico Zamora, personal interview.

10. As quoted in David Jordan, "Argentina's Military Government," p. 59.

11. Alberto Grimoldi, personal interview, as was already quoted in the Proceso chapter (chapter 4).

12. Uniting the military was stated as a central rationale for the war by many of the people the author had the opportunity to speak to, including many a previous military official (who preferred to remain anonymous) and several people closely associated with the military as well as several academics including Professor Cavarozzi.

13. Gary Wynia, "The Peronists Triumph in Argentina," p. 16.

14. General Eduardo Esposito (Ret.), personal interview.

15. David Pion-Berlin, "Military Breakdown and Redemocratization in Argentina," p. 213.

16. A good analysis of the political economy of the Brazilian military regime in which this point is clear can be found in Albert Fishlow's "A Tale of Two Presidents."

17. Of course, a communist-style nationalization of private property would result in a renewed ability to redistribute. For a variety of historical and cultural reasons as well as the current world situation, communism is not here considered an alternative.

18. For example, Guido di Tella, vice-minister of economics toward the end of

the Martínez de Perón government, now feels it essential to open the economy to world competition and to rationalize the state.

19. Manuel Herrera, personal interview.
20. Jorge Donoso, personal interview.
21. Jorge Vives, personal interview.
22. See Adrián Guissarri, "La Argentina informal," for a discussion of the unofficial economy.
23. Juan Carlos Rua, personal interview.
24. William Grant, personal interview.
25. Eduardo de Zavalía, personal interview.
26. Eduardo de Zavalía, personal interview.
27. José Luís Falcó, personal interview.
28. Juan Manuel Castillo, personal interview.
29. Juan Manuel Castillo, personal interview.
30. *Unión Industrial Argentina*, annual publication, p. 28.
31. *Unión Industrial Argentina*, annual publication, p. 28.
32. Manuel Herrera, personal interview.
33. Manuel Herrera, personal interview.
34. Jorge Donoso, personal interview.
35. Steven Darch, personal interview.
36. Jorge Donoso, personal interview.

7

The Menem Presidency and the Break with the Past

From One Democratic Government to Another

Carlos Saúl Menem came to power in July 1989. The process of coming to power and the circumstances that surrounded the transfer resembled those present throughout the breakdown period. Everything pointed to the prospect that the Menem government would be similar to all of those of the preceding decades.

In July 1989 the economy was a disaster. Inflation was running at a rate of 200 percent per month. There was no investment and an enormous capital flight. The political side of the transfer of power was also very destabilizing—the economic crisis forced the Alfonsín government to resign six months before the end of its term and gave Menem no choice but to take the reins of power early. Moreover, there was no constitutional or legal process for doing this; with both the outgoing president and vice-president resigning, the president of the senate should theoretically have been appointed interim president. The understanding among the political parties and the major social actors that allowed Menem to come to power in this manner was fashioned on those alliances between the corporatist entities typical of the breakdown period.

The few factors that were clearly different at the time actually pointed to a deterioration over the breakdown period. Although Menem was elected with deep support, it was overwhelmingly concentrated in the working classes; he would later use this to his advantage, but at the time this source of support was seen as forcing the bourgeoisie into an openly antagonistic disposition with all the associated consequences. These fears were reinforced by the fact that Menem was elected on a very populist, albeit vague, platform; Menem claimed to be the inheritor of Juan Perón's mantle, made frequent references to "social justice," and advocated a unilaterally called moratorium on foreign debt payments. Most scary of all, Menem often complained of an international conspiracy against the country. As his campaign advanced, he refrained from even these vague pronouncements and facile policy programs; instead, he visited popular neighborhoods, promised to be understanding, and asked for his supporters to have faith in him. Many feared that this man would revert back to the Peronism of half a century past, that is, to an explicit corporatist structure.

Apart from the traditional populist supporters, many Argentines at the time feared that Menem's government would result in the final coup de grace against the country, that this signified not merely a perpetuation of past crises but an actual degradation of the traditional, tragic cycle. By July 1989, many Argentines had made plans for permanently emigrating.

What was to occur during the following years was close to the opposite of these early and dire predictions. Under Menem, there seems to be a clean break with the past. The corporatist structure continues to crumble on all fronts. The corporatist entities grow increasingly irrelevant and divided. The power brokers grow more cohesive and rational. Democracy is further taking root as all political competitions now occur within this arena. Redistributions and subsidies, the driving forces behind the past alliances, are being eliminated. As a result, investment is on the rise, capital is being repatriated, and foreign investors are beginning to return. A new stage of Argentine history, assuming a momentum for continuing changes, has begun.

The Menem government has so far profited from the weakened corporatist structure in order to further destroy it and implement its own rational and comprehensive policies. The privileged position Menem had with the (Peronist) working class facilitated his defense against attacks from the CGT and has further forced the weaknesses of this entity to the fore. Given this freedom from attacks by workers and unions, the government has implemented policies, the first in over two decades, that are not geared toward redistributing income from certain sectors of the economy, or corporatist groups, to others. In an economic restructuring, there are clearly those that experience windfall taxes or gains, but there is neither an attempt nor a need to create an alliance, to buy popularity in order to ensure continued legitimacy. As much as is feasible for an economy in obvious and deep-rooted flux, the rules of the economic and political games have remained fixed during the past four years; increasingly, it is the marketplace that determines winners and losers, not government policies.

Finally, it must be added that Menem has thus far avoided the time-consistency pitfalls into which the governments already studied fell. Painful structural changes have not been postponed but were begun on the first day of Menem's government; halfway through his mandate, more structural changes have been effected than during all the preceding governments together. At the same time, the financial system has not allowed Argentina to postpone the major costs of the restructuring to some future date; the piper will not have to be paid at some future date as he had in 1980. Foreign government debt has actually decreased from the high in 1989. National government debt has also decreased as the government has consistently run a primary budget surplus (including state-owned companies) since the beginning of 1991. Private companies as well have avoided the debt trap of the late 1970s. As a result, real interest rates are significantly lower than during the Martínez de Hoz period and banks are on much more stable footing.

It is unclear whether Menem, during his campaign, had envisioned forcing such a radical restructuring of the Argentine economy around liberal free-market lines. This anticipation seems unlikely. Before assuming the presidency, Menem had been the governor of a small and poor province, La Rioja. His administration was well known for an overgrown and inefficient state apparatus. Whenever unemployment went up in his fief, he simply hired more civil servants. Menem was willing to sell his support to Alfonsín (one of the few Peronists to do so) for federal government subsidies that went clearly against all free-market principles. When Juan Sourrouille and José Luis Machinea finally tried to limit provincial spending, Menem found ways of avoiding the limitations. If, however, despite all of this, Menem had always planned to implement the policies that he eventually did, then it was an act of political genius to turn the tables upon the nationalist-oriented economic groups after gaining their confidence and support.

A more likely hypothesis, however, is that Menem realized he had no alternatives. An overtly corporatist structure could not be revived—the government would neither be able to control the corporatist entities nor would it be able to find the funds to buy support. After so much economic stagnation and given the defensive postures on the part of all economic actors, populist policies were no more feasible—there was nothing to redistribute to the nationalist classes. Finally, after all the havoc of the preceding governments, it was no longer possible to accept slow stagnation as had the presidents during the impasse period. Either Menem was to effect rational and market-based policies or else the country would continue to sink without any recourse.

Assuming this last hypothesis is correct, that Menem chose to restructure the economy because he felt he had no alternatives, then the Menem government offers the greatest evidence possible that something did change during the twenty-three years studied, that the corporatist structure did indeed fall apart. Whatever the reason, something has changed. By 1989, Argentina had sunk terribly low, but at least it had found a bottom; now, after so much destruction, was the time to begin creating once again.

The Bunge y Born Basis for Restructuring

Menem came to power with worker support. The bourgeoisie had two reactions. First, it tried to defend itself economically: It increased prices to augment immediate profits and exported as much capital as possible. Second, the bourgeoisie attempted to influence policy in order to protect its interests. It should be noted that this was done more by individual economic actors than by corporatist entities or trade groups. The situation was simply too mercurial for the development and use of "official" channels of communication.

At the same time, it was increasingly clear that Menem had to gain the bourgeoisie's confidence if a complete melt-down of the economy was to be avoided. Menem was forced to reassure the monied classes. It was also clear to everyone, as it had been for much of the breakdown period, that a restructuring of the economy was necessary if growth and stability were to be assured for the longer term, changes that required at least the acquiescence of the bourgeoisie.

It was with these goals that the newly elected president turned to the Argentine multinational Bunge y Born (B&B), a company also eager to affect policy in order to defend its own interests. The company is owned by Argentines but is a multinational conglomerate. Further, this massive holding group was quite different from the typical capitane de la industria in that B&B had minimal dependence on state contracts or on special protectionist measures. The B&B holding company, for example, held no interests in large construction companies depending on state contracts. B&B had vast agricultural interests, but, due to the industrial companies and the vertical integration of the agricultural products, was generally not associated with the SRA. In sum, B&B was the best Argentine company with which to work. It was not associated with any corporatist entity and, given the multitude of subsidiaries and affiliates, was familiar with the problems facing many economic groups. As the group, despite its diversity and size, was not a capitane de la industria, it was not dependent on direct or indirect state funding. Indeed, quite the contrary; in one way or another B&B had traditionally been forced to subsidize the tentative alliances of the past. During the period studied, it suffered tremendously, losing a great deal of its relevance and importance in the Argentine economy. On a political level, Menem could not be too easily criticized for selling out either to foreigners or to a nationalist policy, given the peculiar characteristics of the B&B empire.

In a series of meetings prior to taking office, Menem listened to the company's chief economists, each of whom analyzed an aspect of Argentina's economic predicament. A great deal of emphasis was placed on elucidating longer-term and structural problems that went beyond a simple stabilization. The team was largely successful at convincing the new president. It was clear that gaining the support of the bourgeoisie was essential before anything else could be effected. Although it was widely reported that Menem was holding meetings with B&B, this was not enough to counterbalance Menem's deserved reputation for profligacy and populism. The president had to do something more concrete and symbolic than merely hold meetings and claim that he was convinced of the liberal ideology. After all, both Videla and Onganía claimed to have been convinced as well.

Upon assuming the presidency, Menem appointed several Bunge y Born economists and executives to the ministry of economics. Most important, Manuel Roig, a leading B&B executive, was appointed minister of economics. In order to further reassure the liberal sectors of the economy, Menem named Alvaro Alsogaray, the leader of the conservative UCD party and stalwart of the liberal classes, as Argentina's chief foreign debt negotiator; this was an ideal position from which he could reassure the international community of the new government's economic seriousness. When Manuel Roig died after less than a week in office, Menem replaced him with another B&B executive, Nestor Rapanelli.

From these very first days of the new presidency, one sees tremendous differences from the preceding governments. Although a full-blown alliance was not consummated between the government and some groups of corporatist entities, it was immediately made clear that the government was allied with the business community. This alliance contrasts markedly with the initial period of all of the previously studied governments during which time attempts were made to satisfy and reassure all groups. This time, the business community was clearly, immediately, and intimately linked to the government. It might be claimed that Menem had no choice but to seek the support of the bourgeoisie as the country was in the throes of economic breakdown, but this is exactly the point: The breakdown of corporatism necessitated a shift in course of action.

The appointment of Rapanelli also signified a second change from preceding governments in that it showed a willingness, if not an outright desire, on the part of Menem to look outside of the traditional Peronist entourage for political allies. Whereas Onganía named fellow Catholic Salimei, Perón appointed Gelbard from the Peronist CGE, Videla appointed fellow liberal Martínez de Hoz, and Alfonsín appointed party apparatchik Grinspun, Menem immediately sought the support of the traditionally anti-Peronist upper bourgeoisie. The importance of this cannot be underestimated. The failure of corporatism had been associated with demanding corporatist entities, each of which had close contacts with the power broker in government. These close contacts translated into contradictory and costly measures geared toward offering each of these groups tangible economic advantages. The fact that Menem has been willing to break with groups having privileged contacts resulted directly in his greater ability to impose constraints on the corporatist entities. For this reason B&B was an ideal company as it was not associated with any group.

The president simultaneously cut contact with the various factions of the Peronist Party. As no leading Peronist gained a position with the president's cabinet and were to be increasingly exiled within the party structure as well, this further closed off the government to the lobbying of corporatist entities.

In the short term, this facilitated restructuring the economy from the start of the government. In the longer term, this change would preempt an "internal" policy coup. One analyst explained the situation in the following manner:

> The choice of Cabinet members . . . is very much the result of individual choice by a President who as the months have gone on has increasingly tended to centralize power in his own hands—even proposing, at one stage, to move his offices across the road from the Casa Rosada to the Banco de la Nación.[1]

All in all, it was an auspicious beginning.

Rapanelli's economic plan itself, referred to as the Plan BB, did not include anything unexpected. It had two goals: It was geared toward stabilizing the economy and made sweeping calls for a fundamental restructuring of the state sector. This combination allows comparisons with the Austral Plan, and indeed, to lesser degrees, with all the plans announced during the breakdown period. The central difference lay in the fact that the restructuring was not to be postponed to a second, later phase of the plan, and that it was actually implemented. Instead, the economic restructuring was actually promoted to the detriment of the stabilization program.

> We wanted to set up a framework within which the economic restructuring would take place. It seemed less important to concentrate solely on stabilization, which was a technical problem accomplished many times in the past, than to focus on setting up a structure through which to reform the state, at which no one had ever been successful. The economic laws that were passed during the first months of the government set up just such a framework which, I am quite sure, will result in the first major overhaul of the state sector.[2]

The economics ministry had two laws passed during the last trimester of 1989 that were to lay the groundwork for the economic restructuring and stabilization. These laws, the Law for the Reform of the State and the Law Regarding the Economic Emergency, were far reaching themselves. Between the two of them, they gave the executive branch the power to take all measures necessary to stabilize the economy, to privatize the majority of state enterprises, to suspend all direct and indirect state subsidies to the private sector, and to reorganize the financial sector.[3] An outline of the whole economic restructuring was developing within the ministry, and these first plans would continue to serve as the basis for the restructuring for several years to come. An outline offered by a member of the original economics team, Orlando Ferreres, is shown in Figure 7.1.

Apart from their contents, these two initiatives represented a break with the past in several fundamental ways. First and possibly most important, the economic plan was stipulated in law. All of the economic programs thus far studied had merely been decreed by the president and the minister of economics, sometimes with the collaboration of the corporatist entities. Krieger Vasena and Martínez de Hoz, as befits military governments, announced their plans with few concerns for legitimizing them; neither plebiscites nor laws had to be passed. Perón signed the Compromiso Nacional with the CGT and the CGE, justifying the corporatist structure (although neglecting many entities) but bypassing more general or overall public support. The Austral Plan was merely announced in June 1985 over the radio and television without any prior consultation or legislation. In stipulating the plan in law, Rapanelli legitimized the plan while reinforcing the democratic structure. This was the first time that society's freely elected representatives approved a plan. It would not be possible in the future for individuals to claim, falsely, that they did not originally agree to the plan in a shift akin to that of individuals who first implicitly supported a military coup only to later claim, on moral grounds moreover, that the military should never intervene in politics. The legislative process also implicated the other major political parties (all of which voted for the laws) as well as the various factions within Peronism.

These two laws had a second extremely important effect. In having the outline of his economic program stipulated in law as well as gaining clear and strong powers to implement economic policy, Menem ensured that he would have a longer period of relative freedom in making policy than had his predecessors. It had always been the case that the executive was able to enforce certain constraints on society and the corporatist entities at the very beginning of their governments—people were willing to make sacrifices in order to regain state stability. Once some semblance of stability returned, however, individuals and groups resisted these constraints, often through sympathetic members of the power broker in government. By clearly and explicitly winning support for special powers, this relative freedom was effectively extended. As long as the laws were not repealed, Menem would have free rein to advance the restructuring of the state described in these two laws.

Interestingly, the fact that the plan was openly discussed and developed in conjunction with major economic forces, as was inevitable for the laws to be passed by Congress, further broke down the corporatist structure. As the firms began to realize that the government was conscientious of their needs and was open to public dialogue, there was less of a need for the corporatist entities. The economic actors did not feel the need to mobilize support and to force open channels of inconspicuous communication. The democratic process exposed to the sunlight the political process of negotiation between the government and major economic actors, a fact that rendered the old vertical and more secretive structure increasingly obsolete.

Figure 7.1 Economic Restructuring, Years 1 to 7

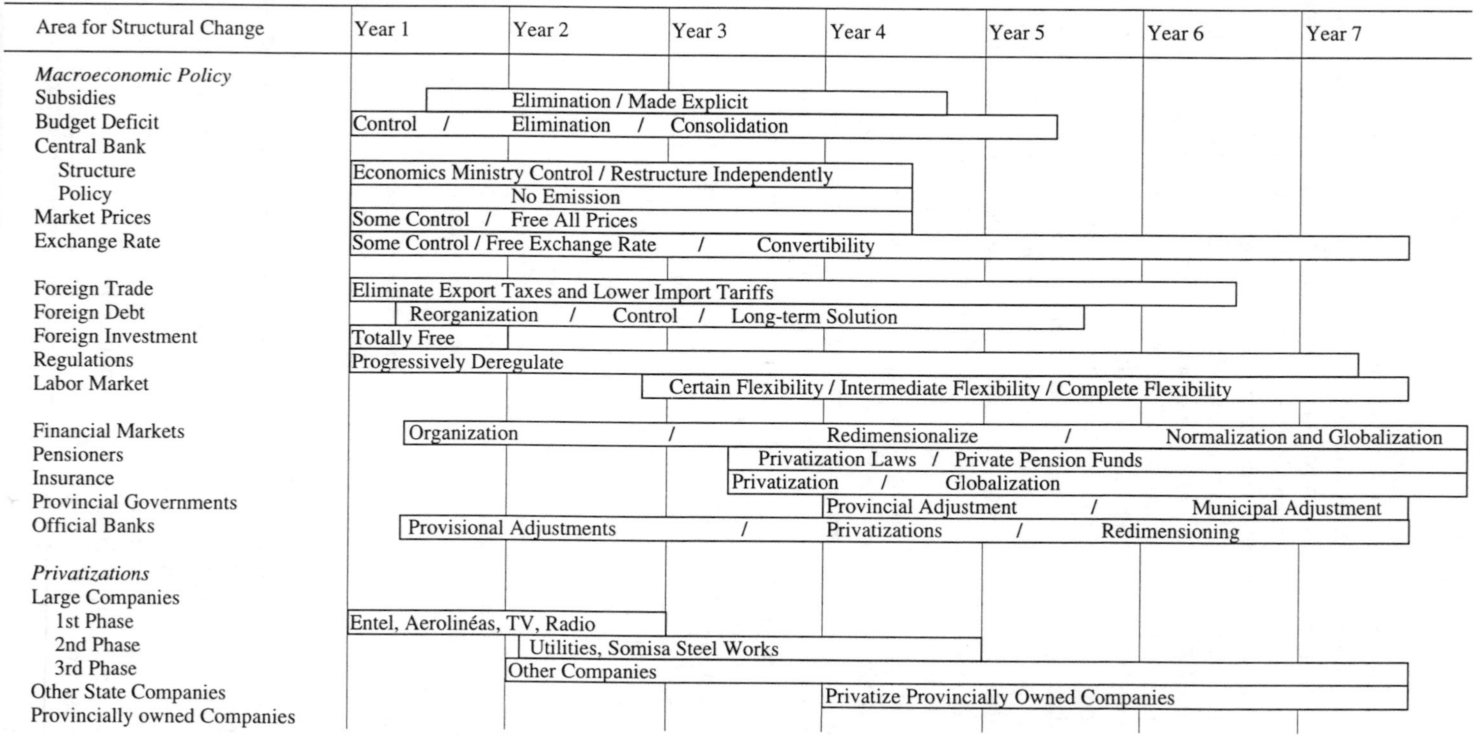

Area for Structural Change	Year 1	Year 2	Year 3	Year 4	Year 5	Year 6	Year 7
Macroeconomic Policy							
Subsidies		Elimination /	Made Explicit				
Budget Deficit	Control /	Elimination	/ Consolidation				
Central Bank							
Structure			Economics Ministry Control / Restructure Independently				
Policy			No Emission				
Market Prices	Some Control /	Free All Prices					
Exchange Rate	Some Control / Free Exchange Rate	/	Convertibility				
Foreign Trade	Eliminate Export Taxes and Lower Import Tariffs						
Foreign Debt	Reorganization /	Control /	Long-term Solution				
Foreign Investment Regulations	Totally Free						
Labor Market	Progressively Deregulate		Certain Flexibility / Intermediate Flexibility / Complete Flexibility				
Financial Markets	Organization		/	Redimensionalize	/	Normalization and Globalization	
Pensioners			Privatization Laws / Private Pension Funds				
Insurance			Privatization / Globalization				
Provincial Governments	Provisional Adjustments		Provincial Adjustment	/	Municipal Adjustment		
Official Banks			Privatizations	/	Redimensioning		
Privatizations							
Large Companies							
1st Phase	Entel, Aerolinéas, TV, Radio						
2nd Phase		Utilities, Somisa Steel Works					
3rd Phase		Other Companies					
Other State Companies				Privatize Provincially Owned Companies			
Provincially owned Companies							

Figure 7.1 (con't.)

Area for Structural Change	Year 1	Year 2	Year 3	Year 4	Year 5	Year 6	Year 7
Restructuring of the State Apparatus							
Laws and Regulations	Basis: Restructuring / Laws to Support /			Convertibility Law			
	Emergency Laws / Stabilization /			Laws to Reform Central Bank			
Social Net		Emergency Measures to Reduce Expenditures / Reorganization and Rationalization					
Justice and Education			Reform Justice System / Total Reorganization of Education System				
National Defense	Schedule and Study Restructuring + Cut Costs / Emphasize National Security and International Missions						
Government Institutions					Consolidation of New Institutional Order		
Relations Between Federal, State, and Municipal Governments			Reformulate Relationship Among Jurisdictions				

Source: Based on data from Ferreres y Asociados, Buenos Aires 1992.

Armed with these laws, the government made clear its intention of following through with the structural changes. The privatizations of Aerolinéas Argentinas and Entel (the national telephone company) were announced within months of Menem's taking office, and offers for the companies were solicited. Early in 1990, both companies were privatized. Given the continuing economic crisis (hyperinflation was to return after the privatization was announced) and tremendous national risk, the prices offered for the companies were low. There was little bidding competition, and there is widespread evidence that the companies were worth more than was actually paid for them. Moreover, there was little progress made toward ensuring that there would be competition in the private sphere so that public monopolies were not simply replaced with private ones. These failures occurred with a backdrop of rumors of corruption. All the same, these initial privatizations must be seen as rampant successes.

In privatizing Entel and Aerolinéas Argentinas, the best-known state companies, Menem set the precedent for future privatizations. After so many years of resistance to privatization from so many sectors including the Peronist party itself, these precedents were extremely important. Their symbolism was similarly significant—both national and international capital realized that Menem was serious. In the longer term, the government could go back and reinforce the regulatory structures so as to strengthen the consumers' position.

Rapanelli's stabilization measures included a series of policies to reduce the deficit. Export taxes were increased on both industrial and agricultural exports. Public utility rates were drastically increased, and a set of temporary taxes, similar to those of the Austral Plan, was also effected. It was also hoped that the deficit would decrease with the Olivera-Tanzi effect. Just as was the case with the Austral Plan, the exchange rate was pegged to the dollar, at a ratio of 650 australs to one dollar. A price freeze was not instituted, but a far looser price "agreement" was made with the leading national industries.

The open debate and legislation that surrounded the economic plan allowed greater leverage regarding the state restructuring, but only at the cost of greater difficulty in stabilizing the economy, however. Regarding the price freeze, for example,

> instead of the isolated technocratic conditions that characterized the preparation of the Austral Plan, a climate of deliberation between the economic policymakers, the other areas of government, and the large companies existed. This context conspired against *fait accompli* political actions. Managers, anticipating government decisions and with a presentiment of a possible price freeze, were able to increase prices substantially in the very days that the economic policy was being formulated.[4]

The stabilization program also had several other weaknesses. As usual, the increases in utility rates, ranging from 800 percent to 1000 percent, decreased the deficit but augmented inflation. The economics team also allowed the monetary base to expand rapidly. Insufficient headway regarding the budget deficit had been made. Ironically, the buoyant export market for traditional agricultural products caused a large influx of dollars, further monetarizing the economy. The economy was weak and the government was not taking sufficient action to stabilize it. As a self-defense mechanism, Argentines bought dollars and thus undermined the stabilization.

Interest rates in local currency had to be sky high to attract any investors. In and of itself, this level caused further pressure on the monetary base as the weekly interest payments were added to the monetary stock. It also increased the government's budgetary pressures because the government was still running a deficit and continued to refinance past debt. Against this backdrop, the government made a blunder in further shifting emphasis from stabilization to long-term restructuring by reducing export taxes and consequently accepting a higher budget deficit. In the same vein, the government began discussing a radical new plan that would forcibly convert short-term debt into dollar-denominated long-term debt; these open discussions once again provoked greater instability in the short term as capital flight grew.

As a result of the policymaking process and the fragile state of the economy, the stabilization program resulted in complete failure. Inflation began to mushroom. A return to hyperinflation was clearly on the horizon. The failure was reminiscent of the corporatist breakdown period. There were two significant differences, however. First was the speed with which it occurred. Menem was allowed to place much of the blame on inherited economic problems, something neither Alfonsín could do toward the end of his presidency nor could Videla do in 1980. The short time span also preempted any true possibility of a regime change—there simply had not been enough time to choose a new power broker. "There was a lot of talk of a coup at the end of 1989, but . . . the return of inflation happened so quickly that everyone, including the military, was unsure what to do."[5] For similar reasons, Menem still had a great deal of relative freedom that allowed him to react with decision and determination. The rapid return of inflation might also have had a psychological effect on the president and his closest advisers. The economic situation was mercurial and deeply rooted so it required serious and prolonged attention if this government were to stay in power and if Argentina were to resume growth and recreate political stability.

The second peculiarity regarding this period of economic instability was the fact that Menem never began to doubt his chosen course of policy. Indeed, one could say that this was the first time that stabilization was sacrificed for restructuring. "Hyperinflation was exploding around him, but he never took his foot off the accelerator, never withdrew his support for his advisers."[6] The return of hyperinflation actually reinforced Menem's conviction that this was the correct policy. Efforts were redoubled to ensure continued work on privatizations as well as several other structural changes to the state. The president realized that even greater constraints had to be forced upon the unions, which had contributed to the inflation with their wage increase, as well as upon business, which had increased prices as the price agreement went into effect. Far from being dissuaded by the return to hyperinflation, the president thought the restructuring had to be intensified.

The return of hyperinflation, therefore, had no fundamental consequences. The work on the privatizations continued, as did plans for the restructuring of the state. With the failure of the initial stabilization aspect of the economic plan, however, the economics team, and particularly the minister of economics, had been discredited. A clean attempt at stabilization was necessary.

On 15 December 1989 Nestor Rapanelli was replaced with Antonio Erman Gonzalez. The new minister was a long-time ally and friend of the president who had had little experience outside Menem's little provincial fief, La Rioja. Menem looked to further concentrate the power of the executive in his own hands in order to ensure greater insulation from lobbying activities from various interest groups and from factions of his own party. The change in economics teams did not represent a change in policy, however. Many members of the original group remained in Menem's government to promote continuity and offer expertise; for example, Orlando Ferreres, the secretary for economic coordination, remained within the government in a variety of positions including adviser for the privatization of military companies. A new precedent was created: Economics ministers were not replaced to facilitate a change in policy but rather replaced so that short-term costs could be tolerated without jeopardizing the overall economic plan. Rapanelli took the blame for the inflation and acted as the scapegoat, but the economic program marched forward. Ministers of economics, after all, could be replaced at this point; the economic plan could not.

Stabilizing the Economy

Gonzalez's task was to stabilize the economy while continuing the structural changes. On 18 December 1989, the new minister announced his first policies. He eliminated all controls on foreign exchange, freed the exchange rate, and abolished the price agreement; in sum, all principal markets were freed. In order to consolidate Rapanelli's actions, Gonzalez further reduced export taxes, as had been foreseen. These measures were hailed as historic. Many people thought that Argentina had not seen such open markets in over half a century. Particularly surprising was the completely free exchange rate. The structural changes were occurring at an unheard-of pace.

The dark side, however, was the persistent economic instability. Hyperinflation continued unabated. The economic chaos began to spill over for the first time into the political arena as looting began in several cities, Rosario most prominently. Although the restructuring was to take priority over stabilization, the two had to move more in tandem than had been the case; no one, Argentine or foreigner, would have the confidence to invest in Argentina with hyperinflation and looting.

At the base of the instability was the uncontrollable budget deficit. Despite all of the measures taken by the government, the deficit could not be controlled as there were simply too many outstanding debts that the government had to continuously refinance. Even given a primary surplus, the state had to continue to pay previous debts. By this time, the only source of credit the government could tap was the forced (but interest-paying) reserve requirements on certificates of deposits contracted at all banks. Given the rising inflation rate and general instability, the interest rates needed to attract investors, by all measures, were astronomical. For the same risk considerations, the certificates of deposit, or *plazo fijos* as they are called in Argentina, had a very short duration, generally a single business day; no matter how fast the inflation rate accelerated, the real debt would remain constant as interest rates on all outstanding debt instantly adjusted.

These high-interest–bearing plazo fijos were having a destabilizing effect on the economy. The high real rate of return was causing a tremendous increase in the money supply, which only augmented the inflationary spiral. These factors were the base of the hyperinflation and the economic instability. Of course, the exorbitant interest rates the government was being forced to pay resulted in a self-perpetuating explosion of debt, and hence further interest payments. These financial components of the government budget grew precipitously both as a percentage of the total budget and of the GNP until they were beyond the government's grasp; no gradual or traditional policy would bring the situation back under control except for some type of bankruptcy, something that was not an alternative for a government that wants to renew faith in Argentina.

The president announced a special plan on New Year's Day. The so-called Plan Bonex, after having been discussed on a theoretical level for several months, took effect immediately; all the plazo fijos were immediately nationalized and transformed into ten-year, dollar-denominated bonds with interest payable every six months. In one fell swoop, the government slashed the monetary base by 60 percent for the M2 and 15 percent for the M1.[7] At the same time, the government eliminated almost all of its short-term debt and replaced it with long-term bonds carrying far lower obligations. The impetus behind the monetary growth as well as behind the continued budget deficit was eliminated. By confiscating money, demand in the economy was also slashed, a fact that further reduced inflationary pressures. It must be added that despite the blow to the sanctity of the austral (the Bonex Plan was in effect an illegal confiscation of liquid assets), the plan was inevitably going to result in a strong currency; individuals would have to sell, due to the monetary tightness and the elimination of savings, dollars amassed over the years in order to pay for essential consumption, and companies would have to sell dollars in order to pay for wages. The strong currency would further battle inflation as import prices would at least stabilize (and in reality actually declined) in austral terms for a significant period of time.

The Plan Bonex was appropriate for all the goals set: Stabilize the economy (meaning reduce inflation) and offer the government some breathing space to effect more fundamental changes regarding the budget. There was a cost to the Plan Bonex—the government had in essence stolen individuals' savings in the local currency and lent them to the state. As a result, the government's credit rating plummeted; no one would any longer trust the government with loans. The few individuals who still had australs would have all the reasons in the world to convert them into dollars. The circumstances created by the Plan Bonex, as would repeatedly be the case under Menem, forced the government to put its own house in order. Gonzalez got a reprieve from the tremendous debt burden, but at the cost of completely closing off access to local capital to finance a budget deficit. Now, the government had to make sure expenditures and revenues were in line.

As was clearly necessary, a string of measures were taken to further reduce the fiscal deficit and to limit the growth of the money supply during the first days of the new year. Almost all state purchases were suspended, and all ministers, it was announced, would have to seek Gonzalez's approval for any fiscal outlays. At the beginning of February, public utility rates were increased across the board by close to 100 percent. On 4 March, further fiscal measures reflected the commitment to cutting the deficit. Gonzalez suspended the payment of all public contracts; for the first time ever, a government affronted the capitanes de la industria, which suffered tremendously with this measure—they would not be paid their fat fees for public works. Further, a 5 percent increase in export taxes and several other minor modifications were also implemented.

In a further contrast with the lack of stringency of the Austral Plan, the economics team ensured that monetary policy was similarly stringent; it would be disastrous if inflation returned, despite all the sacrifices and damage to credibility, because credit continued to flow. Rediscounting of debt was strictly limited on the part of the Central Bank and by the private financial institutions. The central government did all that was possible to simultaneously tie the hands of the provincial governors. Further, the promises not to print money in order to finance the deficit were kept. The Central Bank did, however, begin to purchase dollars in a move calculated to foster faith in the national currency, despite the fact that this purchase resulted in growth in the money supply.

The results of this agglomeration of measures, which can be

cumulatively referred to as the Bonex Plan, were positive. On the economic side, the government budget was cut during the first quarter of 1990 by 43 percent compared to the same period the year before.[8] More important, 1990 was marked with a significant and continuous primary (excluding debt payments) budget surplus, as can be seen in Figure 7.2. By April, the inflation rate began to decrease substantially.

Figure 7.2   Government Budget Surpluses, 1990 (excluding debt service)

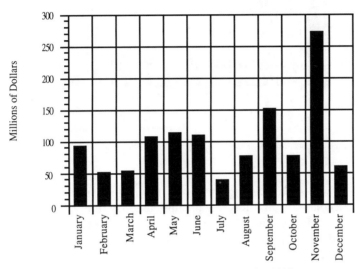

Source: Based on data from *Economist Intelligence Unit* 1990.

The Plan Bonex was inevitably going to cause a recession as local demand was literally confiscated. Only the Central Bank's buying of dollars counteracted this, and minimally so during the first months. In essence, Gonzalez willingly pushed the country into a recession in order to combat inflation. During the twenty-three-year period studied in the body of this book, never once had the government actively implemented policies that would result in a recession, until now. For the first time, in other words, the government was not attempting to "buy" support for its policies through an active economy. Moreover, the dimensions of the recession were noteworthy: "a big, big recession, a collapse basically."

> The gross domestic product, measuring the value of newly produced goods and services, has shrunk by more than 10 percent since last summer, and the unemployment rate has almost doubled in the last year to more than 10 percent. Virtually all of the rise was a result of layoffs and cutbacks in the private sector.[9]

Figure 7.3   Monthly Inflation Rate, 1990

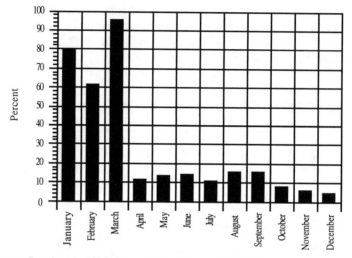

Source: Based on data from *Economist Intelligence Unit* 1990.

Gonzalez was therefore highly successful in that he was able to stabilize the economy. Inflation fell precipitously (Figure 7.3), and the budget deficit was being reined in. Exchange rate policy became extremely important. On the one hand, the government wanted a strong austral in order to ensure that there was continuous downward pressure on inflation; international competition would be used in a manner very similar to that during the Martínez de Hoz period. At the same time, Gonzalez wanted to gradually encourage reactivation of the economy, for until installed capacity was being used, new investments would not be forthcoming. Gonzalez therefore kept the exchange rate stable, despite the lower but continuing inflation, in a dirty free-float; that is to say, the exchange rate was determined by the market, but the government intervened in the foreign currency exchanges.

Instead of having to sell dollars to defend the austral, however, Gonzalez was actually able to buy significant quantities of dollars—for the reasons explained above, the Plan Bonex ensured in and of itself a strong austral for a significant period of time. So that this situation would not backfire at some later date when people no longer needed to sell dollars, the Central Bank kept its hard currency reserves as a guarantee for local currency—as the guarantee grew, so did confidence in the austral. In this way, Gonzalez increased the money supply for reactivation and simultaneously shored up confidence in the austral.

As a consequence of continuing, albeit lower, inflation and a stable exchange rate, the real value of the austral climbed significantly; this situation is comparable to the tablita phase of the Martínez de Hoz economic program. The rapidity of the increase in value of the austral was impressive: "What it took the tablita to do in about two years, Menem has done in a few months."[10] Again, the increasing real value of the austral was used as a mechanism to combat inflation. The decrease in the real exchange rate is represented in Figure 7.4. As it had been for Martínez de Hoz, this policy proved to be Gonzalez's Achilles heel. This time, however, the economic plan would not terminate with the economic minister's tenure.

A year would pass however, before the real exchange rate would have increased to an indefensible level. That year afforded Gonzalez and the whole economics team time to continue with the structural transformation. The economy was opened to foreign competition as tariffs were reduced significantly; this policy of forcing local producers to compete with international ones was the corollary, as it had been during the tablita, of a stable exchange rate. A closed economy would all too easily allow underlying inflationary pressures to continue. At the same time, this was an integral part of the structural changes that were to bring Argentina into the fold of the world economy.

Figure 7.4   Real Exchange Rate, 1990 (1986=100)

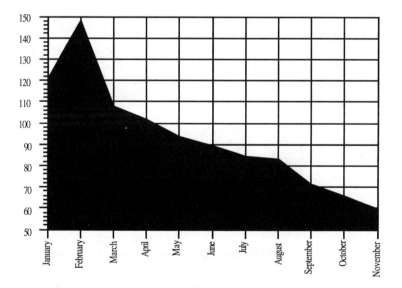

Source: Based on data from *Economist Intelligence Unit*. Derived by deflating actual exchange rate by the difference between Argentine and U.S. inflation rates.

A deep-rooted restructuring of the state began. In coordination with the International Monetary Fund and the World Bank, the Argentine government started rationalizing government services. People were fired from every single major government service. Even the military was forced to cut expenditures in half; during the breakdown period, the military governments would for obvious reasons not implement such policies, while civilian governments never felt secure enough to force such reductions. One government service was a notable exception to this across-the-board downsizing: the DGI, the Argentina counterpart to the Internal Revenue Service. This last service actually saw its payroll grow as a major attempt was made to crack down on tax evasion and the underground economy.

Privatizations continued with full force. It was during Gonzalez's time at the helm of economic policy that both Aerolíneas Argentinas and Entel were privatized. Moreover, the government worked to privatize less politically important companies as well, a fact that reveals the commitment to reform the economy and not just to receive kudos for superficial and minimal attempts. Secondary oil properties, the Buenos Aires zoo, several roads, and railroad lines as well as other public services have all been privatized. Gonzalez made sure that companies were constantly being prepared for privatization. This also meant initiating restructurings and even firing workers before the companies were to be privatized. Although the companies that remained in the government's portfolio were not paradigms for efficiency, they were being run far better than they had been during previous governments.

On a political level as well, Menem was forcing structural changes that further broke down the old corporatist structure. Many of the economic plans were implemented to the chagrin of the CGT. In the face of CGT opposition, Menem first encouraged a split, similar to that which happened under Krieger Vasena, in the union organization. Saúl Ubaldini, an old-guard Peronist, led the CGT-Azopardo while a more amenable ally of Menem, Guerino Andreoni, became the head of the CGT–San Martín. After a few months of letting the two organizations coexist, Menem granted legal status only to Andreoni's union group. More important, the government, in one way or another, rewarded those unions loyal to Andreoni, hence avoiding the pitfall into which the Onganía regime fell. "The food-workers union is a member of the CGT–San Martín, although we still keep cordial relations with Ubaldini. The major reason is that we get advantages this way—it is advantageous for the workers."[11] Simultaneously, the government legislated restrictions on the ability to strike in crucial sectors of the economy, including large sectors of the state apparatus.

A showdown was in the making, which exploded in September 1990. The Buenos Aires section of the Entel workers' union struck upon the announcement that wage increases offered by the company management had not been authorized, as was necessary, by Gonzalez. Menem fully supported his minister; the president immediately fired several of the leaders of the strikers while offering some advantages to the national telephone workers' union in a successful bid to prevent an expansion of the strike across the nation. After two weeks, the striking workers gave up their struggle against the government without having any of their demands satisfied. The defeat of the dissident unions was as complete as any during the corporatist breakdown period.

All of the other corporatist entities were already in a far weaker position. Menem reinforced this through the open policymaking process and by implicating society at large as well as the other political parties in the economic plan through legislation. Most important, however, was the fact that subsidies were no longer offered; government policy was explicitly devoid of attempts to redistribute income from one group to another. This eliminated the stimulus that fostered the power of the corporatist entities. Policy is geared now toward reinforcing the inducements and the constraints offered by the market: Companies are offered the carrot of higher sales and profits if they invest and increase productivity, and are threatened with the stick of lower profits and even bankruptcy if they do not. The inducements and constraints are subsequently geared toward individual economic actors instead of economic groups. This is also best evidenced with the union situation.

Menem did not treat all labor unions in the same fashion but rather offered different inducements and constraints to various unions. This has led to a further deterioration of the CGT as well as the other entities. Concretely, Menem offered advantages to the CGT–San Martín over the CGT-Azopardo. In the longer term, the government implicitly assured higher wages to those unions willing to increase productivity and cut excess labor, as reflected in the push for a smaller but more efficient (productive) public sector. The CGT–San Martín was willing to take advantage of such a situation whereas Ubaldini preferred to conserve jobs even if wages lagged. As the different unions reacted to the stimuli offered by the government in divergent manner, the cohesion of the corporatist entity disintegrated. When the CGT once again merged, the dominant ideology was clearly that of Andreoni. Unions are increasingly willing to play by the rules of the market, and where they are not they will slowly be forced to do so.

The same has been occurring, it must be emphasized, with all of the corporatist entities. The individual members of the SRA will benefit from a more open economy to the extent productivity is increased through investment. The restructuring of the economy offers opportunities to most members of the CGE as well as those of the UIA as the gradual opening of the internal market combined with subsidized capital goods allows many industries to improve in efficiency. Indeed, despite the growing commitment to an open economy, a traditionally liberal or UIA goal, it is the national bourgeoisie that has invested most in the recent period.[12] This activity reflects its aggregate belief that profit opportunities await, although some industries, such as consumer electronics, are almost certainly doomed no matter how much is invested.

It would be wrong, however, to believe that the changes being wrought in Argentina are due solely to government policy of which society at large tacitly approves. Indeed, one of the most fundamental changes from the past is the fact that the population itself, with the political agenda more and more out in the open instead of behind the dark doors of the corporatist institutions, is forcing the government to take certain actions. Far from a growing resistance to reforming Argentine politics and economics, society at large is forcing the government to do more, to be more efficient. This is often to the dismay of the government.

This new tendency first manifested itself regarding indignation over corruption. At the beginning of February 1991, the whole cabinet came under pressure and scrutiny over reports of high-level corruption in the government. In particular, the U.S. ambassador publicly complained of requests for payments from the Argentine subsidiary of a U.S. multinational, Campbell Soup Company's Swift-Armour division, which needed a permit to import machinery in order to increase capacity at a meat-processing plant.[13] A great many rumors, which proved to be true, also circulated regarding the need for "special payments" for all of the privatizations.[14] Corruption has been a long-time problem in Argentina, and although it is not possible to tell whether corruption during the Menem government has been any worse than in the past, what has changed is the ability to hide it so completely. The old corporatist structure allowed deals to be consummated behind closed doors, between the leaders of power brokers and corporatist entities that were long used to such shenanigans. Moreover, the leaders of both groups benefited, some from the graft itself, the others from the state favors they bought. A bystander, even if he did get wind of the particular deals, could do nothing; given the corporatist structure, he was dependent on the very people on whom he should have squealed. This situation has changed. Cases of corruption are coming out, and individuals, both from the government and the private sector (as was the case in the Campbell episode) are coming forward, even if anonymously.

> This company used to benefit from certain contacts that would have to be considered "corrupt." Most large companies did—just look how many received, almost miraculously, tax credits that they did not deserve. This is no longer the case. Now we are on the guard against corruption, as it would almost inevitably imply increasing our costs, not increasing subsidies or profits.[15]

The corruption scandal in the upper echelons of the state caused a crisis that spilled over into the economic sphere. The reports of corruption lit the tinder that was furnished by the overvalued currency. A growing feeling of insecurity precipitated a run on the austral, which fell by about 100 percent over two days (from about 6000 to close to 11,000 to the dollar). In retrospect, it seems as though the government was not overly preoccupied with the economic side of this crisis as it provided a clean method of realigning the austral while saving face—it could all be blamed on Erman Gonzalez and blatant corruption. It was under these circumstances that Gonzalez was forced to resign within weeks of the first leaks of the Campbell Company affair. Another scapegoat was deemed necessary and was sacrificed for the sake of the economic policy. Once again, this dismissal did not represent a change in policy so much as a change in faces, at least at the economics ministry; Gonzalez was shortly to reappear as minister of defense with the express goal of facilitating the privatizations of military companies.

One thing did change, however. The economic policy, no matter how rational, was not going to bring the hoped-for results unless it was implemented well. Argentina's image, and, hence, its future, rested in large part on making sure that the market forces applied to everyone. Not only was the state to be reduced in size, but the resources it continued to control were supposed to be well managed. Rough justice privatizations, in which the country's assets were sold for below market value and through which public monopolies were merely replaced with private ones, would no longer be acceptable. Now that Menem had proven his determination and his belief in a free-market system, more emphasis was being placed on the efficiency of the restructuring.

The foreign minister, Domingo Cavallo, a Harvard-trained economist known for the Cavallo Plan during the Proceso, was transferred to the economics ministry to replace Gonzalez on 29 January 1991. The new minister was the first during the Menem government with a strong background in macroeconomic policy and had long been involved in implementing and studying public affairs. Cavallo would become responsible for changing the emphasis of the economic plan, from ramrodding makeshift policies to constructing an efficient and stable state and market economy.

Cavallo and the Convertibility Plan

This change in ministers of economics was fraught with dangers, in many ways far more so than the transfer from Rapanelli to Gonzalez. When the latter took over, hyperinflation had already returned, due to no fault of his own. Further, Gonzalez took over a mere five months after Menem was inaugurated, a period when it was easier to brush aside economic setbacks. Cavallo faced the potential of a return to hyperinflation. The drop of the austral would inevitably cause an inflationary spike as imported products increased in price and as stores increased prices to preempt the foreseen inflation (indeed, stores generally doubled prices overnight). The inflationary pressures were further augmented by the public utility rate increases. The faster inflation would inevitably cause some capital flight, reduce tax revenues (the Olivera-Tanzi effect in reverse), and generally instill tensions. If the tensions fed on each other, hyperinflation would return with disastrous effects for the economic plan and political stability generally. Something akin to a legitimacy crisis could have developed if the economic plan were discredited in the public's eye.

None of the dire possibilities came to pass, however; between Cavallo's astute stewardship from his first days and the public's faith in the economic plan, hyperinflation did not return. Indeed, in the days after the crisis the austral actually recovered some of its lost ground, rising to about 9000 to the dollar; in a country in which the currency long had only one way to go, this was little short of a miracle. Inflation did go up, but only slightly. Stores slowly reversed large chunks of their prior price increases. The continued calm and stability was in many ways a tremendous test for the Menem presidency; it became clear overnight that people and particularly business leaders had a fundamental faith in the country's new economic course.

Menem used the crisis as a pretext for giving the new economics minister even more power than his already weighty predecessor; the crisis, far from retarding the economic transformation, was used as a pretext to speed it up. After implementing a few measures geared toward consolidating the short-term economic stability, including public utility price increases ranging from 25 percent to 50 percent,[16] attention was turned toward finding a new umbrella under which the economic plan and, more important, the restructuring, would occur.

The central component of Cavallo's economic plan was the Convertibility Law, passed during the first weeks of his tenure. The law states that the Central Bank has to buy australs whenever the currency fell to 10,000 australs to the dollar; in essence, the value of the Argentine currency was guaranteed. Within months, this value would act as a fixed exchange rate. Apart from the rate, however, the exchange market remained free and unified. Unlike most fixed exchange-rate regimes in the past, there were neither limits on converting currency nor differentiated rates for different types of transactions. In order to give the law credibility and power, it stipulated that the Central Bank could not issue any money unless backed by hard currencies—the bank could only do so by buying dollars (or other strong currencies) in the open market. The monetary base was to be completely backed by hard reserves; a run on the local currency would not reduce the government's power to defend the exchange rate but would only result in a shrinking money supply and growing recessionary pressures.

It must be emphasized that Cavallo's Convertibility Law created an extremely rigid exchange-rate regime, far more so than had ever been done in the past. In contrast with the tablita, heretofore the most rigid exchange regime, the exchange rate was fixed from the first day and stipulated in law; unlike the past, the government would have to ensure a precipitous decline in inflation and was not free to devalue unexpectedly. In a symbolic move, the law foresaw the creation of a new currency at the beginning of 1992, the peso, that would replace 10,000 australs and hence would be valued at parity with the dollar.

The most important consequence of the Convertibility Law was the fact that the government was forced to continue with the restructuring; as had been the case with the Plan Bonex, in taking such a large risk the government was forced to live up to its commitments or else face certain and total failure. The government would not be able to backtrack on the steps already taken regarding the deficit, opening the economy, and eliminating regulations; quite the contrary, it would have to push forward.

> From a strictly macro-economic point of view, the adoption of a rigid rule such as that of the convertibility regime was possible only because the preceding adjustment and budgetary restructuring processes had been sufficiently profound so as to assure overall economic consistency.
>
> All the same, the functioning of the economy within a framework of total monetary conversion, in many ways comparable to the gold standard, implies strict limits for both the public and private sectors.[17]

The Convertibility Law shared many other characteristics with the preceding phases of Menem's economic restructuring apart from putting the government into a make-or-break situation. In particular, the convertibility plan represented a further move toward open policymaking in which other parties were not only informed but even implicated. In so doing, the convertibility plan continued the process of strengthening the democratic institutions and further breaking with the corporatist past when power brokers forced into opposition had to try to overthrow the government. Similarly, the open nature of the law eliminated any advantages that particular companies or corporatist entities could gain by being privy to government policy; special contacts with the government were less and less valuable, rendering the old structures of the corporatist entities increasingly hollow and powerless.

The most important aspect of the Convertibility Law, however, was the increasingly clear implementation of both inducements and constraints on individual economic actors and the economy as a whole. The free market itself offers increased profits for those who invest well, bankruptcy for those who lag behind in a changing economy. The whole Menem period can be seen as a move toward ensuring that individual economic actors feel these stimuli and react appropriately to them. Cavallo has attempted to magnify them in an ever more explicit and powerful manner without, one hastens to add, causing the time-consistency problems present during the Proceso.

The most prominent inducement Cavallo offered was a booming economy. As had been the case during past governments, reactivation of the economy in the short term was possible because of the large amount of installed but unused productive capacity. Reactivation was facilitated by capital repatriation and large flows of foreign investments that flooded the stock market—as the Central Bank bought the incoming dollars, money supply (backed by these hard currencies) swelled, and local demand increased. The economic stability and the fixed exchange rate also facilitated a boom in credit, which, in turn, was used to fund spending.

The other stimuli Cavallo was able to offer were all in one way or another tied to stability and future prospects for the country. In essence, Cavallo tried to substantiate the growing belief that Argentina was beginning a long-term growth period during which time those that invested stood to profit tremendously. Cavallo advanced work already started under his predecessors to create a free-trade zone in the Southern Cone through the so-called Mercosur initiative. Through Mercosur, Argentine companies would have free access to well over 100,000,000 consumers in Brazil and other, smaller countries; the larger potential market for products was yet another inducement offered.

The constraints forced upon the economic actors resulted primarily from the combination of a fixed exchange rate and an extremely open economy, as they had under Martínez de Hoz. Local manufacturers had to control costs in order to continue to compete with imports. This pressure on local manufacturers grew, as it had during the tablita, with time as inflation continued, albeit at very low levels; with the fixed exchange rate, any increase in prices results in a weaker competitive position compared with imported goods. This restriction, as had been the case during the Martínez de Hoz years, has proven to be powerful medicine in controlling inflation and, even more notably, wholesale prices, as can be seen in Figure 7.5. There are secondary constraints as well. Mercosur offers, for example, not only potential for those that are ready to compete but also great risks for those firms that have not honed their competitive capacities; the proximity of Brazil offers little scope for protection for those industrial firms whose prices and quality are not comparable.

Cavallo has realized that structural changes are essential in order to prevent time-consistency problems, as occurred during the Proceso, and in order to ensure that market signals are not distorted. His time at the ministry of economics has been marked by unparalleled structural overhauls that have been accomplished with uncommon precision.

Clearly, Cavallo has had to consolidate the government's finances— convertibility and stability generally are completely incompatible with budget deficits, for example. In this regard, Cavallo has consolidated the budget surplus. Taxes have been increased, most notably through the implementation of a value-added tax currently fixed at 18 percent. At the same time, the overhaul of the DGI, the Argentine tax collection agency, has deepened as new people have been hired and an internal reorganization effected. As a result, the primary budget surplus grew to $800 million for the first quarter of 1992, or 2.2 percent of GNP.

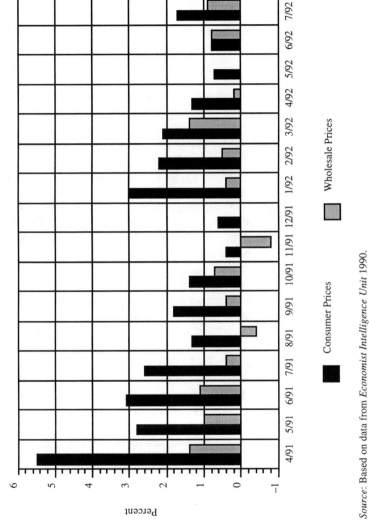

Figure 7.5 Consumer and Wholesale Monthly Inflation Rates Under Cavallo, April 1991–July 1992

■ Consumer Prices   ▨ Wholesale Prices

Source: Based on data from *Economist Intelligence Unit* 1990.

Another central aspect of consolidating the budget surplus has been the rationalization of the state apparatus in order to reduce ongoing expenditure. This initiative has mainly taken the form of promoting redundancies among state workers. So far, over 120,000 unnecessary state workers have been fired. This move resulted in savings of $292 million in 1991, saved $518 million in 1992, and is expected to save $572 million in 1993 compared to personnel costs without restructuring.[18]

Many deregulatory measures were legislated in order to ensure the efficient working of the market. The most important of these related to the labor market. Argentina inherited from Perón's first government a rigid labor market in which firing workers was difficult and extremely costly. Moreover, the union structure encouraged wage increases that went beyond increases in productivity. Cavallo has been successful in reversing much of this: The labor market is far more fluid, eliminating redundancies is cheaper and easier to effect, and wage increases are increasingly tied to changes in productivity. In other spheres, foreign trade was completely deregulated by abolishing all of the traditional government regulations that included, for example, requiring the use of official ports and limiting freedom to choose foreign merchant marine. Regarding agriculture, all the regulatory boards, leftovers from Perón's first stint in government, were abolished. A plethora of other, less important regulations was also abolished.

Privatizations have also marched forward, although slightly behind schedule. By late 1993, all state companies should be privatized, with the possible exception of Yacimientos Petrolíferos Fiscales (YPF), the immense Argentine oil company for which congressional approval was only given in November 1992. The privatization of state companies, it must also be noted, is going far beyond what is essential. All utilities and even the post office are currently slated for the auction block. Moreover, the government is slowly creating a regulatory regime in order to control natural monopolies within the private sector. In an implicit recognition of the poor manner in which the first state companies were privatized, Cavallo has begun to investigate how to force phone rates down. Aerolíneas Argentinas will also be partially reprivatized in the near future after the state reclaimed AA shares owned by bankrupted investors.

Some of the most important advances under Cavallo's leadership have come in the foreign sector, however. At the beginning of 1992, the government was able to negotiate with the International Monetary Fund an Extended Fund Facility (EFF), the international organization's ultimate sign of approval for an economic program. This was the first time in decades that the Argentine government had been able to meet targets stipulated in less rigorous stand-by agreements in order to then clinch an EFF. The EFF offers the Argentine government over $1 billion of open credit. At the same time, the IMF has imposed strict conditions on the government, which, in order to retain the credit, must increase the fiscal surplus, finish privatizing state companies, and reform the pension system. In essence, the IMF agreement offered the government resources to further structural changes while setting high goals for the economic team.[19]

The IMF credit allowed Cavallo to negotiate another breakthrough—on 7 April 1992, Cavallo jointly announced with William Rhodes, the vice-chairman of Citibank, a Brady debt reduction deal. The Brady Plan calls for reducing Argentina's commercial foreign debt load by approximately 35 percent. As the agreement is slowly implemented, Argentina's part of the debt crisis will finally be closed. Clearly, finding new credit for both the government and private industries will be facilitated. In reaction, Moody's, the U.S. credit-rating agency, has raised Argentina's risk rating from a B3 to a B1.

During all of these changes, society at large has supported the economic restructuring. On Sunday, 8 September 1991, Argentines were called to the polls for an interim election. A significant proportion of the legislature and the governorships were contested. The election had been given a plebiscitary connotation well before election day. It would be on this fateful day that Menem's bold strategy would be supported or else destroyed by the voters.

The results were little short of a landslide for Menem. The Peronists won outright in every district except Córdoba (where Angeloz was reelected), the city of Buenos Aires (where de la Rúa was victorious), and the province of Neuquén (where the provincial party gained office). It must be noted, moreover, that both Angeloz and de la Rúa strongly supported the general economic policy; the two suggested that the policies could be implemented more efficiently and less painfully but did not disagree with liberalizing the economy. This victory, it should be emphasized, was not so much a general victory for the Peronists as it was for Menem himself. Several of the victorious candidates ran as "Menemists" rather than on the official Peronist ballot; for example, Carlos Reuteman in Santa Fe and "Palito" Ortega in Tucumán were asked to run to ensure that Menem could find support for his particular policies and not merely for the still relatively vague Peronist banner in these provinces. To another pivotal position, that of governor of the state of Buenos Aires (by far the most important), Eduardo Duhalde, Menem's former vice-president, was elected. In sum, the Peronist Party developed into a more powerful and far more cohesive organization.

At first this landslide victory was used as a mandate to force even further changes. Restructuring of the state deepened and the DGI was given awesome powers in tax collection. Budget surpluses actually surpassed projections agreed to with the IMF. It was also during this time that the EFF and the Brady debt reduction plan were negotiated. Slowly, however, the government began to rest on its laurels. Menem encouraged his closest allies to advance proposals to change the constitution that would allow Menem to be reelected. Coming up against resistance, one faction of his government even suggested that certain economic bargaining chips could be offered in order to clinch a compromise with the Radicals. Sensing that his minister of economics also had political ambitions that probably would include the presidency, Menem began to ostracize Cavallo (who, being a top-quality macroeconomist known for precision and intellect, would not be nearly so easily replaced as his predecessors). As a result of all of this, certain economic proposals were meeting greater resistance in Congress: An important tax overhaul that would shift the tax burden from labor to corporate profits while giving more revenue to the federal government over the provinces, the so-called IEPE, was rejected; privatizations continued but a few months behind schedule; approval for the privatization of YPF (the only company for which express approval is necessary) arrived in November 1992.

Nine months after the last elections, on 28 June 1992, residents of the city of Buenos Aires were called back to the polls to elect a senator. De la Rúa ran in this election too as the Radical candidate against Avelino Porto, the government's candidate. Most notable about this election was the fact that the two leading candidates both supported the economic plan. The movement toward the center of the political arena that marked the end of the corporatist breakdown period is clearly continuing and is resulting in greater stability. The election was far from irrelevant, however. For a series of reasons, the election became something of a plebiscite not on the general economic policy but on Menem's attempts to get reelected on, once again, the issues of corruption, on the speed and quality of the economic restructuring, and on the state of social programs such as education and justice. Yet again, Argentine society went beyond accepting the economic plan, but actually encouraged the government to be even more vigilant in efficiently and honestly restructuring the economy: De la Rúa humiliated the government's candidate by receiving 49.9 percent of the vote compared to Porto's 31.7 percent. *Clarín*, an Argentine newspaper, explained that de la Rúa's support came from "those who, without opposing the current economic programme, are critical of the administration's image and want the government to make corrections."[20]

The last time there had been such a clear and powerful public outcry against Menem was during the Campbell corruption scandal. The changes wrought by society at large were notable—privatizations were henceforth far better executed, a new and extremely capable minister of economics was appointed, and restructuring was deepened. This outcry as well, it seems, is having widespread positive effects.

Most visibly, the time scale for the economic plan has once again been pushed forward. The privatization of the state merchant shipping company ELMA, for example, was delayed just before the election from July to November 1992; just after the election in June, however, the privatization was once again pushed forward to mid-August.[21] Finding a resolution to the financial conflict between the various levels of government has taken on a new urgency, and although a permanent resolution is being sought several measures have been taken to put added pressure on the provinces. In August 1992, for example, responsibility for funding most of the railroad deficits was forcibly passed on to the relevant provinces. Although declarations can be deceiving, it seems as though Menem has at least postponed the idea of reelection. If he still harbors such desires, at least he is clear that, despite all the fundamental changes, costly economic compromises could just as easily destroy him as they did Alfonsín.

It seems as though the destructive corporatist entities have been replaced by an electorate that is convinced of the need for stability and growth as well as cognizant of the sacrifices such goals require.

Looking Toward the Future

At the time of this writing, the continued support of Argentine society is essential. In many ways, the economic restructuring is entering its most tenuous and difficult phase. Although an enormous amount of fundamental and often painful restructuring has been effected, this process has been softened by the booming economy. In 1990 stability returned, itself a tremendous enticement for the Argentine population; the subsequent two years ushered in rapid growth, as can be seen in Figure 7.6, and lower unemployment. This growth, however, as was the growth during the first years of all of the economic plans during the breakdown period, was easy, almost inevitable—stability and renewed confidence quickly allowed existing industrial capacity to come back on-line as demand grew, particularly when credit was once again available. The increases in GNP and industrial production reflect a recovery from depressed levels instead of fundamental and underlying growth. Now that the "easy" growth is over, new growth is contingent exclusively on investment; until new and large flows of investment arrive, growth will be minimal and incomes for all economic groups will be stable.

The reader will realize that it was exactly at this juncture that the economic plans, and often the governments themselves, self-destructed during the breakdown period. The Cordobazo and the relaxation of the economic plan under Videla are the clearest examples. Both Perón and Alfonsín started facing political tensions after the easy stabilization aspects of their economic platforms, at which point they were unwilling to continue with restructuring. The lack of growth forced new political battles and brought the return of instability.

Is this process again to be the destiny of Argentina? Quite simply, no; I hope that, the reader has become convinced of this. Both the political and economic causes of the cyclical crises of Argentine political economy have been resolved for the foreseeable future. More important still, the destructive dynamic that had so long existed between politics and economics, allowing problems in one to reinforce those in the other, has been broken.

Figure 7.6   GDP and Industrial Output Growth Rates, 1990–1993

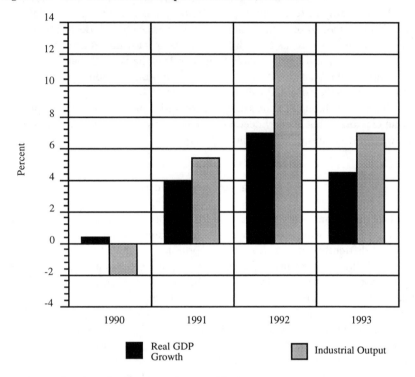

Source: Based on data from *Latin American Monitor*.
Note: Figures for 1992 are preliminary; figures for 1993 are estimates.

Most obvious and most important, democracy has been consolidated in the ten years since the end of the last military regime. The political changes analyzed in the preceding chapter—redefining the military's role in society, fostering cohesive parties, reinforcing the democratic apparatus, and destroying the corporatist structures—have all continued to a point from which there is no return. A coup is inconceivable. All the political parties have far more to lose than to gain by turning their backs on the democracy. And even the individual economic actors have more to lose from a reversion back to all politics; here, too, the changes outlined in the preceding chapter have been consolidated.

The economic conditions for the recurring crises have also been eliminated. The most tangible representation of this is the absence of a budget deficit—on the contrary, today there is a surplus. This shorthand for the changes hides, however, the extent and profundity of the changes that have been wrought. The majority (in revenue terms the vast majority) of the state's economic activities has been turned over to the private sector through privatizations; Entel, once a perpetual drain on the state's finances, now is an important payer of taxes. The state apparatus has been completely overhauled, despite the fact that much remains to be done: The Federal government has fired 200,000 workers and has permanently reduced its expenditure on personnel by approximately 20 percent.[22] Tax revenues have been increased, and the DGI rendered far more efficient. Whole regulatory agencies have been decreed out of existence, as have the senseless regulations that they monitored. The easy phase of the economic plan has passed, but unlike during the past governments, the easy phase was not wasted—a real restructuring has taken place, and, moreover, one without time-consistency problems.

Clearly, at least for the medium term, there will no longer be the spillover between economic and political turmoil: Argentina's overall country risk has significantly diminished, thus posing a far smaller impediment to investment; the economic restructuring, which is allowing Argentina to live within its means for the first time in decades, preempts the need to force a radical change in government composition or policy in order to protect individual incomes. The Argentine Paradox has been resolved for the foreseeable future and shows no signs of returning.

What does this mean for the future? This is clearly far more difficult to say. It is in this sense that much remains to be done. In early 1992, Cavallo, with at least tacit agreement from Menem, announced that Argentina was beginning a period of huge growth, that the "Argentine Miracle" was about to begin. New investment would surge forward, and growth rates approaching 10 percent per year were attainable, according to the minister. A new dynamic was to replace the old destructive one: Economic growth would foster political stability that would further encourage investment. His prognoses were premature, even if they are ever to be proved correct. Much remains to be done before an Argentine Miracle can occur.

Most concretely, the creation of a working market must be completed. The labor laws, still extremely stringent for a developing country, must be relaxed. Similarly, wages, now artificially high in dollar terms with the fixed exchange rate, will have to be reduced to bring them more in line with international standards. Remaining market-suffocating regulations will have to be ditched while others are developed to regulate certain areas of the economy such as private monopolies. At some point, the exchange rate will have to be realigned and possibly left to market forces.

More important, however, the restructuring of the state must continue. The ongoing tug-of-war between the federal government and the provinces must be resolved permanently and more equitably. A resolution to the loss-making government pension scheme must be found. The current tax-sharing scheme, through which taxes are basically equally shared between all of the provinces and the central government, allows too many resources to be wasted by the local governments, which have lagged behind in restructuring.

Stronger internal controls must be put into place to limit corruption and attract capable civil servants. Thus far, emphasis has justifiably been placed on cutting costs in an attempt to sanitize the state's finances; now, quality must be fostered in the state apparatus.

This is clearly occurring, particularly since Cavallo's appointment, in all areas of the government under the jurisdiction of the economics ministry. The DGI and customs inspectors, as examples, have become quite efficient and reliable organizations. Much more remains to be done in the other areas of government, most notably those of health, justice, and education. The market mechanism, now firmly in place, is able to offer carrots and sticks to ensure efficient short-term actions on the part of economic actors. In the longer term, however, the attractiveness of Argentina as a country in which to invest (the carrot), rests in producing a well-trained and capable work force and a just legal system. Right now, these longer term conditions are far from assured. Apart from having reduced costs in the short term, a necessary step to consolidate the stability, the government has done little to redefine and to overhaul the tasks of these departments. Government investment in the infrastructure must be increased and rendered more efficient. For example, the Argentine government currently spends tremendous resources on the university system (which is a regressive form of social spending) at the cost of primary schooling; the long-term viability of the economy as well as encouraging a more just distribution of income is contingent on reversing this. Despite some changes in the legal system, such as allowing for the first time oral (as contrasted to written) testimony, delays are still rampant, costs high, and judicial independence questionable.

Finally, patience is needed, something very difficult to maintain with the end of the easy part of the economic plan. Argentina had developed a terrible international reputation. Many companies and individuals, Argentine and foreigners alike, have lost fortunes in Argentina. The country has changed fundamentally, but prolonged stability and proof that the rules of the game are set are needed in order to convince potential investors. Only when the conclusions of this book are proved and a chapter of Argentine history is closed for good will there be greater confidence in investing in the country. This patience is warranted: If the changes are consolidated as described above, and if attempts to artificially prime the economy or redistribute income are resisted, there truly could be an Argentine Miracle. "This time the sacrifice has value," claimed government propaganda posters posted in August 1992, and it is true.

If the government gives into temptations to spend the gains already garnered—for Menem's reelection, for a redistribution of income, or for anything else—the consequences will not be immediately disastrous. There has been enough economic restructuring that hyperinflation will not easily return. Incomes will not in the near future double or become halved overnight. Political violence is nonexistent and certainly cannot return quickly. New wars or military coups are not feasible. The country would simply stagnate. In the longer term, the lack of growth could foment renewed social tensions that eventually could drag the country through yet another cathartic period. But such an outcome is far away.

For right now, the Argentine Paradox has been resolved—there is no longer a recurring government legitimacy crisis. This calm affords Argentina an opportunity to paint a different future, one in which the destructive dynamic is replaced by one that fosters growth. This future is possible, but not certain. If turning back is no longer possible, continuing to move forward is far from assured, but the opportunity is there. Investment flows, although not as strong as had been hoped for this stage of the economic plan, are growing. Investment for 1992 is on course for being 40 percent higher than the abysmally low levels of 1991, and another 30 percent increase is expected in 1993, assuming the current economic policy is maintained.[23]

Another period of Argentine history is over. With a bit of luck and a lot of persistence, a new, much brighter chapter might now begin. It is far from certain—it will never be completely understood how a country with tremendous potential has had such a contorted past. But at least now, with the end of the breakdown period, Argentina has the possibility of defining the characteristics of the next period of its history. It just might be that the Argentine Paradox will be replaced with the Argentine Miracle.

Notes

1. Peter Calvert, "Argentina: Goodbye to Peronism," p. 174.
2. Orlando Ferreres, personal interview.
3. Pablo Rojo with Armando Canosa, "El programa de desregulación del gobierno argentino," p. 30.
4. Juan Carlos Torre, "Argentina: Il ritorno del Peronismo," p. 122, my translation.
5. Juan Carlos Herrera, personal interview.
6. Alberto Grimoldi, personal interview.
7. Mario Damill and Roberto Frenkel, *Hiperinflación y Estabilización*, statistical appendix.
8. Mario Damill and Roberto Frenkel, *Hiperinflación y Estabilización*, p. 49.
9. Floyd Norris, "Argentina's Painful Path to Efficiency."
10. Roberto Frenkel, personal interview, August 1990, when the austral was approximately 6000 to the dollar.
11. Juan Carlos Rua, personal interview.
12. Norman Peagam, "Argentina: Menem Ditches the Dogma," p. 25.
13. See Shirley Christian, "Bluntly Put, Graft Is Rife."
14. These rumors were corroborated by one member of the government to whom the author spoke; for obvious reasons, the individual spoke on the condition of anonymity.
15. Personal interview, requested anonymity.
16. See Nathaniel C. Nash, "Argentina's Markets Back Economic Plan."

17. Pablo Rojo with Armando Canosa, "El programa de desregulación del gobierno argentino," p. 35.

18. Héctor Domeniconi et al., "Hacia un estado moderno," p. 22.

19. *Economist Intelligence Unit* Country Report, #2, 1992, pp. 8–10.

20. *Clarín* as quoted in *Latin American Monitor*, August 1992, p. 1037.

21. *Latin American Monitor*, August 1992, p. 1039 and June 1992, p. 1027.

22. Héctor Domenicone et al., "Hacia un estado moderno," p. 22.

23. *Economist Intelligence Unit*, #2, 1992, p. 5.

Appendix A

Presidents and Ministers of Economics, 1966–1992

Date and Means of Presidential Accession	President	Minister of Economics	Type of Regime	Alliance
1 May 1958 Elected	Arturo Frondizi	Emilio Del Carril (5/1/58–6/24/59) Alvaro Alsogaray (6/25/59–4/26/61) Roberto Alemann (4/26/61–1/12/62) Carlos Coll Benegas (1/15/62–3/26/62) Jorge Wehbe (3/26/62–4/6/62)	Impasse Period	—
29 March 1962 Military coup	José Guido	Federico Pinedo (4/6/62–4/25/62) Alvaro Alsogaray (4/30/62–12/10/62) Eustaquio Méndez Delfino (12/10/62–5/15/63) José Alfredo Martínez de Hoz (5/21/63–10/12/63)	Impasse Period	—
12 October 1963 Elected 7 July 1963	Arturo Illia	Eugenio Blanco (10/12/63–8/5/64) Juan C. Pugliese (8/19/64–6/28/66)	Impasse Period	—
29 June 1966 Military coup	Juan Carlo Onganía	Jorge Salimei (6/29/66–1/3/67) Adalbert Krieger Vasena (1/3/67–6/11/69) José Dagnino Pastore (6/11/69–6/17/70)	Military	None Industrial Industrial
18 June 1970 Elected by military	Roberto Levingston	Carlos Motano Llerena (6/18/70–10/15/70) Aldo Ferrer (10/26/70–5/28/71)	Military	Populist Populist

229

Date and Means of Presidential Accession	President	Minister of Economics	Type of Regime	Alliance
26 March 1971 Internal group	Alejandro Lanusse	Juan Quillici (6/1/71–10/11/71) Jorge Wehbe (10/13/72–5/24/73) Cayetano Licciardo (10/11/71–10/13/72)	Military	None (Praetorianist) None (Praetorianist) None (Praetorianist)
25 May 1973 Elected 11 March 1973	Héctor Cámpora	José Ber Gelbard (5/24/73–10/21/74)	Peronist	Populist
15 July 1973 Interim president	Raúl Lastiri	José Ber Gelbard	Transitional	Populist
12 October 1973 Elected 23 September 1973	Juan Perón	José Ber Gelbard	Peronist	Populist
1 July 1974 Ascended from vice presidency upon husband's death	Isabel Martínez de Perón	José Ber Gelbard Alfredo Gómez Morales (10/21/74–6/2/75) Celestino Rodrigo (6/2/75–7/19/75) Pedro Bonanni (7/22/75–8/11/75) Antonio Cafiero (8/14/75–2/3/76) Emilio Mondelli (2/3/76–3/24/76)	Peronist	Populist Populist Conservative/ Reactionary None None (Praetorianist) None (Praetorianist)
24 March 1976 Military coup	Jorge Videla	José Alfredo Martínez de Hoz (3/29/76–3/28/81)	Military	Liberal
29 March 1981 Elected by military	Roberto Viola	Lorenzo Siguat (3/29/81–12/21/81)	Military	None (Populist tendencies)
22 December 1981 Internal coup	Leopoldo Galtieri	Roberto Alemann (12/22/81–6/30/82)	Military	Conservative
1 July 1982 Military coup	Reynaldo Bignone	José Dagnino Pastore (6/2/82–8/24/82) Jorge Wehbe (8/25/82–12/7/83)	Military	None (Praetorianist)

Date and Means of Presidential Accession	President	Minister of Economics	Type of Regime	Alliance
10 December 1983 Elected 30 October 1983	Raúl Alfonsín	Bernardo Grinspun (12/10/83–2/19/85)	Radical (Democratic)	None (Populist tendencies)
		Juan Sourouille (2/19/85–4/4/89)		None
		Juan Pugliese (4/4/89–5/26/89)		None (Praetorianist)
		Jesus Rodriguez (5/26/89–7/8/89)		None (Praetorianist)
8 July 1989 Elected 14 May 1989	Carlos Menem	Miguel Roig (7/8/89–7/14/89)	Peronist (Democratic)	None
		Nestor Rapanelli (7/16/89–12/14/89)		None
		Antonio Erman Gonzalez (12/15/89–1/31/91)		"Reform"
		Domingo Cavallo (1/31/91–)		"Reform"

Appendix B

Interviews

All interviews were conducted in Buenos Aires. I conducted four trips for the purposes of this study, one during July and August 1990 (funded by a Woodrow Wilson School Grant), the second during December of the same year, the third during September 1991, and the final one in August 1992. All the interviews were conducted during these times. Many of the people listed were interviewed on more than one occasion. No distinction, however, has been made regarding the number of sessions with the individual or the date of the interviews. The first two interviews were tape-recorded. Subsequently, I chose to take handwritten notes in the hope of getting more candid comments. Almost all of the interviews were in Spanish, and hence the translations are my own. Regarding some issues, the interviewees were offered confidentiality, a fact that at times forced me to not fully ascribe the source of a particular point in this work.

Needless to say, the following is not an exhaustive list of the people with whom I spoke but rather is limited to those discussions that were previously arranged for the explicit purpose of this research. Casual and social conversations, many of which proved to be useful, have not been included, as those individuals did not give me the express permission to include them in this study.

Almansi, Aquiles A.	Professor, Centro de Estudios Macroeconomicos de Argentina
Avila, Jorge C.	Director, Macroeconomica
Bacqués, Pablo J.	Executive Director, The American Chamber of Commerce in Argentina
Ball, Ernest E.	The Lynnhaven Group (on mission in Argentina related to an IMF study)

Balvé, Alberto	Opus Dei representative
Boero, Guillermo Estévez	Congressman, Socialist Party
Bourbon, Héctor Pérez	Assistant on the General Legislation Commission (Peronist)
Broda, Miguel Angel	Private economist, Broda y Ascociados
Camaña, Dante	Congressman, Partido Justicialista; President, Food Workers' Union (Sindicato Gastronómico)
Canavese, Alfredo Juan	Professor, Centro de Investigaciones Económicas, Instituto Torcuato di Tella
Carballo, Carlos	Vice-Minister of economics under Menem
Carrizo Carricante, Adolfo	Attorney
Castillo, Juan Manuel	President, la Confederación General Económica
Cavarozzi, Marcelo	Professor, Centro de Estudios de Estado y Sociedad
Darch, Steven	President, J. P. Morgan, Argentina
de Pablo, Juan Carlos	Private economist
de Zavalía, Eduardo	President, Sociedad Rural Argentina
Distel, Rodolfo	Fundación Arturo Illia para la Democracia y la Paz (Radical think tank)
di Tella, Torcuato	Director, Instituto Rodriguez
Diz, Alfredo	President of the Central Bank under Videla
Donoso, Jorge	Assistant to the Executive Vice-Presidency, Siderca (Techint group)
Eckstein, Jorge	Industrialist, property developer
Esposito, Eduardo	General (Ret.)
Falco, José Luís	Associate, la Confederación General Económica
Ferreres, Orlando J.	Vice-Minister of Economics under Menem (under Rapanelli), director of economic advisory firm
Frenkel, Roberto	Centro de Estudios de Estado y Sociedad

Garnero, Ugo	Assistant to Congressman Lamberti, Partido Justicialista (Peronismo de las Bases)
Giorgio, Luis A.	Director of Monetary and Financial Studies, Central Bank, Menem government
Golonbek, Claudio	Fundación para la Investigación Económica Latinoamericana
Grant, William	Economics Officer, United States Embassy, Buenos Aires
Grimoldi, Alberto L.	Secretary of Industry under Videla, Vice-President of Central Bank under Galtieri, also in Krieger Vasena's economic team
Grinspun, Bernardo	Economics minister under Alfonsín
Hampton, Carlos E.	President, Comega (agricultural producers, processors, and merchants)
Herrera, Juan Carlos	Fundación de Estudios Contemporáneos (Peronist think tank)
Herrera, Manuel E.	Secretary, Unión Industrial Argentina
Klein, Guillermo W.	Vice-Minister of Economics under Videla, other government positions prior to that
Krieger Vasena, Adalbert	Minister of Economics under Onganía
Lagorio, Ricardo Ernesto	Secretary of Argentine Foreign Service, Menem government
Martínez de Hoz, José Alfredo	Minister of Economics under Videla
Molina, Eduardo	Vice-President of Congress, various positions under Alfonsín
Mora y Araujo, Manuel	Private pollster, sociologist at Instituto Torcuato di Tella
Oklander, Mario	Secretary, Confederación General de la Industria
Presman, Jorge	Centro de Estudios para el Cambio Estructural (Radical)
Raidman, Laura	Attorney (Unión Centro Democratico)

Raidman, Federico I.   President, Ingefir, S.A., construction firm

Robben, Antonius   University of Michigan (in Argentina doing field research on military)

Rodrigues, Carlos   Centro de Estudios Macroeconómicos de Argentina

Rua, Juan Carlos   Union secretary, Radical Party

S. de Kaplan, María Alejandra   Assistant to the President of the General Legislation Commission (Congress), Radical Party

Schvarzer, Jorge   Centro de Investigaciones Sociales Sobre el Estado y la Administración

Sourrouille, Juan   Minister of Economics under Alfonsín

Stuhlman, Luis   Vice-Minister of Social Welfare under Alfonsín, currently at Fundación para el Cambio en Democracia

Szewach, Enrique   Fundación para la Investigación Económica Latinoamericana

Tagliaferri, José Luis   Responsible for institutional relations, Ministry of Economics under Cavallo

Torre, Juan Carlos   Instituto Torcuato di Tella

Ubaldini, Saúl E.   President, Confederación General de Trabajo (de la Republica Argentina)

Uriarte, José A.   Subgerente General, Banco Central under Menem government

Vives, Jorge   Director of Strategic Planning, Massalin Particulares (Philip Morris subsidiary)

Zamora, Federico   Congressman, Unión Centro Democratico

Bibliography

Newspapers and magazines were frequently consulted. In particular, *La Nación* was read on a quotidian basis during my visits in Argentina. *Clarín*, *Paginas/12*, and *The Buenos Aires Herald* were also read regularly and proved very helpful. Of course, I also tried to keep track of articles on Argentina in the international press, notably in *The New York Times*, *The Financial Times*, and *The Economist*. Some business studies were also frequently consulted: The Economist Intelligence Unit's Argentina Report, Carta Ecónomica from Broda y Asociados, the reports from Ferreres y Asociados and the *Latin American Monitor*. No attempt has been made to include the articles from all of these sources, however, unless they have been cited in the notes or were considered of particular value.

Acevedo, Manuel, Basualdo, Eduardo M., and Khavisse, Miguel, *¿Quién es quién?* Editorial 12, Buenos Aires, 1991.

Acuña, Carlos H., and Golbert, Laura, "Empresarios y politica (parte I)," *Boletín Informativo Techint*, #255, Noviembre/Diciembre 1988.

———, "Empresarios y politica (parte II)," *Boletín Informativo Techint*, #263, Mayo/Agosto 1990.

Alexander, Robert L., *Labor Relations in Argentina, Brazil, and Chile*, McGraw Hill, New York, 1962.

American Chamber of Commerce, *President Menem's Administration, The First Two Years: A View from the Private Sector*, Buenos Aires, 1991.

Argentine-American Chamber of Commerce, *The New Argentina*, New York, 1991.

Arnaudo, Aldo A., "El programa antiinflacionaria de 1973," *Desarrollo Económico*, April 1979.

Arriagada, Genaro, *Pinochet: The Politics of Power*, Allen & Unwin, Boston, 1988.

Ayers, Robert L., "The 'Social Pact' as Anti-Inflationary Policy: The Argentine Experience Since 1973," *World Politics*, July 1976.

Azpiazu, Daniel, Basualdo, Eduardo M., and Khavisse, Miguel, *El nuevo poder económico en la Argentina de los años 80*; Editorial Legasa, Buenos Aires, 1986.

Baily, Samuel L., "Argentina: Search for Consensus, " *Current History*, November 1966.

Balvé, Beba C., and Balvé, Beatriz S., *El '69: Huelga Politica de Masas*, Contrapunto, Buenos Aires, 1989.

Barreiro, Ernesto, "If Menem Falters in Argentina. . . ," *The New York Times*, 23 March 1990.

Bergquist, Charles, *Labor in Latin America: Comparative Essays on Chile, Argentina, Venezuela, and Colombia*, Stanford University Press, Stanford, 1986.

Bergstein, Jorge, *El "Cordobazo"*, Cartago, Buenos Aires, 1987.

Bilder, Ernesto A., "El Plan Gelbard," *Problemas del Desarrollo*, May 1977.

Bonelli, Eduardo C., "Vaguedades y pasos firmes al comenzar el segundo año," *La Nación*, 15 July 1990.

Braun, Oscar, and Joy, Leonard, "A Model of Economic Stagnation—A Case Study of the Argentine Economy," *The Economic Journal*, December 1968.

Buchanan, Paul G., "State Corporatism in Argentina: Labor Administration under Perón and Onganía," *Latin American Research Review*, Spring 1985.

Business Week, "Can Argentina's Economic Changes Survive?" 21 July1980.

Bustamente, Jorge E., "Quizá Martínez, pero sin hoz," *Ambito Financiero*, 9 October 1990.

Calvert, Peter, "Menem's First Crisis," *The World Today*, August 1990.

———, "Argentina: Goodbye to Peronism," *The World Today*, March 1991.

Calvo, Guillermo A., "Fractured Liberalism: Argentina Under Martínez de Hoz," *Economic Development and Cultural Change*, April 1986.

Camilion, Oscar, *The Argentine Crisis*, Council on Foreign Relations, New York, 1990.

Cammack, Paul, "Brazil: Redemocratization and the Lessons of Populism," in *Social Change in Contemporary Brazil*, edited by Geert Banck and Kees Koonings, Center for Latin American Research and Documentation, Amsterdam, 1988.

Canitrot, Adolfo, "La experiencia populist de redistribución de ingresos," *Desarrollo Económico*, October–December 1975.

———, *La viabilidad económica de la democracia: Un analysis de la experiencia peronista 1973–1976*, CEDES, Buenos Aires, 1978.

———, *Teoría y practica del liberalismo: Politica antiinflacionaria y apertura económíca en la Argentina, 1976–1981*, CEDES, Buenos Aires, 1980.

Carciofi, Ricardo, *La desarticulación del pacto fiscal: Una interpretación sobre la evolución del sector publico Argentino en las dos ultimas decadas*, CEPAL, Buenos Aires, 1989.

Cardoso, Fernando Enrique, "On the Characterization of Authoritarian Regimes in Latin America," in *The New Authoritarianism in Latin America*, edited by David Collier, Princeton University Press, Princeton, 1979.

———. "Entrepreneurs and the Transition Process: The Brazilian Case," in *Transitions from Authoritarian Rule: Comparative Perspectives*, edited by Guillermo O'Donnell, Philippe Schmitter, and Laurence Whitehead, Johns Hopkins University Press, Baltimore, 1988.

Cardoso, Fernando Enrique, and Faletto, Enzo, *Dependency and Development in Latin America*, University of California Press, Los Angeles, 1979.

Cavarozzi, Marcelo, *Peronism and Radicalism: Argentina's Transition in Perspective*, The Wilson Center Latin American Working Papers, Washington, D.C., 1985.

———, "Political Cycles in Argentina since 1955," in *Transitions from Authoritarian Rule: Latin America*, edited by Guillermo O'Donnell, Philippe Schmitter, and Laurence Whitehead, Johns Hopkins University Press, Baltimore, 1986.

Cavarozzi, Marcelo, and Grossi, María, *De la reinvención democrática al reflujo politico y la hyperinflación*, CEDES, Buenos Aires, 1989.

Chalmers, Douglas A., "The Politicized State in Latin America," in

Authoritarianism and Corporatism in Latin America, edited by James M. Malloy, University of Pittsburgh Press, Pittsburgh, 1977.

Christian, Shirley, "Menem's Reforms Provoke Backlash," *The New York Times*, 14 October 1990.

———, "Peronist Workers Rebel in Argentina," *The New York Times*, 22 March 1990.

———, "Bluntly Put, Graft Is Rife: U.S. Envoy Speaks Out," *The New York Times*, 22 March 1990.

Cohen, Alvin, "Revolution in Argentina?" *Current History*, November 1967.

Collier, David, "Overview of the Bureaucratic-Authoritarian Model," in *The New Authoritarianism in Latin America*, edited by David Collier, Princeton University Press, Princeton, 1979.

Collier, David, and Collier, Ruth Berrins, "Who Does What, to Whom, and How: Toward a Comparative Analysis of Latin American Corporatism," in *Authoritarianism and Corporatism in Latin America*, edited by James M. Malloy, University of Pittsburgh Press, Pittsburgh, 1977.

———, *Shaping the Political Arena*, Princeton University Press, Princeton, 1992.

Collier, Ruth Berrins, and Collier, David, "Inducements Versus Constraints: Disaggregating Corporatism," *The American Political Science Review*, December 1979.

Confederación General Económica, *El Documento CGE-CGT: Acuerdo social*, press release, Confederación General Económica, Buenos Aires, 1971.

———, *Coincidencias programaticas del plenario de organizaciones sociales y partidos politicos*, press release, Confederación General Económica, Buenos Aires, 1972.

———, *Declaración conjunta de la Confederación General del Trabajo y de la Confederación General Económica de la Republica Argentina*, press release, Confederación General Económica, Buenos Aires, 1972.

———, *Acta del Compromiso Nacional*, press release, Confederación General Económica, Buenos Aires, 1973.

Corradi, Juan E., *The Fitful Republic: Economy, Society, and Politics in Argentina*, Westview Press, Boulder, 1985.

Cortes, Rosalía, *Conflict and Inflation in Argentina, 1966–1980*, Institute of Social Studies, The Hague, 1985.

Crouch, Colin, "Trade Unions in the Exposed Sector: Their Influence in Neo-Corporatist Behaviour," in *Labour Relations and Economic Performance*, edited by Renato Brunetta and Carlo Dell'Aringa, Macmillan, London, 1990.

Dahl, Robert A., *Polyarchy*, Yale University Press, New Haven, 1971.

Damill, Mario, and Frenkel, Roberto, *Hiperinflación y estabilización: La experiencia Argentina reciente*, CEDES, Buenos Aires, 1990.

———, *Malos tiempos: La economía Argentina en la decada de los ochenta*, CEDES, Buenos Aires, 1990.

de Hoyos, Ruben, "Argentina and the Soviet Union: International Relations in Three Stages," in *Great Power Relations in Argentina, Chile, and Antarctica,* edited by Michael A. Morris, Macmillan, London, 1990.

de Pablo, Juan Carlos, *La politica antiinflacionaria en la Argentina, 1967–1970*, Amorrortu, Buenos Aires, 1970.

———, "Inversión, liberalismo y populismo," *Desarrollo Económico*, April 1978.

———, *Economía política del Peronismo*, El Cid Editor, Buenos Aires, 1980.

———, "Economic Policy Without Political Context: Guido, 1962–3," in *The*

Political Economy of Argentina, 1946–1983, edited by Guido di Tella and Rudiger Dornbusch, Macmillan, London, 1989.

de Pablo, Juan Carlos and Martínez, Alfonso José, *Argentina: Thirty Years of Economic Policy (1958–87)*, unpublished manuscript, 1988.

de Riz, Liliana, *Retorno y derrumbe: El ultimo gobierno peronista*, Mexico City Folios Ediciones, 1981.

———, "Política y partidos. Ejercicio de análysis comparado: Argentina, Chile, Brasil y Uruguay," *Desarrollo Económico*, January 1986.

———, *La Argentina de Alfonsín: La renovación de los partidos y el parlemento*, CEDES, Buenos Aires, 1989.

———, Partidos políticos y perspectivas de consolidación de la democracia: Argentina, Brasil y Uruguay, CEDES, Buenos Aires, 1991.

Díaz-Alejandro, Carlos F., *Essays on the Economic Development of the Argentine Republic*, Yale University Press, New Haven, 1970.

di Tella, Guido, *The Economic Policies of Argentina's Labour-Based Government, 1973–1976*, The Wilson Center Working Papers, Number 47, Washington, DC, 1979.

———, *Argentina Under Perón, 1973–76: The Nation's Experience with a Labour-based Government*, St. Martin's Press, New York, 1983.

———, "Argentina's Economy Under a Labour-based Government, 1973–6," in *The Political Economy of Argentina, 1946–1983*, edited by Guido di Tella and Rudiger Dornbusch, Macmillan, London, 1989.

di Tella, Guido, and Dornbusch, Rudiger, "Introduction: The Political Economy of Argentina," in *The Political Economy of Argentina, 1946–1983*, edited by Guido di Tella and Rudiger Dornbusch, Macmillan, London, 1989.

di Tella, Torcuato S., *Corporatism and the Political Party System in the Argentina Transition*, manuscript.

———, "¿La Argentina de hoy es Italia de 1970?" an interview with Jorge Halperín in *Clarín*, 19 June 1988.

———, *Latin American Politics*, University of Texas Press, Austin, 1990.

Domenicone, Héctor, Gaudio, Ricardo, and Guibert, Armando, "Hacia un estado moderno: El programa de reforma administrativa," *Boletin Informativo Techint* #269, January–May 1992.

Dornbusch, Rudiger, "A New Chance for Argentina," *Challenge*, January 1986.

———, "Politicas de estabilización en los paises en desarrollo: ¿Qué hemos aprendido?" *Desarrollo Económico*, July 1986.

———, "Argentina after Martínez de Hoz," in *The Political Economy of Argentina, 1946–1983*, edited by Guido di Tella and Rudiger Dornbusch, Macmillan, London, 1989.

Dornbusch, Rudiger, and de Pablo, Juan Carlos, *Deuda externa e inestabilidad macroeconómica en la Argentina*, Editorial Sudamericana, Buenos Aires, 1988.

Economist, "Brazil and Argentina: Bankshut," 9 February 1991.

Economist Intelligence Unit, Argentina: A Country Profile, London, 1990, 1991, and 1992.

Epstein, Edward C., "Politicization and Income Redistribution in Argentina: The Case of the Peronist Worker," *Economic Development and Cultural Change*, July 1975.

———, "Antiinflation Policies in Argentina and Chile, or, Who Pays the Cost?" *Comparative Political Studies*, July 1978.

———, "Control and Co-optation of the Argentine Labor Movement," *Economic Development and Cultural Change*, April 1979.

———, "Recent Stabilization Programs in Argentina, 1973–86," *World Development*, August 1988.

Fanelli, José María, and Frenkel, Roberto, *Argentina's Medium Term: Problems and Prospects*, CEDES, Buenos Aires, 1989.

Fernández, Julio A., "Crisis in Argentina," *Current History*, February 1972.

———, "The Crisis of Authority in Argentina," *Current History*, January 1974.

———, "Political Immobility in Argentina," *Current History*, February 1976.

Fernández, Roque B., "La crisis financiera Argentina: 1980–1982," *Desarrollo Económico*, April 1983.

———, *What Have the Populists Learned from Hyperinflation?* CEMA, Buenos Aires, 1990.

Ferrer, Aldo, "The Argentine Economy, 1976–1979," *Journal of Interamerican Studies and World Affairs*, May 1980.

Filippini, Mariano, and Olcese, María Angélica, "Transitional Economic Policies, 1971–3," in *The Political Economy of Argentina, 1946–1983*, edited by Guido di Tella and Rudiger Dornbusch, Macmillan, London, 1989.

Fishlow, Albert, "A Tale of Two Presidents: The Political Economy of Crisis Management," in *Democratizing Brazil*, edited by Alfred Stepan, Oxford University Press, New York, 1989.

Fodor, Jorge, "Argentina's Nationalism: Myth or Reality?" in *The Political Economy of Argentina, 1946–1983*, edited by Guido di Tella and Rudiger Dornbusch, Macmillan, London, 1989.

Frenkel, Roberto, "Salarios industriales e inflación: El periodo 1976–82," *Desarrollo Económico*, October 1984.

Gerchunoff, Pablo, "Peronist Economic Policies, 1946–55," in *The Political Economy of Argentina, 1946–1983*, edited by Guido di Tella and Rudiger Dornbusch, Macmillan, London, 1989.

Gerchunoff, Pablo L., and Vicens, Mario, *Gasto publico, recursos publicos y financiamento en una económia en crisis: El caso Argentino*, Instituto Torcuato Di Tella, Buenos Aires, 1989.

Germani, Gino, *Authoritarianism, Fascism, and National Populism*, Transaction Books, New Brunswick, 1978.

Grinspun, Bernardo, *La evolución de la economía argentina desde diciembre 1983 a septiembre de 1989*, Ediciones Radicales, Buenos Aires, 1990.

Grossi, María, and Gritti, Roberto, "Los partidos frente a una democracia difícil: La evolución del sistema partidario en la Argentina," *Crítica y Utopía*, Winter 1989.

Guadagni, Alieto Aldo, "Economic Policy During Illia's Period in Office, 1963–6," in *The Political Economy of Argentina, 1946–1983*, edited by Guido di Tella and Rudiger Dornbusch, Macmillan, London, 1989.

Guissarri, Adrián, *La argentina informal: realidad de la vida economica*, Buenos Aires Emece, 1989.

Hamilton, Nora, *The Limits of State Autonomy*, Princeton University Press, Princeton, 1982.

Heymann, Daniel and Navajas, Fernando, "Conflicto Distributivo y Deficit Fiscal: Notas sobre la Experiencia Argentina, 1970–1987, *Desarrollo Económico*, October, 1989.

Hirschman, Albert O., "The Turn to Authoritarianism in Latin America and the Search for Its Economic Determinants," in *The New Authoritarianism in Latin America*, edited by David Collier, Princeton University Press, Princeton, 1979.

Humphrey, John, *Capitalist Control and Workers' Struggle in the Brazilian Auto Industry*, Princeton University Press, Princeton, 1982.

Huntington, Samuel P., *Political Order in Changing Societies*, Yale University Press, New Haven, 1969.

Jelin, Elizabeth, "Labour Conflicts Under the Second Peronist Regime, Argentina 1973–76," *Development and Change*, April 1979.

Jordan, David C., "Argentina's New Military Government," *Current History*, February 1970.

————, "Argentina's Bureaucratic Oligarchies," *Current History*, February 1972.

————, "Authoritarianism and Anarchy in Argentina," *Current History*, January 1975.

————, "Argentina's Military Government," *Current History*, February 1977.

Kahler, Miles, "Orthodoxy and Its Alternatives: Explaining Approaches to Stabilization Adjustment," in *Economic Crisis and Policy Choice: The Politics of Adjustment in the Third World*, edited by Joan M. Nelson, Princeton University Press, Princeton, 1990.

Kaufman, Robert R., "Corporatism, Clientelism, and Partisan Conflict: A Study of Seven Latin American Countries," in *Authoritarianism and Corporatism in Latin America*, edited by James M. Malloy, University of Pittsburgh Press, Pittsburgh, 1977.

————, "Industrial Change and Authoritarian Rule in Latin America: A Concrete Review of the Bureaucratic-Authoritarian Model," in *The New Authoritarianism in Latin America*, edited by David Collier, Princeton University Press, Princeton, 1979.

————, "Liberalization and Democratization in South America: Perspectives from the 1970s," in *Transitions from Authoritarian Rule: Latin America*, edited by Guillermo O'Donnell, Philippe Schmitter, and Laurence Whitehead, Johns Hopkins University Press, Baltimore, 1986.

————, "Stabilization and Adjustment in Argentina, Brazil, and Mexico," in *Economic Crisis and Policy Choice: The Politics of Adjustment in the Third World*, edited by Joan M. Nelson, Princeton University Press, Princeton, 1990.

Kenworthy, Eldon, "Argentina: The Politics of Late Industrialization," *Foreign Affairs*, April 1967.

Knowles, Christopher, "Revolutionary Trade Unionism in Argentina: Interview with Augustin Tosco," *Radical America*, May–June 1975.

Kohli, Atul, "Introduction," in *The State and Development in the Third World*, edited by Atul Kohli, Princeton University Press, Princeton, 1986.

Krell, Eduardo, "Re: ¿Cual es el bonche en Argentina?" *Phoenix*, Article 1231, 4 December 1990.

Krieger Vasena, Adalbert, *El programa económico argentino*, 1967/69, Academia Nacional de Ciencias Económicas, Buenos Aires, 1988.

Landi, Oscar, "La tercera presidencia de Perón: Gobierno de emergencia y crisis política," *Revista Mexicana de Sociologia*, October 1978.

Landsberger, Henry A., and McDaniel, Tim, "Hypermobilization in Chile, 1970–1973," in *The State and Development in the Third World*, edited by Atul Kohli, Princeton University Press, Princeton, 1986.

Latin America Monitor, vol. 9, 1992.

Latin American Securities Limited, *Argentina: A Look at the Stock Market and Economy*, London, 1990.

Linz, Juan J., *The Breakdown of Democratic Regimes: Crisis, Breakdown, Reequilibration*, Johns Hopkins University Press, Baltimore, 1978.

Mainwaring, Scott, "Authoritarianism and Democracy in Argentina," *Journal of Interamerican Studies and World Affairs*, August 1984.

Mallon, R., and Sourrouille, J., *Economic Policymaking in a Conflict Society: The Argentine Case*, Harvard University Press, Cambridge, 1975.

Malloy, James M., "Authoritarianism and Corporatism in Latin America: The

Modal Pattern," in *Authoritarianism and Corporatism in Latin America*, edited by James M. Malloy, University of Pittsburgh Press, Pittsburgh, 1977.

Mann, Arthur J., and Schulthess, Walter E., "Long-run Expenditure Constraints in Argentina," *Public Finance Quarterly*, January 1986.

Martínez de Hoz, José Alfredo, *Bases para una Argentina moderna, 1976–80*, Editorial Emece, Buenos Aires, 1981.

———, "La privatización de las empresas del estado," *Ambito Financiero*, 19 December 1985.

———, "Las cico "C" de la economía," *La Nación*, 15 March 1987.

———, "La apertura exportadora y la apertura importadora," *Ambito Financiero*, 15 February 1988.

———, *Diez años después*, manuscript, 1976.

Maynard, Geoffrey, "Argentina: Macroeconomic Policy, 1966–73," in *The Political Economy of Argentina, 1946–1983*, edited by Guido di Tella and Rudiger Dornbusch, Macmillan, London, 1989.

Maynard, Geoffrey, and Willie van Rijcheghem, "Stabilization Policy in an Inflationary Economy—Argentina," in *Development Policy—Theory and Practice*, edited by Gustav F. Papanek, Harvard University Press, Cambridge, 1968.

Merkx, Gilbert W., "Sectoral Clashes and Political Change: The Argentine Experience," *Latin American Research Review*, Summer 1969.

———, "Argentina: Peronism and Power," *Monthly Review*, January 1976.

Ministerio de Economía, *Memoria: 29–3–76 al 29–3–81*, Argentine Ministry of Economics, Buenos Aires, 1981.

Mora y Araujo, Manuel, "La naturaleza de la coalición alfonsinista," in *La Argentina Electoral*, edited by Natalio R. Botana et al., Editorial Sudamericana, Buenos Aires, 1985.

———, *Liberalismo y democracia*, Manatiel, Buenos Aires, 1988.

Mouzelis, Nicos, "On the Rise of Postwar Military Dictatorships: Argentina, Chile, Greece," *Comparative Study of Society and History*, October 1986.

Munck, Ronaldo, with Ricardo Falcon and Bernardo Galitelli, *Argentina: From Anarchism to Peronism*, Zed Books, London, 1987.

Nación, "Dirigentes peronistas proclaman a Menem como conductor estratégico," 29 July 1990.

Nash, Nathaniel C., "Argentina's Markets Back Economic Plan," *The New York Times*, 5 February 1991.

Norris, Floyd, "Argentina's Painful Path to Efficiency," *The New York Times*.

O'Donnell, Guillermo, "Corporatism and the Question of the State," in *Authoritarianism and Corporatism in Latin America*, edited by James M. Malloy, University of Pittsburgh Press, Pittsburgh, 1977.

———, "State and Alliances in Argentina, 1956–1976," *The Journal of Development Studies*, October 1978.

———, "Reflections on the Patterns of Change in Bureaucratic-Authoritarian States," *Latin American Research Review*, Winter 1978.

———, *Bureaucratic-Authoritarianism*, Institute of International Studies, Berkeley, 1979.

———, *Notas para el estudio de procesos de democratizacion politica a partir del estado burocrato-autoritario*, Estudios CEDES, Buenos Aires, 1979.

———, "Tensions in the Bureaucratic-Authoritarian State and the Question of Democracy," in *The New Authoritarianism in Latin America*, edited by David Collier, Princeton University Press, Princeton, 1979.

———, *Bureaucratic Authoritarianism*, University of California Press, Berkeley, 1988.

————, *Argentina, de nuevo*, Working paper #152, The Kellogg Institute, University of Notre Dame, Notre Dame, 1991.

O'Donnell, Guillermo, and Schmitter, Philippe C., *Transitions from Authoritarian Rule: Tentative Conclusions About Uncertain Democracies*, Johns Hopkins University Press, Baltimore, 1986.

Ostiguy, Pierre, *Los capitanes de la industria*, Editorial Legasa, Buenos Aires, 1990.

Palomino, Héctor, "Les syndicats dans les premières années du gouvernment constitutionnel," *Problèmes d'Amérique Latine*, 4° Trimestre, 1986.

————, "Las corporaciones están entre nosotros," *El Bimestre Politico y Económico*, Julio/Agosto 1987.

Peagam, Norman, "Argentina: Menem Ditches the Dogma," *Euromoney*, September 1990.

Petrecolla, Alberto, Unbalanced Development, 1958–62," in *The Political Economy of Argentina, 1946–1983*, edited by Guido di Tella and Rudiger Dornbusch, Macmillan, London, 1989.

Pion-Berlin, David, "Military Breakdown and Redemocratization in Argentina," in *Liberalization and Democratization in Latin America*, edited by George A. López and Michael Stohl, Greenwood Press, New York, 1987.

————, *The Ideology of State Terror: Economic Doctrine and Political Repression in Argentina and Peru*, Lynne Rienner Publishers, Boulder, 1989.

Portantiero, Juan Carlos, "Political and Economic Crises in Argentina," in *The Political Economy of Argentina, 1946–1983*, edited by Guido di Tella and Rudiger Dornbusch, Macmillan, London, 1989.

Potash, Robert A., *The Army and Politics in Argentina, 1928–1945: Yrigoyen to Perón*, Stanford University Press, Stanford, 1969.

————, *The Army and Politics in Argentina, 1945–1962: Perón to Frondizi*, Stanford University Press, Stanford, 1980.

Przeworski, Adam, "Some Problems in the Study of the Transition to Democracy," in *Transitions from Authoritarian Rule: Comparative Perspectives*, edited by Guillermo O'Donnell, Philippe Schmitter, and Laurence Whitehead, Johns Hopkins University Press, Baltimore, 1988.

Randall, Laura, *An Economic History of Argentina in the Twentieth Century*, Columbia University Press, New York, 1978.

Ranis, Peter, "The Dilemmas of Democratization in Argentina, *Current History*, January 1986.

Rock, David, *Argentina: 1516–1982*, University of California Press, Berkeley, 1985.

Rodriguez, Carlos Alfredo, *Macroeconomics of the Public Sector Deficit: The Case of Argentina*, manuscript, 1991.

Rojo, Pablo, with Canosa, Armando, "El programa de desregulación del gobierno Argentino," *Boletin Informativo Techint* #269, January–May 1992.

Roth, Roberto, *Los Años de Onganía*, La Campana, Buenos Aires, 1980.

Rouquié, Alain, "Demilitarization and the Institutionalization of Military-dominated Politics in Latin America," in *Transitions from Authoritarian Rule: Comparative Perspectives*, edited by Guillermo O'Donnell, Philippe Schmitter, and Laurence Whitehead, Johns Hopkins University Press, Baltimore, 1988.

Rudolph, James D., editor, *Argentina: A Country Study*, published by the United States Government as Represented by the Secretary of the Army, Washington, D.C., 1985.

Sachs, Jeffrey, "Curing Argentina's Illness," *The Boston Globe*, July 16, 1989, p. A1.

———, "Social Conflict and Populist Policies in Latin America," in *Labour Relations and Economic Performance*, edited by Renato Brunetta and Carlo Dell'Aringa, Macmillan, London, 1990.

Schmitter, Philippe C., "Still the Century of Corporatism?" *The Review of Politics*, January 1974.

———, "Sectors in Modern Capitalism: Modes of Governance and Variations in Performance," in *Labour Relations and Economic Performance*, edited by Renato Brunetta and Carlo Dell'Aringa, Macmillan, London, 1990.

Schvarzer, Jorge, "Cambios en el liderazgo industrial argentine en el periodo de Martínez de Hoz, *Desarrollo Económico*, October 1983.

———, *Martínez de Hoz: La lógica política de la política económia*, CISEA, Buenos Aires, 1983.

———, "Restricciones a la política económica en la década del ochenta en la Argentina, *El Bimestre Politico y Económico*, Marzo/Abril 1987.

Schvarzer, Jorge, and Sidicaro, Ricardo, "Empresarios y estado en la reconstrucción de la democracia en la Argentina," *El Bimestre Politico y Económico*, Septiembre/Octubre 1987.

Scobie, James R., *Argentina: A City and a Nation*, Oxford University Press, New York, 1971.

Sheahan, John, "Economic Politics and the Prospects for Successful Transition from Authoritarian Rule in Latin America," in *Transitions from Authoritarian Rule: Comparative Perspectives*, edited by Guillermo O'Donnell, Philippe Schmitter, and Laurence Whitehead, Johns Hopkins University Press, Baltimore, 1988.

Sidicaro, Ricardo, "Trois ans de démocratie en Argentine (1983–1986)," *Problèmes d'Amérique Latine*, 4° Trimestre, 1986.

Skidmore, Thomas E., "The Politics of Economic Stabilization in Postwar Latin America," in *Authoritarianism and Corporatism in Latin America*, edited by James M. Malloy, University of Pittsburgh Press, Pittsburgh, 1977.

Slaastad, Larry A., "Argentine Economic Policy, 1976–81," in *The Political Economy of Argentina, 1946–1983*, edited by Guido di Tella and Rudiger Dornbusch, Macmillan, London, 1989.

Smith, Peter H., "Argentina: The Uncertain Warriors," *Current History*, February 1980.

Smith, Tony, "The Underdevelopment of Development Literature: The Case of Dependency Theory," in *The State and Development in the Third World*, edited by Atul Kohli, Princeton University Press, Princeton, 1986.

Smith, William C., "Reflections on the Political Economy of Authoritarian Rule and Capitalist Reorganization in Contemporary Argentina," in *Generals in Retreat*, edited by Philip O'Brian and Paul Cammack, Manchester University Press, Manchester, 1982.

———, *Authoritarianism and the Crisis of the Argentine Political Economy*, Stanford University Press, Stanford, 1989.

Snow, Peter G., *Political Forces in Argentina*, Praeger, New York, 1979.

Sociedad Rural Argentina, *Mensaje para le dirigencia Argentina*, Sociedad Rural Argentina, Buenos Aires, 1988.

Stepan, Alfred, "Paths Towards Redemocratization: Theoretical and Comparative Considerations," in *Transitions from Authoritarian Rule: Comparative Perspectives*, edited by Guillermo O'Donnell, Philippe Schmitter, and Laurence Whitehead, Johns Hopkins University Press, Baltimore, 1988.

———, *Rethinking Military Politics: Brazil and the Southern Cone*, Princeton University Press, Princeton, 1988.

Szusterman, Celia, "The 'Revolución Libertadora,' 1955–8," in *The Political*

Economy of Argentina, 1946–1983, edited by Guido di Tella and Rudiger Dornbusch, Macmillan, London, 1989.

Taliercio, Robert R., Jr., *Only the People Will Save the People: The Crisis of Change and Continuity in Peronism, 1976–1989*, a senior thesis presented to the Woodrow Wilson School, Princeton, 1990.

Thompson, John, "Argentina Economic Policy Under the Onganía Regime," *Inter-American Economic Affairs*, Summer 1970.

Torre, Juan Carlos, "Argentina: Il ritorno del Peronismo," in *Dalle Armi alle Urne*, edited by Giuliano Urbani and Francesco Ricciu, Il Mulino, Bologna, 1991.

Turner, Frederick C., "The Aftermath of Defeat in Argentina," *Current History*, February 1983.

Uchitelle, Louis, "Argentina's Painful Path to Efficiency," *The New York Times*, 14 May 1990.

Unión Industrial Argentina 1990, Unión Industrial Argentina, Buenos Aires, 1990.

Valenzuela, Arturo, and Valenzuela, J. Samuel, "Party Oppositions Under the Chilean Regime," in *Military Rule in Chile*, edited by Arturo Valenzuela and J. Samuel Valenzuela, Johns Hopkins University Press, Baltimore, 1986.

Vilas, Carlos M., "El populismo latinoamericano: Un enfoque estructural," *Desarrollo Económico*, October 1988.

Villanueva, Javier, "Evolución de las estrategias de desarrollo económico en el periodo de posguera," *Desarrollo Económico*, April 1981.

Villareal, Sofía, Palomino, Mirta, and Itzcovitz, Victoria, "Les organizations patronals argentines face au Gouvernement Démocratique," *Problèmes d'Amérique Latine*, 4° Trimestre, 1986.

Waisman, Carlos H., *Reversal of Development in Argentina: Postwar Counterrevolutionary Policies and Their Structural Consequences*, Princeton University Press, Princeton, 1987.

Whitehead, Laurence, "Internationalization Aspects of Democratization," in *Transitions from Authoritarian Rule: Comparative Perspectives*, edited by Guillermo O'Donnell, Philippe Schmitter, and Laurence Whitehead, Johns Hopkins University Press, Baltimore, 1988.

Wiarda, Howard, *Corporatism and National Development in Latin America*, Westview Press, Boulder, 1981.

Wynia, Gary W., "Illusion and Reality in Argentina," *Current History*, February 1981.

———, "The Argentine Revolution Falters," *Current History*, February 1982.

———, *Argentina: Illusions and Realities*, Holmes and Meier, New York 1986.

———, "The Peronists Triumph in Argentina," *Current History*, January 1990.

———, *The Politics of Latin American Development*, Cambridge University Press, New York 1990.

———, "Argentina's Economic Reform," *Current History*, February 1991.

Yuravlivker, David E., "Political Shocks, International Reserves and the Real Exchange Rate—The Argentine Case," *Journal of International Money and Finance*, December 1987.

Zablotsky, Edgardo Enrique, *An Economic Theory of Autocracy: A Public Choice Theory on the Causes and Economic Consequences of Military Coups D'Etats*, unpublished manuscript.

Index

247

About the Book and Author

Since the mid-1960s, a series of governments has come to power in Argentina promising political stability and economic growth. Despite immense popular support and great variations in their structures and economic policies, however, all but the current one have failed. Seeking to understand Argentina's spiral downward from its auspicious beginnings, Erro analyzes these governments and identifies a set of factors that impeded the effective implementation of economic policies and political consolidation in the 1966–1989 period.

Then turning to the Menem government, Erro demonstrates that Menem, originally expected to revert to Peronism, is actually breaking the traditional cycle and implementing policies that are allowing democracy and political/economic stability to take root. The book concludes with an assessment of the Menem government's chances for long-term success.

Davide G. Erro works for a multinational corporation while continuing research at the Woodrow Wilson School for Public and International Affairs, Princeton University.